Individualism in Early China

Individualism in Early China

*Human Agency
and the Self in
Thought and Politics*

Erica Fox Brindley

 University of Hawai'i Press
Honolulu

© 2010 University of Hawai'i Press
All rights reserved
Printed in the United States of America
15 14 13 12 11 10   6 5 4 3 2 1

Library of Congress Cataloging-in-Publication Data
Brindley, Erica.
  Individualism in early China : human agency and the self in thought and politics / Erica Fox Brindley.
    p. cm.
  Includes bibliographical references and index.
  ISBN-13: 978-0-8248-3386-2 (hardcover : alk. paper)
  ISBN-10: 0-8248-3386-4 (hardcover : alk. paper)
    1. Individualism—China—History. 2. Self (Philosophy)—China—History. 3. Philosophy, Chinese—To 221 B.C. 4. Philosophy, Chinese—221 B.C.–960 A.D. I. Title.
  B824.B74 2010
  126.0931—dc22
                                                            2009042973

University of Hawai'i Press books are printed on acid-free paper and meet the guidelines for permanence and durability of the Council on Library Resources.

Designed by Josie Herr
Printed by The Maple-Vail Book Manufacturing Group

For my loving parents,
Monica and Tom

Contents

Preface ix

Acknowledgments xiii

Introduction xv

CHAPTER ONE Individual Agency and Universal, Centralized Authority in Early Mohist Writings 1

CHAPTER TWO Centralizing Control: The Politics of Bodily Conformism 29

CHAPTER THREE Decentralizing Control and Naturalizing Cosmic Agency: Bodily Conformism and Individualism 54

CHAPTER FOUR Two Prongs of the Debate: Bodily Agencies vs. Claims for Institutional Controls 77

CHAPTER FIVE Servants of the Self and Empire: Institutionally Controlled Individualism at the Dawn of a New Era 104

CHAPTER SIX Conclusion 121

Postscript: A Note on Chinese Individualism, Human Rights, and the Asian Values Debate 131

Notes 137

Works Cited 189

Index 201

Preface

> The state successfully transformed the idea of individualism into a synecdoche for a negative West, as the discourse surrounding this meaning began to play an important role in China's reinvention of the power relationship between East and West, as well as that between the state and its intelligentsia. In other words, the state had a political stake in presenting the idea of individualism to its people as *un-Chinese*.
> —Lydia H. Liu, "Translingual Practice"[1]

Chinese culture is often characterized as a culture of obligation rather than individual freedom. This characterization is not just a stereotype; it is rooted in various nineteenth- and twentieth-century constructions of Chinese identity, as such an identity is compared to that of the "West."[2] Such a characterization affects scholarship, diplomacy, and public policy. For example, the modern Chinese state, among other Asian contemporaries, has resisted paying attention to charges of "universal human rights" violations on grounds that such rights are bound up in culturally specific views on individualism—views that are incompatible with traditional "Asian values."[3]

Given that policy decisions and international relations depend greatly on whether or not Chinese or Asian values are compatible with individualism, it would seem that the issue would be of considerable scholarly importance. Furthermore, given the wealth of scholarship on human rights in Asia and the "Asian values" question, one would think that understanding the nature of Chinese individualism might be central to determining the extent to which Western-style human rights are relevant to Asian traditions and contexts.[4] Yet relatively few scholars directly address the specific notion of individualism in China or Asia, and they especially do not discuss it at length in historical context.[5] An exclusively European and American concept, "individualism" remains, for most scholars, an icon in the development of Western thought and institutions.[6]

Individualism in modern times has greatly influenced social and political institutions, views of the self, and liberal, democratic values associated with the universal rights of man and human rights.[7] In such contexts it is invariably construed as a particular development of ideals and movements specific to Enlightenment Europe that traces its origins to earlier Greek and Judeo-Christian traditions. Given its close associations with European cultural and historical identity, some scholars of China have been apprehensive about using such a concept to analyze the history of China and East Asian cultures. They contend that definitions of individualism in contemporary European and American contexts do not exactly correspond to the various views on the individual that obtain in Asian history.[8] They point to China's deep involvement with Confucian values as defining individual obligations to one's family *so as to overshadow* the importance of the self. Rather than be found guilty of misappropriating or mistranslating individualism, many scholars of China avoid the topic altogether, or they assume that the concept of the individual is simply not relevant to a society imbued with communitarian values and a penchant for interpersonal relations.[9]

Such a view might appear reasonable on the surface, but when one closely examines the imperatives of cross-cultural analysis, translation, and comparison, its flaws begin to emerge. Indeed, proponents of this view refuse—in the name of being historically precise—to use the term "individualism" when referring to ideas outside of the Western context, not even as a heuristic tool. But, I contend, terms with specific histories, such as "science," "religion," "philosophy," "self," "cosmos," etc., can and should be effectively used outside of their original historical and linguistic contexts for comparative and interpretive purposes. To cut off the use of a perfectly good term and analytic device simply out of allegiance to a presumed original context or a single tradition is to deny concepts their potential to change, adapt to new contexts, and facilitate the translation of other cultures and the past.

The taboo against redefining concepts such as "individualism" for hermeneutical purposes encourages thinking about concepts as fixed, unchanging entities, rather than as fluid, living representations of fleeting human agendas and thought.[10] It is untenable because even within its so-called "original" context in the West, the concept of individualism assumed many forms and was constantly being contested and redefined.[11] To isolate individualism in terms of a single definition and context actually misunderstands the dynamic, contextual, and fundamentally unstable nature of such concepts in any historical tradition.

Given how eager people in the West are to apply what they term "universal human rights" to China, it is imperative that scholars pursue a serious, nuanced study of individualism in China. Furthermore, they must not so readily accept the idea of its absence and irrelevance throughout Chinese history. To do the latter only makes the gap between indigenous Chinese views on the individual and "human rights" views—which clearly embrace a concept of the autonomous, free individual—appear more unbridgeable than necessary. As a result, the argument that countries such as China should embrace human rights becomes a matter of Western chauvinism and imperialism, of Westerners forcefully imposing their enlightened ethical notions about individual prerogatives on a morally bereft "other," whose tradition seems devoid of such concepts. However, as many Asia watchers and scholars are aware, and as this book will help clarify, Chinese culture and history is far from lacking illuminating concepts that address the powers and prerogatives of the self as individual.[12]

In this book I claim that various forms of individualism—defined conveniently now as ideals that value certain inborn and inalienable prerogatives and powers of the individual—can be found in East Asian cultural traditions. Through a detailed look at many attitudes toward individual autonomy and one main form of individualism in early China, I correct misconceptions about the insignificance of the individual in Chinese history and intellectual cultures. My goal is to re-orient the reader's attitudes toward the individual in Chinese history so that he or she might be able to re-evaluate the special and distinct types of Chinese as well as Euro-American–style individualisms.

What are the distinct flavors of Chinese and Euro-American individualisms? As C. B. Macpherson wrote when discussing "possessive individualism" in seventeenth-century England:

> Its possessive quality is found in its conception of the individual as essentially the proprietor of his own person or capacities, owing nothing to society for them. The individual was seen neither as a moral whole, nor as part of a larger social whole, but as an owner of himself.[13]

This type of individualism focuses on an individual's possessive claims to uniqueness and autonomy from one's surroundings. Such a notion—which serves as one of the many ancestors to current concepts of individuals and their rights—differs significantly from early Chinese conceptions of individualism that I present in this book. In early China, the individual is always situated within a larger familial, social, and cosmic whole. Such a "holistic" individualism emphasizes the individual from within a complicated and ever-changing web of relationships with people, objects, and events.[14]

Because it stresses achievement through individual relationship to others and not freedom through individual separation from others, such a concept of the individual necessarily jogs our current conceptions of what it means to be free, autonomous, and independent beings.

In highlighting forms of Chinese individualism as alternatives to certain Euro-American–style forms, I do not intend to recommend such individualisms as correctives to modern Western liberalism, but as powerful perspectives that can enhance our pre-existing views of the self in society, reminding us of our interdependence with others and our desired connections with our larger environments.[15] Most fundamentally, I write this book so that we might reconceive the value of the individual and human agency in classical, early Chinese thought, which has implications for the entire Chinese tradition. I hope such an exercise will help pave the way for a more culturally sensitive approach to modern conceptions of human rights, individualism, and freedom for contemporary China as well as other cultures influenced by the early traditions of China.[16]

Acknowledgments

This project has assumed more than a dozen different guises, and working on it has undoubtedly taken its toll on many individuals besides myself. I am indebted to all the great mentors, guides, friends, and family members in my life who gave critical input and who helped support me emotionally, intellectually, and financially over the years. Most recently, I thank my colleagues at Penn State who have read through and provided useful feedback on the manuscript during the final stages, especially On-cho Ng. On-cho was able to emphasize that Pat Crosby at the University of Hawai'i Press might be open to such a topic. I thank him for all his patience and advice. Indeed, he was right about Pat, whom I thank for judiciously shepherding this book through the bowels of the review process and seeing to it that it would be ready for the press. Anonymous reviewers also provided comments that considerably benefited the manuscript. I am grateful to the two reviewers who took the time to provide substantial, detailed, and relevant comments, and I hope that what they find here addresses their concerns as adequately as possible.

Penn State has provided an especially supportive environment for writing and conducting research. The History Department was able to grant ample funding that facilitated the publication of this book. And the university has given me colleagues both in and beyond my home department who serve as my role models, sources of support, and friends.

I also wish to thank colleagues at other universities who examined, commented on, and influenced all or parts of this manuscript earlier on: Yuri Pines, Roger Ames, Miranda Brown, Michael Nylan, Donald Munro, Steve Angle, Robert Eno, and Gideon Yaffee. Yuri Pines took on a special role, not just as a trusted specialist in early Chinese history, but as a constructive critic who was able to point out strategies for drawing out the manuscript's strengths and effectively working on its weaknesses.

At the earliest stages of this project, Willard Peterson and Michael Puett walked me through the conceptual processes associated with writing a book.

They spent many hours with me discussing key issues relevant to human agency in early China. I thank Willard Peterson for sparking my interest in early Chinese intellectual history and being my devoted teacher ever since my junior year at Princeton. I am grateful also to Michael Puett for joining Peterson as my trusted advisor while I was working on my PhD and for helping shape some of my most fundamental approaches to the study of intellectuals and their ideas from a historical framework. Without these two mentors, I would not be the type of scholar that I am, and I thank them for the many fruitful discussions we have shared over the years.

Other professors have also been formative to me. Andrew Plaks and colleagues attending his reading groups in classical Chinese helped strengthen my critical analysis of original texts. Professor Yü Ying-shih was unfailingly supportive. And Professors Tang and Yüan inspired me as an undergraduate, helping me develop foundational linguistic skills necessary for my line of work. In Taiwan, I especially thank Cai Biming and Wang Ronglin for their instruction in classical Chinese and Taiwanese. I am also grateful to the Chiang Ching-kuo Foundation for financing a year of my dissertation writing.

While I cannot name them all individually here, many friends have been there for me through some very trying years while I was writing this book and waiting for news concerning its publication. I thank them for being such vital supports. I also thank my family as my deepest source of strength and inspiration: my sisters Bianca and Becky, my husband Derek and daughter Claire, my in-laws MeiMei, Carol, and Galen, and my parents Monica and Tom.

Parts of chapter one were originally published as "Human Agency and the Ideal of *Shang Tong* (Upward Conformity) in Early Mohist Writings," *Journal of Chinese Philosophy* 34.3 (September 2007): pp. 409–425. Many thanks to the *Journal of Chinese Philosophy* and Blackwell Publishing for allowing me to reproduce these sections.

Introduction

The imperial beginnings of China tell a story not just of concrete changes in state structure, policy, and military power but also of important developments in ideology. Well before the First Emperor of the Qin proclaimed sovereignty over a unified empire in 221 BCE, the concept that all should be united under a single great cosmic authority had clearly begun to take root in religious and intellectual circles as well as in political discourse.[1] Alongside this focus on a unified authority that extends beyond and helps shape individual behaviors, a widespread debate on universal human nature (*xing* 性) began to locate cosmic authority and power in all humans from birth, helping usher in movements that viewed the individual body as a key source of empowerment.[2] This book introduces the development of early Chinese beliefs that link universal, cosmic authority to the individual in new and interesting ways, indeed in ways that might sometimes be referred to as individualistic. In addition, this book also illustrates how such ideological and religious beliefs developed alongside and potentially helped contribute to larger sociopolitical changes of the time, such as the centralization of political authority and the growth in social mobility of the *shi* (士 educated elite) class.

Much twentieth-century scholarship on early Chinese thought and religions focuses on single authors—the "great men" of ancient China—and on certain aspects of their philosophies. While the writings I examine are most certainly worthy of deep philosophical analysis, it is important to approach them not just as philosophical texts but as historical artifacts as well. Indeed, I hope to show that these texts can provide us with valuable insights into the changing religious, philosophical, and sociopolitical discourses of the period. This is possible, especially since "religion," "philosophy," and "politics" were not separate categories of intellectual inquiry in ancient China. The intellectuals who composed and compiled such texts would have been deeply involved for their livelihoods in seeking (or rejecting) official appointment through their ability to discuss and provide solutions to certain religious and philosophical problems, as well as political conditions and state affairs. I therefore aim to move beyond what we can know about a single author and his "philosophical" work to a discussion of how the ideas and political-religious beliefs represented in various authors' works changed from period to period and fit into the general political and social climate of the times.[3]

The ancient sources to be examined in this book are representations of specific modes of culture and systems of knowledge embedded within contemporary social institutions and political agendas. By asking how certain ideas connect groups of authors from roughly the same epoch to each other, I abandon a singular focus on the transmission of ideas strictly according to distinct "schools" of thought and focus instead on thematic continuities and discontinuities during certain increments of time.[4] This approach allows me to illustrate how diverse intellectual lineages influenced each other, shared or did not share certain basic orientations, and were similarly implicated in the broader intellectual, religious, social, and political world of a particular era: the Warring States (453–221 BCE) and early imperial periods (221– ~100 BCE).[5]

Starting with the writings of the early Mohists (fourth century BCE), I analyze many of the major writings through the early second century BCE such as those of Laozi, Zhuangzi, Xunzi, and Han Feizi, as well as anonymous authors of both received and excavated texts. I show how changing notions of human agency affected prevailing attitudes toward the self as individual. In particular, I demonstrate the onset of ideals that stress the power and authority of the individual, either as a conformist agent in relationship to a larger, cosmic whole, or as an individualistic agent endowed with inalienable cosmic powers and authorities. I then go on to show how distinctly internal (individualistic), external (institutionalized), or mixed (syncretic) approaches to self-cultivation and state control emerged in response to such ideals. As I explore the nature of early Chinese individualism and the various theories for and against it, I also reveal the ways in which authors innovatively adapted new theories on individual power to the needs of the burgeoning imperial state at the end of the Warring States and in the Qin and early Han empires.

Approaches to the Study of Individualism in China

In past studies that examine the role of the individual in China, scholars have framed questions and established values in such a way that China comes out lacking in comparison to the "West."[6] Max Weber was perhaps one of the

Introduction

most influential thinkers to embrace this biased approach. In his book on the religions of China, Weber wields evidence from Chinese culture and history to prove his point about the "non-existence of modern capitalism in China."[7] Weber's chief arguments for such a point are grounded in his view that the cultures of Northern Europe and China each defined individual motivation and personal ideals differently. For Weber, the Puritan individual acted according to a "supramundane orientation," which derived from the Puritan rational ethic. This supramundane religiosity shaped individuals so that they looked favorably upon the acquisition of material wealth (for the purposes of storing up for the hereafter), and this attitude served to drive the growth of modern capitalism.[8] The Chinese people, on the other hand, lacked a transcendent, divine orientation that cast the individual and his or her strivings beyond this world. According to Weber, then, the Chinese lacked a sense of individual autonomy from mundane powers and concerns that the Puritans possessed, so that the Chinese, unlike the Puritans, were not inclined to engage in activities conducive to modern capitalism.[9]

Aside from making utterly fallacious claims about Chinese views of the individual and his or her proclivities toward capitalistic activities, Weber also makes use of a biased method of inquiry. Weber's approach defines a problem according to parameters of discourse that are relevant for only one of the two cultures being compared—that of the Puritans in Europe. He uses the other culture, in this case China, to provide a contrastive, negative background—or to demonstrate a lack within those parameters. This is like posing questions such as, "Why did China not develop 'science'?" or "Why were there no 'philosophers' in China?" when both "science" and "philosophy" are defined strictly according to historical developments and categories stemming from either Renaissance or Enlightenment Europe or classical Greece.[10] The only way for China to have emerged favorably according to such parameters would be for it to have duplicated Renaissance or Enlightenment Europe and classical Greece, which because of its obviously different history, it did not do. Because Weber seeks out an identical likeness according to the Western model, he fails to achieve a fair or adequate means of comparing China with Europe.

Weber's approach is characteristic of much of twentieth-century Western scholarship on China.[11] Scholars who engage in this comparative method almost invariably end up celebrating one culture by denigrating another—or neglecting serious study of the "secondary" culture altogether. They arrive at their conclusions from a positive examination of one culture according to its own vocabulary alongside a negative and/or superficial examination of the other based on conceptual categories that are by definition foreign to it. Such a self-centered and self-congratulatory method does not facilitate a deeper understanding of other cultures according to their own cultural contingencies, vocabularies, conceptual frameworks, and historical developments.

Other scholars of the past thirty years have looked into the question of authority associated with the self in China in what Paul Cohen calls more "China-centered" ways.[12] Roger Ames, Henry Rosemont, and W. T. de Bary in particular have contributed much to current understandings of the Confucian self as "person"—which, Ames states, is not associated with "a notion of discrete and isolated 'self,'" but is "alternatively articulated in a robust sociological language."[13] Such statements demonstrate that scholars recognize the importance of the self in Confucian traditions as articulated according to its own core emphases and themes. Moreover, the conclusion that the "self" in Confucian thought cannot be understood in terms of a "discrete and isolated 'self'" is entirely in line with the general sense of "individual" highlighted in this book.

However, as Ames' citation shows, much of the scholarship concerning the self in early China not only focuses more exclusively on Confucian thought, but it also insists upon translating "self" as "person," and not "individual."[14] While such a translation is justified on many counts, it can be understood to suggest that Eastern and Western modes of thought are entirely distinct and non-overlapping and that the notion of the "individual" does not and has never existed in China.[15]

Much scholarship that directly addresses the notion of the "individual" in China still clings to a narrow definition of individualism, leading to an unbalanced presentation and comparison of the changing roles of the individual in both Chinese and Western cultures. For example, Chad Hansen acknowledges the problem by demonstrating that the term "individualism" is culturally defined according to "Western-style individualism."[16] However, rather than focusing on what "Chinese-style" visions of the individual might entail, and thereby establishing a means of cross-cultural, cross-historical translation, Hansen confines himself to a narrowly conceived definition of individualism. His conclusion, that "[w]e may justifiably generalize that there is no individualism in Chinese philosophy,"[17] leaves the reader with a picture of a conceptual world in China that either lacks its own integrity regarding fundamental issues of human concern, or seems utterly alien from our own so that translation becomes an exercise in futility.

Some philosophers do, however, include the "individual" as a worthy arena of discussion. Irene Bloom speaks of the merits of "individuals" when discussing a religious change in early China "from prognostication to 'virtue,' from external controls and influences over human affairs to self-control and 'moral force' on the part of living individuals."[18] While she does not go so far as to discuss "individualism" in such a context, Bloom outlines an interesting development concerning an "inward-turn" that seems to justify the use of the term "individual."

In the same volume as Hansen's article on individualism, Yü Ying-shih argues along very different lines.[19] He at once acknowledges the European provenance of the concept of individualism while attempting to show that certain types of individualism, defined differently from the kind embodied in Weber's Puritan ethic, appeared at various points throughout Chinese history. By tweaking the definition of individualism a bit, he shows us that one can arrive at interesting examples of it in China's past. But this approach, while significantly more revealing about China than Hansen's or Weber's, still attaches itself to the solipsistic approach to individualism that it is trying to overcome. This is because the historical and intellectual moment that Yü highlights, that of the so-called Neo-Daoist movement in medieval China, constitutes an extraordinary and uncommon moment in the general history of China.[20] The fact that Yü felt compelled to point to the phenomenon in China that most closely resembles a European and American definition of individualism suggests that his very choice of topic is still constrained by an earlier, unbalanced manner of framing the debate on individualism in China.

Michael Nylan pursues another approach in arguing—essentially contra Yü—that the label "individualism" is not appropriate even for medieval times. Nylan's analysis of later Han and Wei-Jin intellectual and political practices sheds detailed light upon the contingencies and factors associated not with "individualism," but with what she calls "studied 'unconventional' behavior designed to establish group identity.'"[21] Her analysis is potently China-centered, and her arguments against calling such a trend "individualistic" are well worth considering. However, such arguments primarily rely on a comparison of the Chinese situation with a single definition—deemed "basic"—drawn from Western contexts (deriving from Alexis de Tocqueville).[22] Not interested in redefining "individualism" for the Chinese case, Nylan assumes a fundamental contradiction between Western "individualism" and certain Wei-Jin phenomena, such as a "heightened emphasis on family interests," a lack of "emphasis on maximum responsibility," or the absence of a belief in "the natural equality" of all individuals.[23] By maintaining a strict definition of "individualism" that only appears to fit the Western model in which it arose, Nylan strikes down potentially meaningful comparisons with relative ease. While she offers an interesting account of Han and Wei-Jin intellectual trends, she does not delve beyond casual comparisons.

Certainly, one of the fundamental tasks of the scholar of a different culture or time period is to analyze and thereby translate what is unknown by highlighting its similarities with and differences from what is already known. Methodological orientations that stress only a lack of something do not always provide balanced, convincing arguments that help us learn more about others as they existed from within their own cultural contexts. They stress difference at the cost of similarity. Often, they imply that such difference is bad, as it is associated with what is inferior, less sophisticated, less enlightened, or even stunted in development. Similarly, analyses that emphasize Chinese difference do not pursue the comparison such that so-called "foreign" terms like "individualism" might make sense within the context of Chinese views on the self.

As suggested so far, I do not believe we can completely throw out the term "individual" with reference to early Chinese concepts of self. This is especially apparent when we wish to talk about a particular emphasis on the self in early Chinese thought that goes beyond the "irreducibly interpersonal" self of Confucianism, as Ames describes so thoroughly in his work.[24] As we will see, the type of self as "individual" outlined in this book implies a certain type of agency, authority, and power accorded to one's person, in and of itself. Because the term "individualism" in English better conjures up such characteristics, I contend that "individualism" is a good fit and is clearly preferable over the less familiar term "personalism" in such cases.[25] As a consequence, I necessarily speak of "self" as "individual" rather than "person," and analyze "self" in a slightly different light than that of the bulk of scholarship on this topic.

This book therefore takes a different approach from much of the pre-existing scholarship on the self or on the topic of "individualism." I follow upon Yü's model but take it one step further, allowing room for the texts themselves to help shape the very definition of individualism that I will use. Rather than constrain myself to narrow definitions that will bind me exclusively to one or another cultural context, I invoke the concept of individualism at its broadest level to encompass two key criteria: (1) a belief that individuals possess any number of positive prerogatives or powers in the world by virtue of their existence as individuals, and (2) a belief that individuals can achieve their ideals through the use of their own autonomous, or self-inspired, authority of some kind. These two criteria are not unrelated to current American conceptions of individualism and might be said to satisfy at a minimal level what it means to be an individual in American culture.[26]

Introduction

They may thus serve as a general foundation or touchstone of similarity for more culturally specific notions of individualism that emerge out of the Chinese context.

The reader might object that the very invocation of the terms "individual" and "individualism" suggests an argument for the ultimate similarity or sameness of the Chinese tradition with that of the modern West. I contend, however, that it does not. Rather than argue for sameness, I propose that we change our typical conceptions of Enlightenment "individualism" to accommodate processes and clusters of concepts that are mostly foreign to it, but similar only in a most general way. By this, I refer to the fact that in cultures of ancient China and modern America alike, authors generally address issues related to individual empowerment, authority, control, creativity, and self-determination, yet they do not necessarily package these crucial aspects of individualism in the same way.[27] Focusing on what is unique about early Chinese thinking on these topics gives us a means of understanding particular "Chinese" discussions of and respect for the self, rather than giving us a chance to dismiss the Chinese belief system as purely conformist and devoid of interest in the self and its powers of control.

Historical Background: A Growing Awareness of Individual Agency

Changing conceptions of authority and the individual in Warring States China were deeply intertwined with large-scale sociopolitical developments that date from the Warring States period to the period of the first unified empires of the Qin (221–207 BCE) and Han (202 BCE–220 CE). The two most important sociopolitical developments connected to the ideological changes this book traces are the rise of meritocratic practices and ideals—during which the older, *zong-fa* 宗法 kinship polity (or "kin-based order") of the Zhou began to disintegrate—and the crafting of an increasingly centralized, bureaucratic political structure—out of which the notion of a universal empire emerged.[28] Admittedly, one can construe these two developments as merely different aspects of the same transformation: the replacement of the early Zhou system of royal and kinship-based authority with a more centralized, bureaucratic order.[29]

In the Warring States period, a new method of state administration was being developed and adopted by many states of the interstate sphere. This method relied increasingly on bureaucratic and meritocratic rather than kinship-based determinations of power and spheres of authority. One main aim of this method was to centralize the state by creating and increasing the number of administrative units or commanderies and districts (*jun* 郡 and *xian* 縣) over which the central regime had direct control.[30] In addition, centralizing states, unlike their predecessors of the Spring and Autumn period, opened up many positions, including some of their highest governmental positions, to a new class of men who had not previously been part of the ruling class or the hereditary aristocracy.[31] They did this by introducing meritocratic practices, allowing men who had hailed from a group of lower-level court functionaries and retainers, the *shi* 士 stratum, or educated elite stratum of society, to become more socially mobile than before.[32] Once they became more socially mobile, such people (many of the authors whose writings we will examine in this book stem from this group) were apt to think of themselves as agents with increasing amounts of control over their own lives and futures.

As the Warring States period progressed, members of the *shi* stratum became more physically mobile as well as socially mobile. As "merchants of ideas" rather than lifelong and loyal supporters of regionally centered aristocratic lineages, *shi* men of a variety of religious, political, and cultural interests traveled from state to state to sell their ideas and expertise to rulers. Even Confucius seems to have participated in this marketing aspiration, as he is cited to have proclaimed that he would rather sell a valuable piece of jade (symbolizing the value of the gentleman and his attainment) than store it away in a box for safekeeping.[33] By the fifth and fourth centuries BCE, aspiring officials, political advisors, and so-called "persuaders" (*shui zhe* 說者) would seek employment irrespective of state affiliation. And likewise, courts and rulers would compete for the best statesmen from a pool of men extending well beyond their own borders. The notion that individuals could decisively affect the general state of order and well-being of a state through official appointment, as well as the idea that they could gain significant personal and material benefits by using their rhetorical abilities and intellectual expertise to gain the ear of an important leader, no doubt contributed to an increased sense of individual agency and control in this period.[34]

Many famous statesmen and a range of diverse experts competed to achieve merit and high positions in society. Great political and military reformers such as Wu Qi, Li Kui, Shen Buhai, and Shang Yang were among the most famous men who served as aides to courts outside of their home court in the fifth and fourth centuries BCE.[35] Other intellectuals as well, such as Confucius, Mozi, and Mencius, were known to have served or given advice to rulers of different states, while still others such as Xunzi and the men at the Ji Xia Academy in the state of Qi, and Xunzi's disciples Li Si and Han Feizi, tried to connect themselves to various courts as more permanent advisors or members of an elite, scholarly institution patronized by the state. As commodities of value in an increasingly fluid and competitive market, the *shi* sought and gained employment in a broadened network of courts, and so their personal expertise, talents, and achievements were up for sale in a way they had never been before in the history of China.

Other changes during the Warring States period helped contribute to the growth of the centralized state, an increase in social mobility, and ultimately an increased sense of personal agency on the part of individuals. One of the most significant social changes was the administrative dissolution of the lineage, which was replaced, first in the state of Qin, with the delineation of nuclear families.[36] This had the result of placing the head of each household within an institutional, administrative framework of direct responsibility toward the centralized state. In addition, agricultural production was heightened by the use of iron technologies throughout the East Asian mainland. Iron dramatically altered military technology, which helped centralizing states engage in new types and scales of warfare.[37] Some states were able to expand military service and incorporate diverse peasant populations into an army-based political body, with the result that peoples of different lineages and types came into more frequent contact with each other.[38] Social mobility was increased through military meritocracies, such as the type employed in the state of Qin since Shang Yang's time (middle of the fourth century BCE), which gave commoners and men of lower ranks greater opportunities for political advancement and leadership. All these factors helped create a society in which persons of greater social variety could appear as important actors in society and politics of the day.[39] In short, increased interactions among peoples and the expanded horizons and needs of the bureaucratized, centralized state allowed more types of people, and greater numbers of them than ever before, to demonstrate agency in the world.[40]

Texts dating from the fourth century BCE provide us with manifest proof of a growing intellectual interest in new ideas on human agency. Intellectuals began concerning themselves with the limits and possibilities of human achievement and control in the world—a world in which the intellectual's own sense of agency and efficacy was probably growing in tandem with the rise in social mobility. Perhaps as a function of rhetorical competition, perhaps through a need to render coherent many divergent ways of thinking, or perhaps, as this book emphasizes, because of the demands of increasingly centralized states, intellectuals began presenting their claims about human agency and potential in terms of universal, cosmic agencies that could unify all individuals and things in the cosmos according to a correlated and systematic network of relationships.[41] Their texts shed light on a widespread debate that addresses human powers in general, universalized terms.[42] Through such debates, intellectuals cast their net more broadly so as to empower, at least in theory, individuals who in previous times might not have been considered relevant to their discussions on the cosmos, society, and the self. These changes in ideological scope mark the genesis of individualistic movements that apply (at least in theory) not just to an elite few but to all individuals universally.

Explanation of Key Concepts

Modes of Human Agency: Conformity and Individual Agency

The central component of individualism in early China, I contend, is individual agency. Throughout this book, I refer to the concept of agency to discuss the power, authority, and potential associated with and attributed to individuals. I distinguish these three aspects of agency from each other in the following manner: one has the power to do something if one can do it; one has the authority to do something if one is authorized or allowed to do it; and one has the potential to do something if it is conceivable that one will attain in the future both the power and authority to do it. Agency connects to all these concepts insofar as it involves action in ways that imply access to certain types of power, authority, and potential. By referring to two different types of agency, as defined below, I provide an interpretive tool for understanding how early Chinese thinkers conceptualized the relationship between the self and idealized—often cosmic, or divine—sources of power and authority in the world.

Standard dictionary entries for the term "agent" often speak of individuals who do not just act but who are motivated to act through either external or internal authorities. One prominent interpretation of the term construes an agent as "one who acts for or in the place of another by authority from him."[43] This meaning views the agent as a medium of authority who carries out an action commissioned from without. Such a meaning is still widely in use, as can be seen in phrases like "travel agent," "CIA agent," "bureaucratic agent," "real estate agent," etc.

Another meaning stresses internal sources of authority and active involvement in authorizing or bringing about change. Henry Rosemont puts it: "Human beings do in fact have ends, and are bestowers of value; this is what it means to be an *agent*, as opposed to an animal or an automaton."[44] An agent in this sense is often defined as "a person responsible for his acts."[45] While the meaning of responsibility is difficult and elusive, I will simply assert here that being responsible for an act is to be accountable or answerable for it.[46] In one sense, a person who is responsible must take possession of or "own up" to his or her acts, referring to the fact that to some extent he or she must identify with or authorize doing it. He or she thus owes an explanation, answer, or account of such an act. This definition of responsibility points to individuals as primary sources or arbiters of authority, as opposed to individuals who serve as instruments of an external command or authority. Agency that is initiated from within the individual and involves individual responsibility thus differs from agency that involves instrumentality or conformity to external authorities. This more individualized agency is what people have in mind when they speak of "free and autonomous agents," "agents of one's destiny," etc.[47]

Contemporary philosophical discourses on action theory define agency in terms of action, and "human agency" as a particular form of action, involvement, or power of involvement in the world. These discourses define agency in fundamental, basic ways; for example, in terms of causation and change, "agents are treated as causes—that is, as initiators of change in the world," and in terms of a power "to initiate action."[48] As causes and initiators of change, agents can act in either passive or active ways, as an agent for another or as an agent of one's own authority.[49] Much of contemporary action theory, however, does not use the term "human agency" to designate passive forms of agency. Concerned primarily with issues of human volition and the role of the will in action, debates mostly revolve around distinguishing "human agency" from passive action of all sorts, whether caused by inanimate objects or passive human beings.[50]

In this study, however, I include both forms of passive and active agencies under the general rubric of agency.[51] I distinguish between the two forms by referring to "conforming agents" as passive agents on the one hand, and "individual agents" as leading, active, or self-determining agents on the other. My primary consideration for distinguishing between these types of agency is the extent to which powers and authorities that motivate behavior are designated as internal or external to the self. Thus, for example, the conforming agent is a person who is authorized by an external source to perform an act and who carries out such an authorization. The individual agent, on the other hand, serves as a source of authority for himself or herself. He or she is autonomous in some matter and relies on his or her own judgment, initiative, and, sometimes, power as a source of authorization for action.

My use of agency in this book thus not only highlights the most primary sense of "agent" as a subject that acts. It underscores the sources of authority and loci of control for an individual's actions—or, in other words, it focuses on the motivations for and influences upon an agent's actions. According to this usage, an agent does not merely act; he or she obtains the authority and sometimes even the power to act either from within or without the individual. So whereas contemporary action theory aims to define the nature of human volition, I follow the cues of ancient Chinese thinkers and aim to identify how sources of authority and power work through and from within agents.[52]

The two heuristic modes of the conforming agent and the individual agent help elucidate early Chinese discourses on the self because they help to clarify boundaries of authority and power, as well as how each functions in relationship to individuals. Conformity points to the mediation of an authority outside the individual, and thus it points to the individual as an *instrument or medium* of a higher authority. Individual agency, on the other hand, points to the initiation or creation of authority within the self, and thus it points to the individual as an important *source* of authority. However, because these two modes do not distinguish between ultimate and proximate sources of authority, it is entirely possible for an individual to act in an ultimately conformist manner even though he or she represents the proximate source of authority over such action. As we will see in the following chapters, many thinkers analyzed in this book at once promote ideals for what might be dubbed "self-determining conformism," or even "conforming self-determination" precisely because they supported a type of individual agency as defined within an overarching framework of conformism to the cosmos.

I use the term "individualism" in this book because certain early Chinese views on the sources of human agency can justifiably be linked with key beliefs generally associated with individualism in some Western traditions. Such Western beliefs include the dignity, freedom, authority, and autonomy of the self or individual. Of these beliefs, the notion of autonomy perhaps reigns supreme as a distinguishing aspect of individualism. In contemporary parlance, for example, autonomy is defined against the notion of conformity, and the two describe a subject's existence either *apart from* (autonomy) or *as a part of* (conformity) a given whole. In this book, I juxtapose conformity with individualism, and do not pit "autonomy" and "conformity" against each other.[53] Rather, I present conformity as an integral part of the early Chinese understanding of what it means to be a fulfilled, empowered, and authoritative individual—autonomous in a different sense. This differs significantly from some current conceptions of conformity and individualism, and it signifies a crucial distinction between certain reigning types of individualisms in contemporary Western cultures and those that pervade the history of Chinese culture.

Typically, conformity implies a lack of individual authority over choice and action. It connotes a lack of uniqueness and a lack of distinctiveness, creativity, and free will, therefore also implying a lack of an individualistic spirit. The conforming agent does not have a strong identity or sense of self-determination, insofar as she or he "forms with," or *con-forms* to what is dictated or already formed beyond or outside the self. Because of the agent's perceived lack of initiative and will, he or she appears to be hollow, or devoid of the necessary spirit for self-determination and creativity. Moreover, such a person is not viewed as a free actor who makes autonomous decisions and behaves according to the unique predispositions of the self.

On the other hand, autonomy is frequently associated with an active agency of the self that initiates change. Autonomous agency represents a cornerstone of contemporary American views on freedom and choice. It is described in terms of individuality, or one's possession of such things as a unique identity, creativity, the personal agency to make decisions, and a free will. Indeed, it points toward many brands of American individualism, since autonomous agents determine their own fate to every extent possible. And, though one might question the soundness of such a belief, the autonomous agent in many discursive models is free from certain external influences.[54] This can be seen in the fact that various individualisms of today generally recast the individual as someone with the potential to be separate and different from one's environment and conventional norms. They empower individuals by emphasizing their ability to make decisions and judgments apart from mundane influences and norms in the world.

Early Chinese forms of individualism do not generally focus on the radical autonomy of the individual, but rather on the holistic integration of the empowered individual with forces and authorities in his or her surroundings (family, society, and cosmos). For early Chinese thinkers, there is no such thing as unfettered autonomy or freedom of will, in line with Kantian notions of the self.[55] While such concepts are considered problematic even in some Western traditions, they nonetheless constitute a core strand of thought that continues to inform contemporary concepts of individualism.[56] In contrast to such a conceptualization, there exists a relative and relational sort of autonomy in early Chinese contexts, a type of autonomy that grants individuals the freedom to make decisions for themselves and to shape the course of their own lives to the fullest degree that they can and should—all from within a complicated and rich system of interrelationships.[57] This type of autonomy, in other words, grants authority to the individual to fulfill his or her potential as an "integrated individual." The goal of such an individual is to achieve authoritativeness as a person while at the same time conforming to certain types of authority stemming from his or her larger environment.[58]

To the extent that these early Chinese views of the empowered and authoritative individual carve out a special space for a person's own autonomy and choice, they should be understood as sharing in some of the most basic ingredients that also make up individualisms in the Western world. Yet the emphasis in the Chinese tradition on the relative autonomy of an individual from within a system of holistic and interconnected processes is quite different from many of the models with which we are most familiar. Rather than view autonomy in relationship to a void (individuals as *ex nihilo*), individuals emerge authoritative and powerful as part and parcel of an interconnected web of forces. Therefore, a crucial back-and-forth tug between the self and the various influences and authorities surrounding it is woven into the very fabric of what it means to be a fully attained and empowered individual.[59]

The Self as Individual

The concept of the self in Chinese history, like that in other cultures, has always been changing and context-dependent. However, a few fundamental differences between the general orientation toward the self in China and that in many contemporary Western circles are worth mentioning.[60] There are two main terms that might be glossed as "self" in Warring States China: *shen* 身, referring to one's person, body, or self; and *ji* 己, referring to the self in a reflexive and emphatic manner as well as to one's actual person.[61] The latter term is straightforward in that it often reflexively points to the self. Otherwise, *ji* does not denote much more than the person who is speaking, or "person" in a simple sense of the individual human being. On the other hand, the former term, *shen*, reveals a critical difference between early Chinese and our own views. This is because the term *shen* connotes the psychophysical aspects of the self as well as certain aspects of personhood. As the body and its attributes are very much a part of what it means to be a person or *shen*, the term tends to refer to a particular, embodied, and experiential entity. This means that other early Chinese concepts, such as *qi* (material force 氣) and the various constituents of a person—one's nature (*xing* 性), psychology (*xin* 心, *qing* 情), spirituality (*shen* 神), and body (*shen* 身, *xing* 形)—are all part of the complicated mixture of "self" that emerges in early China. Of such aspects of the self, this book will focus on the emergence of debates about human nature (*xing* 性) in particular to mark an "individualistic turn" in Chinese intellectual history.

Introduction

Western dualistic thinking of the past few centuries, which came to dominate philosophical and scientific circles since Descartes' time, has traditionally conceived of a self that is disassociated from its psycho-physiological aspects by positing a sharp dichotomy between the mind and body.[62] According to such a tradition, the self was conceptualized in terms of essences or essential characteristics—like that of the "ghost in the machine"—rather than embodied experiences.[63] Such a notion is deeply entangled in the intellectual history of European thought as it was influenced by ancient Greece and Judeo-Christian traditions. These traditions emphasize the existence of absolute truth and essential natures as largely separate, distant, or hidden from the common, everyday experiences of human beings. Such an idea is also expressed very prominently in famous proclamations such as Descartes' "I think, therefore I am," which strips the self down to its most mental, essential, and disembodied nature.[64] Commonplace ideas such as getting to know one's "true self," or taking time to nourish the true needs of the self, all support this notion that the self is an entity that is fundamentally hidden, mental, and estranged from everyday experience and the appearances of everyday life.

Certainly, there were countermovements within the Western tradition, such as the thought of natural philosophers and scientists, who argued vehemently against the prudence of such dualistic thinking.[65] But in the past few centuries, these movements have been in the minority. Only in the last twenty to thirty years has there been a notable rise in philosophical discussions aimed at combating dualistic thinking by joining philosophical inquiry with certain perceived advances in scientific fields such as evolutionary biology, psychology, and neurology.[66] For this reason, and because I believe that Descartes' legacy still reigns in much of contemporary, popular conceptions of the self, I use the disembodied self as a foil which might best highlight differences apparent in the intellectual cultures of ancient China.

Free from such a radical dichotomy between truth/essence and appearance, the early Chinese self is not encumbered by a gross split between mind and body, or between "true" nature and experience. Rather, the early Chinese self is more akin to an organism, which both consists in and emerges out of complex processes occurring inside and outside of it, as it interacts with and relates to his or her environment. In such a way, the concept of the self and person is much more integrated than in certain dualistic Western traditions, as it stands in constant and ever-changing relationship to what occurs both within and without.

To the extent that the self is conceived as more physical, embodied, and dynamic than in dualistic Western thought, the early Chinese self necessarily entails a different definition of the "individual." While there is no clear term in early Chinese that might translate consistently into "individual," such a term facilitates discussion of those aspects of the self that emphasize its particularity within a whole. I therefore use the term "individual" to refer to early Chinese notions of self that concern not so much the subjective, psychological sense of self, but the particular qualities of a person that mark him or her as a single entity capable of exerting agency from within a web of human, social, and cosmic relationships. In other words, I refer to the individual not as an atomistic, isolated, and undifferentiated part of a whole, but as a distinct organism that must serve particular functions and fulfill a unique set of relationships in the worlds of which he or she is a part.[67] The "individual" is thus a unique participant in a larger whole—both integral to the processes that define the whole as well as to the change and transformation that stems from itself and its environment.

CHAPTER ONE

Individual Agency and Universal, Centralized Authority in Early Mohist Writings

In searching for the roots of individualism, we begin with an unlikely source: the writings of the early Mohists. Unlike the Confucian *Analects*—a rough contemporary of the early Mohist writings—which focuses deeply on the cultivation of individual moral autonomy, early Mohist writings underscore the importance of an individual's conformism to Heaven's will.[1] This appears to be a far cry from any notion of individualism with which we might be familiar. Certainly, conformism per se is not equal to individualism. This does not mean that the two must be unrelated or that one cannot serve as the fertile ideological soil for the growth of the other. As this book will demonstrate, conformist ideologies are tightly linked to nascent forms of individualism in early China. To better understand this link, we begin our study with an examination of the ideal of "upward conformity" (*shang tong* 上同) in early Mohist thought.

Even a casual reader of the early Mohist writings will notice that they deviated from the bulk of other contemporary writings by not emphasizing the process of individual self-cultivation.[2] It is not necessarily the case, however, that the early Mohists did not support self-improvement in their writings or that they did not implicitly promote an ideal relating to individual perfectibility. In fact, the early Mohists avidly stood by the notion that the individual is a powerful agent who, by striving in a particular manner to fulfill his or her ultimate responsibilities toward Heaven, might take positive, moral control over the shape and direction of his or her life. Intriguingly, however, the early Mohists promoted such a philosophy on individual agency at the same time as they invoked a strong rhetoric for conformity to authority—in particular, the authority of one's leaders and Heaven above. The apparently contradictory relationship between the early Mohists' concept of upward conformity and their injunctions for individual control and responsibility render their message on human agency subtle and complicated, perhaps even more so than writings for which self-cultivation is an explicit concern.

In what follows, I examine the early Mohist rhetoric on upward conformity to ascertain their views on the limits and parameters of individual agency and autonomous decision-making powers.[3] By exploring what underlies this rhetoric—rooted so deeply in a religious belief about the nature of Heaven's interactions with man—I show how such rhetoric goes hand in hand with encompassing views on individual self-determination and meritocratic government policies. Most relevant for the developments outlined in this book, the rhetoric of upward conformity advocates universal and uniform allegiance to a single higher power—mediated through a political hierarchy. This differs from the views expressed in the Ru (Confucian) circles of the day, which, while ultimately extolling the Dao and Heaven's authority, also allocated a considerable amount of power to cultural forms and moral persons both inside and outside of government service.

The Universal Authority of Heaven and Its Compensatory Powers

Upward conformity as a behavioral ideal is implied throughout the early Mohist corpus and is discussed explicitly in three chapters, each titled "Upward Conformity" 上同 (Upper, Central, Lower).[4] In these chapters, authors outline their program of upward conformity through two types of arguments. On the one hand, they speak of social problems arising from the presence of many diverse judgments (yi 義), or claims on what is right or wrong. Hence, they address the problem of disparate authorities.[5] On the other hand, they discuss solutions to these problems through legalistic and meritocratic measures ensured through upward conformity. However, the main significance of upward conformity revealed in these chapters and, indeed, throughout the early Mohist corpus lies in its imperative for all human action to be based ultimately in one authority—that of Heaven—and only proximately in the people and institutions that support it. Thus the early Mohist ideal of upward conformity is inextricably linked to the early Mohist religious injunction for Heaven's ultimate and exclusive authority in the human realm.[6] Given this idealized role of Heaven, how exactly does Heaven interact with humans such that individuals might conform to its will? And what does such an interaction imply about human agency and responsibility?

For the early Mohists, Heaven is the ultimate source of good, correct, and idealized authority in the world.[7] This authority, not in the least derivative of the human realm, is accompanied by certain powers that Heaven enjoys over both the public and private lives of individuals. On the one hand, Heaven grants life, wealth, and social order; on the other, it sends down death, poverty, and social disorder:

> So, how is it I know that Heaven desires what is just and abhors what is unjust? I say it is because when there is justice, all under Heaven has life; without justice they die. With justice there is wealth; without justice there is poverty. With justice there is order; without justice there is disorder. Therefore, Heaven desires that things live and abhors that they die, desires that they are wealthy and abhors that they are poor, desires their order and hates their disorder. This is how I know that Heaven desires what is just and abhors what is unjust.[8]

Here Heaven is presented as an anthropomorphized entity with desires and strong emotions (such as abhorrence), as well as a capacity to judge and respond to the actions of humans in the world. Such desires and emotions—referred to in the text as "Heaven's will" (*tian zhi* 天志)—hold ethical status and are made manifest to humans through signs of life, wealth, and order. It is through these outward signs that humans can come to know the standards of Heavenly justice (*yi* 義) represented by its will.

The reader should note that in the early Mohist text, Heaven is not the only supernatural power that responds to human actions. Ghosts and spirits (*gui shen* 鬼神) are efficacious (*ming* 明) deities who serve as agents of Heaven's will in the world. While I would like to focus here on Heaven as the ultimate source of justice and morality in the world, it is important to acknowledge that the early Mohists viewed the actions of ghosts and spirits to be in complete agreement with the will of Heaven.[9] Unlike in the *Analects*, where it is shown that bad things sometimes happen to good people and vice versa, and unlike in the newly published bamboo text titled "Ghosts and Spirits," where the author claims that "ghosts and spirits are efficacious in some areas and not efficacious in others," the early Mohists always view divine response as justified according to a system of what is morally right or wrong.[10]

In two of the chapters titled "Upward Conformity," early Mohist authors elucidate the consequences of what happens when humans conform upward but not all the way up to the authority of Heaven: "When the people of the world all conform upward to the Son of Heaven but do not conform upward to Heaven, then disaster will strike and seem never to depart. Nowadays, when harsh winds and bitter rains arrive in torrents, this is due to Heaven's punishing all the people who do not conform upward to Heaven."[11] Hence the ideal of upward conformity is based on the single authority of Heaven and its judgments on right and wrong, good and bad. Since going against this ideal will result in direct punishment from Heaven in the form of natural calamities, it is fair to say that Heaven holds direct, universal, and centralized power over all individuals.

These passages shed light on the fact that the authority of Heaven's justice is all-encompassing and inevitable, insofar as individuals and humans can never really escape from the punishments or rewards that Heaven metes out in accordance with individual action—or even the collective actions of society. But while its authority is such, Heaven's power, or its ability to respond to humans, is actually limited in certain ways. It cannot directly affect what happens in the world, or for that matter, absolutely dictate a course of individual action before it occurs. This power of Heaven is what I call "compensatory power." It is a power solely based on its positive or negative (punitive or encouraging) responses to human action. Because Heaven can only assert its moral desires indirectly by signaling to humans what they themselves should change or uphold, the fulfillment of Heaven's will is actually wholly dependent on individual determination in the world. In this sense, Heaven serves as the ultimate judge and authority over humankind, yet the underlying responsibility for insuring good order in the world lies firmly in the human realm.

Individual Determination of Destiny

The importance of Heaven's retroactive and responsive power in the human world cannot be overlooked, for it provides the basis for Mohist conceptions of individual agency in relationship to Heaven's power of control. This is highlighted for us in the early Mohist chapters "Against [the Concept of Heaven's] Command, 35–37." Sometimes translated as "fate" or "destiny" in the context of Mohist writings, *ming* 命 represents the command (or mandate) of Heaven that pre-ordains and dictates the lives of individuals.[12] For the early Mohists, the concept of *ming* represents an erroneous belief advocated by contemporary Ru rivals. According to their interpretation of Ru belief in *ming*, humans have no power to deny or counteract this all-encompassing Heavenly force.[13] This creates a particularly dangerous situation, early Mohists claim, for if one lacks a sense of agency to change one's fate and shape one's destiny, what incentive would there be for individuals to take control over and change their behavior for the better?

Individual Agency and Universal Authority

It is clear from the text that the issue of individual control constitutes the authors' main concern regarding the concept of *ming*. They claim, "Among the punishments of the former kings, were there ever any that said: 'One may neither request good fortune nor evade disaster; reverence will do you no benefit, and violence will not harm you'?"[14] The rhetorical question begs the reader to answer "no" and to conclude that even the ancient statutes are formulated to encourage individuals to take control of their lives in the hopes of improving them. Thus, to the early Mohists, the concept of *ming* is potently perverse because it obviates the necessity for an individual's claims on agency in the world.[15]

The early Mohists reject *ming* because it negates their religious belief that Heaven hands out incentives and warnings for individuals to improve themselves and change the world for the better. From within this immanent system of divine justice, each individual can choose to act in accordance to Heaven's will or not. The choice to act morally constitutes one's compliance, or conformity, with Heaven's system of justice, but it is a choice that nonetheless lies in the individual's hands.[16] Thus, at this minimal level of choosing whether or not to abide by Heavenly justice, early Mohists underscore the power of individuals to determine their own moral destinies.[17]

As mentioned above, the Heaven of the early Mohists does not command that individuals behave in any particular way. As compensator rather than commander, Heaven distributes punishment and reward according to the actions that individuals themselves decide to take. It does not stipulate beforehand how every individual will act, but sends down punitive and encouraging suggestions as to how they should act. Heaven thus holds individuals accountable for the choices they make.[18] In contrast to the early Mohist representation of *ming*, Heaven allows for human agency by motivating individuals to take control of their own futures according to an immanent, divine, and moral system of rewards and punishments.

Underlying the basic autonomous agency of every individual to decide on a course of action, therefore, is the fact that he or she will either be duly punished for choosing to go against Heaven's will, or will be rewarded for going along with it. In this sense, an individual's choice to conform upward to Heaven constitutes at once the fulfillment of an incentive and the avoidance of Heaven's wrath. Such a choice appeals to an individual's desire for self-preservation and flourishing; at the same time, it appeals to his or her desire to comply with a sacred ideal and fulfill a responsibility or obligation. While these are certainly compelling reasons for one to choose conformity over any other course of action, upward conformity still constitutes a choice. It provides the individual with a means to control his or her future. In contrast, the concept of *ming*, as depicted by the early Mohists, merely dictates how things must and will be for an individual, thereby denying individual choice and control in life.

Personal *Yi* vs. Heaven's *Yi*: Are Individuals Capable of Correct Self-Determination?

In the beginning of the three "Upward Conformity" chapters, early Mohist authors refer to an original state of dysfunctional sociability among humans in which each person stakes out his or her claim on *yi*, or "moral rectitude" (also translated here as "justice"), which happens to differ from the next. The resulting situation is one in which nobody agrees with anybody else and nobody possesses authority over another, regardless of who might be right or wrong. From this original condition of man to possess his or her own personal sense of *yi*, social chaos ensues, and people soon realize that they must agree to conform to a single authority to ensure social order among humans.[19] Do such passages not suggest that individuals, while they ultimately can take possession of their own beliefs and actions, are inherently incapable of deriving a correct view of morality on their own? If so, would this not contradict claims about individual autonomy outlined in this chapter?

Though there is much that is unstated in the early Mohist writings, it is clear that the capability of certain individuals to derive the correct view of morality (i.e., Heaven's *Yi*) is not only possible but imperative for the proper functioning of upward conformity in society.[20] I emphasize here that deriving the correct view of morality is only achieved by *certain individuals*, because, as we will see below, though the people *en masse* might be able to generally apprehend and decide what is right or wrong and who is worthy or not, each of them individually will not necessarily succeed at deriving the correct view on his or her own.[21] This is because the process of arriving at an understanding of Heaven's *Yi*, which in early Mohist thought corresponds to the only correct system of morality, is complicated and requires much concerted effort. Indeed, the condition of original chaos mentioned above suggests that without the proper environmental incentive—namely, worthies and figures of moral authority who might lead from the top of society—very few individuals will expend the effort to arrive at the correct view of morality. The problem, then, is not that individuals do not possess their own autonomy, for everyone can make decisions and judgments of some sort on their own. Rather, it is that in the absence of guidance from moral leaders, not every individual is either willing to or capable of *successfully* arriving at Heaven's moral *Yi*.

In conclusion, though individuals are autonomous agents capable of self-determination, the degree to which they might successfully apprehend Heaven's moral *Yi* differs from individual to individual and, in some instances, is largely dependent on incentives and guidelines that derive from external authorities.[22] This suggests that while only a few individuals are morally autonomous in an ultimate sense (in the sense of their having the ability to arrive at the correct view *ex nihilo,* or utterly on their own), the majority of humans are morally autonomous in an interdependent, or proximate sense.[23] That is to say, most individuals must rely on external authorities of some kind to perfect their autonomous choices about morality.[24]

This leads us to the question of moral motivation. The early Mohists do not provide an explicit account of human nature, and their vision of the sources of morality within individuals is difficult to ascertain from the text.[25] As Zhang Qianfang asserts:

> [T]he source of morality for Mohism seems to lie entirely outside the individual person. A person wants to be good not for the sake of the good itself, but apparently for the hope to reap benefits from acting in accordance with the will of heaven and for the fear of suffering from punishments if he acts to the contrary. At bottom, human beings are selfish and appear to love others only for their own interests. This understanding, derived naturally from Mohism, fails to recognize any dignity inherent in a human being, and is inconsistent with the Mohist teaching that a person is to respect himself and others as ends, not merely as means of his material feeling of pleasures and pains. Thus, although Mozi has formulated a clear overarching principle, which he seeks to apply persistently to practical situations, the Mohist principle seems to lack a solid theoretical foundation.[26]

While I would agree with Zhang that the ultimate source of authority lies outside the individual in Heaven's will, I do not agree that the early Mohists view all individuals as lacking in moral motivation. Certainly, they present carrot-and-stick incentives as powerful tools that shape individual motivations and desires. But, as we will see in sections to come, they also imply that the masses desire true moral leadership based on the principles of Heaven's will. By suggesting that people naturally yearn for a moral Son of Heaven, I believe the early Mohists provide a basis—though indeed not a solid one—for attributing some degree of moral motivation to people themselves.

Deciphering Heaven's Laws: The Role of the "Achieved Man"

There is an even more significant way certain individuals determine the course of their lives than by a mere choice to conform or not to Heaven's will. Because Heaven can prescribe moral behavior for humans only through its compensatory operations, individuals must find a means of interpreting its signs and signals so as to ascertain its ultimate will. They must find a method of attaining knowledge and insight into Heaven that is consistent with its system of punishment and reward in the world. Thus, in early Mohist thought, individuals decide not just whether to comply with Heaven's standards. They also must figure out what such standards are and how one might derive a reliable method for knowing them. The threefold process whereby individuals decide to conform to Heaven's will, find a method of learning about Heavenly morality, and conform to such morality by translating knowledge into action is implied throughout early Mohist writings. Such a process attests to the early Mohist belief in the individual as a thoroughly autonomous agent in both personal and social change.

How do individuals come to understand Heaven's will? Throughout their early chapters, Mohists speak of justice (*yi*) and moral standards (or laws, *fa* 法), both of which ultimately derive authority from Heaven. Justice refers to a more abstract, normative system that humans might apprehend through their study of Heaven's will. The text claims, "Heaven desires justice and despises injustice" and "orders the people of the world to follow the tenets of justice in carrying out affairs."[27] Therefore, Heaven directly sanctions justice in the world. Laws, on the other hand, refer to standard moral injunctions based on justice. As a standard for Heaven's will, laws can be likened to religious tools that are necessary in constructing a blueprint for moral behavior. This is seen in the analogy early Mohists invoke that compares laws to the compass and square, employed by artisans to construct their wares.[28] Like the concrete objects measured and created by circles and squares, laws—as behavioral blueprints—help measure and define moral actions according to Heaven's will. In this way, laws help humans articulate divine justice in the world.

Since Heaven does not communicate its will directly as commandments or positive pronouncements, humans must translate Heaven's compensatory actions into intelligible, prescriptive laws. The following quote demonstrates how Mozi deciphers Heaven's will from an examination of the ancient past:

Individual Agency and Universal Authority

> Mozi said, "Of the sage-kings of the ancient Three Dynasties period, Yu, Tang, Wen, and Wu all abided in Heaven's will and were rewarded for it. Of the violent kings of the ancient Three Dynasties period, Jie, Zhou, You, and Li all went against Heaven's will and were punished for it."[29]

By learning from the positive examples of the good sage-kings and the negative examples of the bad, Mozi deciphers moral precepts through the study and evaluation of history. He correlates events and actions in the human realm with Heaven's systematic, intelligible, and ultimately just responses to them. Hence, his claim: "How do we know that justice means 'that which is correct'? Because when there is justice in the world, then the world is in order, but when there is no justice in the world, then it is in disorder."[30] Here we see that the degree of orderliness in the world serves as both a proof of and measure for Heaven's will and its delineations of justice. But such justice can only be ascertained through a thorough evaluation of real-world events.

Not only do levels of chaos and orderliness serve as a measure for Heaven's will. The early Mohists support the verification of language and, in particular, propositional statements by endorsing a close scrutiny of events and actions and their efficacy in the world:

> Mozi said: " . . . it is necessary to establish criteria.[31] If one's statements are [spoken] without criteria, then . . . one cannot obtain clarity of knowledge in distinguishing between right and wrong, benefit and harm. For this reason it is necessary to test one's words against the three proofs." What do we mean by the "three proofs"?
>
> Mozi has said: "[One's statements must] have a basis, [they must] be derivable [in the present], and [they must] have application. Upon what should one base them? With regards to the highest level of the ruler, one bases them on the affairs of the ancient sage-kings. From what should one derive them? With regards to the lower levels of society, one derives them by analyzing what the people perceive through their eyes and ears. Upon what does one judge applicability? When one puts [one's statements] into practice in administration, one observes whether they strike upon benefit for the state, households, hundred surnames, and people. This is what we mean by saying that there are three proofs for one's statements."[32]

This passage lists the tools an individual may use to uncover the correct "language" of Heaven's will—or the truth and falsity of propositions about it. Historical precedent, raw human perception, and worldly efficacy serve as measures by which all propositions are deemed true or false. Thus, by cross-referencing propositions with a battery of external documentation about reality, the early Mohist translator of Heaven's will can evaluate statements of truth to discern which ones correspond accurately with the true language of divine justice.

The fact that there is a correct method for testing statements demonstrates that tools exist for uncovering the true language of Heaven's will. Though Mozi's criteria for testing the veracity of statements, such as "the affairs of the ancient sage-kings" and "what the people perceive through their eyes and ears," seem to us like loose standards that leave much room for interpretation, in the world of early Mohist hermeneutical sensibilities, there seems to have been little reason to doubt the correlation between such standards and truth. At the very least, early Mohists felt justified in asserting the legitimacy of the correlation. This all demonstrates that Heaven's will is ultimately knowable, but that it is up to individuals to create reliable methods for apprehending it. Thus early Mohists express a kind of "rational positivism" that attests to their underlying belief in the fundamental agency of individuals to decipher Heaven's will.

As the passage above suggests, early Mohist self-cultivation is not only a matter of "obtaining" (*de* 得) standards for determining the veracity of statements (i.e., the conformity of statements with Heaven's will).[33] It is also a matter of putting these standards of inquiry to use in the world. By speaking in one breath about both the possession and use of "tools" that reveal Heaven's will, Mozi shows that one and the same person can obtain and apply Heaven's standards (*fa*) in the world:

> My possession of the will of Heaven is like a wheelwright's possession of the compass or a carpenter's possession of the square. The wheelwright and the carpenter take hold of their compass and square to measure what is round or square in the world. They say: "That which fits these measurements is right; that which does not fit them is wrong." Now the books of the gentlemen of the world are too numerous to be listed, and their sayings too many to be examined in full. Among the highest circles the gentlemen lecture to the feudal lords, and in lower circles they expound to men of honor. And yet on matters of humaneness and justness they are far apart. How do I know this? Because I *obtain* the clear standards of the world to measure them [the moral validity of each person's claims] [italics mine].[34]

The "possession of the will of Heaven," here a cognitive possession, is likened to the possession of a measuring device. The processes of obtaining and applying standards appear as a function of one's cognition, since one and the same individual—Mozi—both obtains "the clear standards of the world" and uses them to "measure" the validity of what others say. Through this cognitive means of obtaining Heaven's standards and subsequently implementing them to gauge the validity of what people say, Mozi mediates Heaven's authority in the world.

The above-mentioned criteria for evaluating the potential correspondence between human language and Heaven's will derive directly from Mozi's own rational and logical faculties, which he uses further "to obtain clarity of knowledge in distinguishing between right and wrong, benefit and harm."[35] Like the person who establishes the compass or carpenter's square as standards for judging the trueness of circles and squares, Mozi uses his knowledge to create a device or methodology that tries to objectify the process of deciphering Heavenly standards.[36] In other words, Mozi's method provides a consistent blueprint for obtaining knowledge about Heaven's will such that individuals need not merely rely on their own subjective judgments. He establishes laws, or positive norms for human behavior derived from Heaven's will, so that others who do not possess his insights into morality can still reap benefits from them.[37]

Though methods of individual self-cultivation are not a central or explicit concern for the early Mohists, they do on occasion speak of the "achieved man" (*xian zhe* 賢者) as an ideal.[38] Interestingly, both wisdom and nobility of character are critical traits presumed to be present in such an individual, so that the early Mohist goals for individual authority are as fundamentally intellectual as they are moral: "How do we know that elevating the achieved is the foundation of government? Because when the noble and wise rule over the humble and stupid, then there will be order."[39] Unlike the *junzi* ideal of the Ru, which mostly aims at impeccable moral aptitude, feeling, character, behavior, and understanding, the achieved man of the early Mohists aims at obtaining correct knowledge about Heaven's truth. Like Mozi himself, such an individual is achieved primarily because of his knowledge of universal laws of justice and his will to do right—in conformity with Heaven—not because of his understanding of ritual truth, moral empathy, and judgments of individual character.

The two individual ideals of wisdom and nobility support the early Mohists' descriptions of an anthropomorphized Heaven. Consider the following example, in which justice, as the standard of good government, is transmitted by a "noble and wise" Heaven:

> Mozi said: "Justice does not emerge from the stupid and base; it must emerge from the noble and wise. How do I know that justice does not emerge from the stupid and base and that it must emerge from the noble and wise? I say: Justice is [the basis of] good government. . . . Now, the stupid and base cannot rule the noble and wise. There must first be the noble and wise, in order that they may then rule the stupid and base. . . . Then who is noble and who is wise? Heaven is noble and wise. Therefore justice in fact emerges from Heaven.[40]

A noble and wise Heaven passes on its characteristics to noble and wise leaders. Thus, the early Mohist idealized individual cultivates himself by achieving the likeness of his highest deity: an intelligent and good Heaven. This comparison of individuals to Heaven is especially appropriate given the imperative of human conformity to Heaven's standards, and it attests to the early Mohists' religious desire that individuals achieve the likeness of Heaven in both form and action.

As demonstrated above, the early Mohists strongly support the acquisition of knowledge (in particular, "Mohist" knowledge) as the means by which an achieved individual accesses and decides on Heaven's standards in society. To them, such decision making constitutes the accurate transcription of objective, divine standards—standards that are to be obeyed by everyone regardless of one's social background.[41] The achieved individual's active decision making, therefore, provides him and others around him with a means of fulfilling the religious ideal of upward conformity to Heaven. Insofar as achieved men use their intellect to create tools that clarify Heaven's standards for others, they render Heaven's will universally accessible to the world.

Individuals such as Mozi use history, world events, and human perception to derive a method for deciphering and knowing Heaven's system of moral justice. Their method lies in the logical deduction of the nature of morality based on the compensatory signs of Heaven's will in the world. It urges one to use rational, cognitive processes to determine what is right or wrong, true or false—not to blindly follow the dictates of traditional authorities such as the Ru and their rites. Thus cognitive analysis and reasoning are key ingredients in early Mohist beliefs on human agency. They form the foundation for an individual's determination of what is right or wrong and how he or she should act. In effect, they give an individual the means to conform to Heaven above and take direct control over the future of society and one's person.

Though self-cultivation is not outlined in detail in early Mohist writings, it exists as a goal in which one strives to attain the dual traits of Heaven itself: wisdom and nobility. The individual who successfully cultivates his wisdom and nobility is able to decipher Heaven's standards for himself and others while conforming upward to them. Wise men such as the ancient sages and Mozi (and thus, presumably, the men who follow him), might be said to have attained the requisite level of cultivation that allows them to serve as decision makers and leaders in history and society. Such men provide uncultivated people and those of lesser cognitive and moral achievements with a means of knowing and conforming to Heaven's authority. Therefore, one might say that achieved men attain the highest levels of individual agency and intellectual-moral autonomy in society.

Types of Upward Conformity: Rulers, Achieved Men, and Mindful Conformists

Early Mohists believe that all people can follow and conform to Heaven's standards. Everybody, from the Son of Heaven to the peasants below, is equally implicated in and has equal responsibility to fulfill the same standards of behavior.[42] But to what extent do the early Mohists view their highest goal—becoming an achieved man—as a universal ideal?

The three parallel chapters on "Elevating the Achieved" provide a strong claim that men of any social class might be considered achieved (*xian* 賢) and able (*neng* 能)—or morally and intellectually cultivated in the early Mohist sense.[43] For example, in ancient times, "Even though [one] might have been a farmer or a craftsman, if he had ability (*neng*) then he was promoted."[44] Ability, as either acquired or innate (the text does not directly distinguish between the two), is not the sole possession of any particular class of people.[45] In a similar passage, early Mohists claim, "[Word of this] reached the ministers of distant and outlying regions, princes in the court, the multitudes of the state, and the peasants of the four borders, who, upon hearing it, all competed to become righteous."[46] These quotes explicitly endorse open competition in ability or moral rectitude among people of most every context and background. They show how the early Mohists promoted equal access to the ideal of bettering the self in accordance with Heaven's will.[47]

Despite their ideal of equal access, early Mohists stipulate—through the notion of a meritocracy—that only a very few men will actually succeed in becoming morally achieved enough to be employed at the highest levels in government.[48] So while early Mohist formulations on self-cultivation strongly support social mobility, the underlying concept of a meritocracy at the same time justifies maintaining a fixed hierarchy in which only a few moral agents, albeit the best ones, reign supreme. This poses a problem with respect to the dictates of upward conformity, which admonish political inferiors to conform to their political superiors. If a person does not rise in the political hierarchy due to lack of moral achievement, to what extent does the notion of upward conformity allow him or her to act as an autonomous agent in his or her development and expression of morality? How is it possible both to maintain one's moral autonomy and conform to one's political superior at the same time?

In the following sections, we examine three different types of upward conformity as integral to the early Mohist politico-religious vision of authority. The first type involves the ruler at the top of the human hierarchy and his idealized role as central mediator of Heaven's authority in the world. The second involves the role of achieved men—ministers and advisors—who, though lower on the political hierarchy than the ruler, nonetheless possess claims to moral authority by virtue of their elevated intellectual and moral status. And lastly, we will analyze the role of the "mindful conformists," or those people whose status in society dictates that they conform upward to political superiors. We will ask whether such conformists must relinquish or maintain their moral autonomy in the process of upward conformity.

The Ruler as Superior Mediator of Heavenly Authority

Early Mohists claim that Heaven's universal standards call for equal conformity and responsibility to dictates that are objective and detached from one's person and position of power. However, it is clear from their statements concerning wise and noble rulers and achieved ministers that some people have more of a claim to the acts of deciphering and issuing Heaven's standards than others, such as the "stupid and base." The rhetoric of universal conformity to Heavenly standards encourages the self-cultivation of any individual. At the same time, it combines with the notion of meritocracy ("advancing the worthy" 進賢) to legitimate authority that conforms to Heaven's will at the top of the political hierarchy. Indeed, we would not understand the full picture of what it means to conform upward if we were only to consider upward conformity as a religious ideal and not also as a concrete, political platform that supports meritocracy and a centralized hierarchy of authority.

The dual themes of the strong, righteous authority of leaders and the obedient conformity of followers permeate the "Upward Conformity" chapters of the early Mohist corpus.[49] Leaders who follow Heaven can serve the people by "arousing benefit and expelling harm"[50] and by "obtaining good people and rewarding them [for it] and obtaining violent people and

Individual Agency and Universal Authority

punishing them [for it]."[51] Special status is accorded to those at the top center who might make use of their intellectual, moral, and religious superiority to lead over and benefit others.[52] Achieved individuals, and especially the Son of Heaven, stand in a privileged position to dictate Heaven's standards to others:

> Furthermore, justice is defined through rulership.[53] It is not the case that one follows orders from below to govern those above; one must follow the orders from above to govern those below. For this reason the common man puts forth his utmost effort to obey in his tasks and never relies on himself to rule. For there are men of the *shi* class to rule over him. Men of the *shi* class put forth their utmost effort to obey in their tasks and never rely on themselves to rule, for there are ministers and high officials to rule over them. . . .[54] The Son of Heaven never relies on himself to rule, for Heaven rules over him. That the Son of Heaven rules over the Three High Ministers, dukes, men of the *shi* class, and common people is clearly known by all *shi* and gentlemen of the world. That Heaven rules over the Son of Heaven is not clearly known by the people of the world.[55]

Political hierarchy serves here as a means for the correct transmission or mediation of Heaven's authority in the world. So while all individuals are equal with regards to what they must ultimately obey (Heaven's standards), they are unequal in terms of with whom they must comply (their immediate superiors). In the end, most people conform to Heaven through the mediation of a human authority more immediately above them. Not all modes of conformity are equal.

The mediation of Heaven's will depends on the expression of human authority from within a political hierarchy. Beginning with an intelligent and noble Son of Heaven, Heaven's truths are communicated downwards, and only sometimes upwards (as we will discuss more below), through a chain of command in a structured hierarchy of control. For everyone except the Son of Heaven, Heaven's standards are ideally mediated through one's superior. The political structure thus serves as an effective roadway upon which the authority of Heaven's standards might travel.[56]

Understanding the way Heavenly authority is mediated in the early Mohist vision of society is important to our understanding of the extent to which authority was associated with individuals in different ways. Early Mohists support a meritocratic form of official appointment to mitigate the problem of political authority that lacks moral legitimacy.[57] In terms of individual authority, a meritocracy implies that those on top are actually the rightful heirs of positions of power and authority.[58] In the early Mohist view, the people on top are not merely those with powerful positions; they possess the most moral authority to know, make decisions about, and propagate Heaven's will:

> Why do we desire just men to be ruling in high [positions]? Because when just men rule on high, the world will be ordered, the Lord on High, the mountains and rivers, and the ghosts and spirits will have officials in charge [of worship], and the myriad people will enjoy great benefit.[59]

The top-heavy dynamic between just leaders and the people below decides the fate of society. Those in high positions, like the Son of Heaven, must serve not just as political leaders but as religious agents of Heaven as well. When such a system functions properly, a position at the top of the hierarchy legitimizes one's merit. The political hierarchy thus becomes an ideal vehicle for mediating Heaven's authority, as it is structured not merely according to politics and social background, but according to a hierarchy of moral goodness and attunement with Heaven's standards.[60]

The early Mohists appear to admit to at least one exception in their notion of meritocracy. The person who holds the most power according to the notion of upward conformity is the Son of Heaven (of the Zhou state). At the top of the human hierarchy, he is the primary moral exemplar whose leadership impinges on the lives of everyone else. Yet it appears that he, and perhaps the ducal lords of other states (rulers in their own rights), are exempt from being promoted or demoted on the basis of merit.[61] Note that in the passage above, the discussion revolves not around the Son of Heaven per se but around "just men" who are to rule in high positions. Instead, the early Mohists simply assert that Heaven rules over the Son of Heaven, and that it is his duty to conform upwards to its will.[62] Though in the text there is no evidence specifically for or against the meritocratic appointment of ducal lords, I will include them in my discussion here under the assumption that as ruler-like entities in their own states, the same logic might apply to them as to the Son of Heaven.

While some authors of the period debated the issue of "yielding the throne" to the best candidate rather than to the heir apparent, the early Mohists did not do so, for perhaps two related reasons.[63] First, if the Son of Heaven and other ducal lords were included in their projected audience, it might have been a matter of self-preservation not to speak about the moral and religious grounds for ousting people in such positions. In this case, early Mohists would have consciously avoided such topics out of political expediency or basic survival in and among the groups of people with whom they were conversing. Second, early Mohists might simply have believed that if policies of meritocratic appointment for the other, upper ranks of court positions were truly instituted, this would be sufficient to ameliorate situations in which the Son of Heaven or other ducal lords did not know about Heaven's will or embody its moral authority in their persons. In such a case, early Mohists would be banking on the idea that moral exemplars close to the ruler would somehow provide a check on the ruler's authority to ensure that Heaven's will prevails in the world. They would therefore not have needed to risk their own survival at court by broaching the topic of a ruler's merit.

The Son of Heaven's position, and that of heads of state in general, appear to be the only positions in the political hierarchy that are not appointed from above according to a system of meritocracy. While the early Mohists seem to project a certain confidence that the Son of Heaven will be ruled by Heaven, as stated in previous citations, it is more likely that such confidence is founded not in their confidence of rulers in general but in their confidence that the system they propose is sound and efficacious as a whole. After all, it is certainly not a coincidence that the early Mohists speak of upward conformity mostly in terms of one's conformity to Heaven or to the just men who surround the ruler at the top, and not singularly to the ducal lord or Son of Heaven. Indeed, there always appears to be someone (high ministers who understand Heaven) or something (Heaven) that prevents the leader at the top center from claiming absolute authority over the people.

So while the Son of Heaven and ducal lords seem to be exempt from meritocratic procedures of appointment and dismissal, they are not to be exempt from their responsibilities to conform upwards to the just laws of Heaven. Even though such men claim positions that are allotted the highest degree of authority and decision-making power in society, their powers to garner the upward conformity of others are contingent upon their ability to respect Heaven's will and actually abide by its authority rather than their own. In the next section, we delve further into the types of limitations constraining the Son of Heaven's authority by looking into the role of wise and noble ministers—or those to whom early Mohist meritocratic principles were to be applied.

The Authority to Advise: Achieved Ministers as Checks on a Ruler's Authority

Though in early Mohist thought everyone must decide whether or not he or she will conform upwards or cultivate himself or herself intellectually and morally, only achieved agents are rewarded positions in the politico-religious hierarchy (below the ruler, that is) and allowed to use their agency to decipher and dictate Heaven's standards for others. Therefore, the Son of Heaven and ducal lords are hardly the only people in the idealized, early Mohist state who should possess the moral authority of Heaven. The leading elite corps of men who support them exert unequal moral control over others despite everyone's fundamentally equal relationship to Heaven's authority.

That moral authority is to be possessed by many men at the top, and not just by the Son of Heaven or ruling figure, can be seen in the fact that the early Mohists view leadership in terms of many people working together as leaders:

> [Heaven desires] that among men those who have strength will work for others, those who understand the Way will teach others, and those who possess wealth will share it with others. It also desires that those above will diligently attend to matters of government, and those below will diligently carry out their tasks.[64]

Here the author shows the necessity of having many people above who will assume leadership roles in government that demand the obedience and conformity of others. He defines strong, centralized leadership broadly—in terms of the advisors who should surround a ruler as well.

By bestowing high rank and political authority upon achieved men, a meritocracy ensures that those who are not ducal lords or the Son of Heaven can join such leaders in the task of government. As the "philosopher kings" and ministers of society, these people at the top hold exclusive authority as the moral intelligentsia in society. But if the Son of Heaven is already "ruled by Heaven" and everybody conforms upward to his virtuous standards, what need is there for the achieved man? What function does the achieved man serve in the early Mohists' view on upward conformity?

In their chapter "Against the Ru," the early Mohists advocate not the mindless conformity of a minister to his lord, but the minister's mindful admonishment of the latter when he is wrong:

> Again the Ru say: "The superior man is like a bell. Strike it and it will sound; do not strike it and it will not sound." But we answer: The benevolent man exerts the utmost loyalty in serving his lord and attains the measure for filial piety in serving his parents. If [those whom he serves] achieve

goodness, he will praise them; but if they have any fault, he will admonish them. This is the way of a minister.[65]

This example shows us that there are cases in which rulers and lords govern correctly not necessarily because they themselves are inherently wise and noble and thus able to know the will of Heaven. Unachieved or fallible rulers can govern correctly by surrounding themselves with achieved men who are not only wise and noble, but who also exercise their moral and intellectual agency to praise and admonish their lords.[66]

While a single figure—that of the ruler—maintains the last decision on matters of government, it is the men surrounding him who can and should shape his decisions in important ways. Ministers and advisors might therefore serve as checks on a ruler's authority by offering sound advice and admonitions when necessary. In such a scenario, the mediation of Heaven's will especially lies in the power of achieved ministers to convey wisdom and morality to their rulers, who, because they are not chosen according to a meritocracy, will sometimes be fallible. Through appraisal of a ruler's actions and decisions, worthy ministers and advisors such as the early Mohists themselves might serve as the human backbone for ensuring that Heavenly standards are transmitted and implemented throughout a state.

In such a role, achieved men qua government officials serve as the ultimate arbiters of Heavenly authority in the realm. Though they do not lay claim to the highest positions in the land (reserved for the ducal lords or the Son of Heaven), they are legitimized through their knowledge of Heaven's will to make critical decisions about law, morality, and public policy that demand the upward conformity of others. And in cases where the ruler is not in tune with Heaven's will, such men admonish him so that he might once more serve as an authentic mediator of moral authority—not a false one. By keeping the ruler and his dictates and laws in line with Heaven, achieved men ensure that the system of upward conformity is unified and grounded in the one true authority of Heaven rather than in an arbitrary system of particularized, personal whims or inclinations. Such men might be said to possess the highest form of moral and intellectual autonomy, insofar as they are the ones who truly hold the key that unlocks Heaven's will in the world. As such, they hold the position of ultimate moral authority in society.

Mindful Conformists and the Authority to Sense Right from Wrong
To the early Mohists, a political hierarchy based on merit helps determine the correct, downward flow of authority and the degree of influence certain

individuals should have in the world. Dominant-subordinate relationships of power form the latticework in which their vision of justice might be transmitted from the moral intellectuals at the top to the "stupid and base" below. The different roles of ruler and minister on the one hand (as official leaders) and subject on the other constitute the two main types of agencies presented in the early Mohist model for the good society. Standing opposite all the men discussed above, whether the Son of Heaven, ducal lords, ministers, or advisors, are the conformists in society, who assume low positions (or no position at all) in the meritocratic hierarchy of government.

An important outcome of meritocratic appointment is that intelligence and moral worth are rewarded through the granting of ever-greater apportionments of political authority. By this means, religious and intellectual expertise is translated into political authority and expressed through the centralized hierarchy of the state. And if those who know better gain higher positions commensurate with their moral and intellectual capabilities, then those who do not know better remain below for a reason. It is precisely these latter people—those who do not fully have the moral or intellectual acumen to decipher Heaven's will and rise in a meritocratic society—who must conform to their political superiors. Whereas the achieved man conforms to Heaven's standards by making decisions about the rectitude of laws and actions, people who are not achieved conform to Heaven's standards primarily as they are filtered through the social hierarchy of command.

Such conformists are individuals who act correctly as the political sphere dictates. While ultimately responsible to Heaven's standards, they express such responsibility through their dutiful behavior toward political authorities who possess the immediate power to punish or reward them:

> Therefore the ancient sage-kings issued statutes and decrees, posting them as rewards and punishments to encourage achieved [behavior] and suppress violence. So men were filial and tender to their parents at home and fraternal and yielding [according to age] to the men of their local communities. Their actions of presiding and residing showed a sense of propriety, their behavior when at home or outside a sense of restraint, and their relations with the opposite sex a sense of the distinctions between them.[67]

Sage-kings serve here as agents of Heaven, issuing statutes and standards and positively governing society through a system of punishments and rewards not unlike the compensatory authority of Heaven itself. Conformists at lower levels of the political hierarchy obey the dictates of the sage-kings and serve loyally according to their public rank of contractual responsibility. Unlike the role of ministers, who might admonish those at the top when they are wrong, there is no hint that people at such lower levels could challenge higher authority, especially not when that authority is deemed to represent Heaven's authority in the world. But in conforming to their political superiors, are such people to relinquish their moral autonomy entirely?

Notably, the early Mohists do not advocate mindless conformity to what is dictated from above, not by any person in society, even the "stupid and base."[68] Instead, they suggest that people in base positions should be mindful that in a truly meritocratic society, they have not yet surpassed their superiors in their knowledge of morality and Heaven's will. Thus the early Mohists do not support completely passive conformity, but rather conformity in response to an individual's active evaluation of who might best understand what is right and wrong. Because relatively unattained individuals are to have a fairly good sense of what could conceivably be right in order for them to accept and condone the moral leadership of another over them, such individuals still need to hold on to their own power of judgment and self-determination. For this reason, it is perhaps more felicitous to refer to this group of actors as "mindful conformists" rather than "conformists."

The early Mohists advocate human participation at each level of society that is both in accordance with the standards of Heaven and the power dynamic stipulated by one's rightful position in the political hierarchy. In such a way, decision-making agents (mostly rulers, ministers, and their advisors) subjugate themselves to the standards of Heaven, yet they never cease to wield the authority of deciphering, using, and transmitting Heaven's will in accordance with their positions in society. Mindful conformists, on the other hand, pay heed to Heaven's authority while mindfully obeying laws and commands as they are mediated through their political superiors. What does this mean? While those at the top make important decisions about what is right and wrong, mindful conformists at the bottom judge, accept, and follow such decisions because and only because they apprehend them to be most probably right—or in accordance with Heaven's will. Note that in this claim, mindful conformists do not figure out for themselves what is right or wrong, but they must nonetheless use their own faculties to apprehend and evaluate whether or not they think their superior is correctly conveying Heaven's will.

This type of moral autonomy of the people below is apparent in certain passages of the text. Intriguingly, early Mohist authors suggest that people have a voice in endorsing or rejecting their leaders based on vague apperceptions of what is right or wrong. According to the author of chapter 13,

"Upward Conformity, Lower," leaders must rely on "securing the sentiments of those below" (得下之情) in order to bring about order in society.[69] But what does a phrase such as "securing the sentiments of those below" mean? Though the author is particularly unclear on this issue, he gives some clues:

> If he on top does not secure the sentiments of those below, then he will not understand [what/whom] the people deem good and [what/whom they] denounce. If he does not understand [what/whom] the people deem good and [what/whom they] denounce, then this means he will not reward good people and he will not punish violent people. By carrying out government that does not reward good people and punish the violent ones, one necessarily brings his state and its mass of people to disorder. Consequently, meting out rewards and punishments without securing the sentiments of those below is something one must carefully watch out for.[70]

The people possess firsthand knowledge of the ethical worth and deeds of those in their community. The leader should rely on the sentiments of "those below" to "understand [what/whom] the people deem good and [what/whom they] denounce."[71] Without such knowledge, the efficacy of laws (in terms of reward and punishment) is jeopardized.

Such a statement assumes that "those below" (*xia* 下), also referred to as the "people" (*min* 民), have the ability to make decisive, correct judgments concerning the ethical worth of the people surrounding them. Moreover, it claims that the people's sentiments should give knowledge of and serve as the basis for higher-level decisions concerning punishment and reward. Though the people do not make the final decision in such matters, their ethical input and feedback are critical to the actual correctness of the decision. Consider the following example: "If he does not understand [what/whom] the people deem good and [what/whom they] denounce, then this means he will not reward good people and he will not punish violent people."[72] In this scenario, the people are not passively conforming to decisions sent down from above; they help determine the justice of such decisions in the first place. In such a way, they too have a say, though limited, in deciding on men of moral and intellectual worth to be promoted in the meritocratic system. In other words, they are to have a voice in who should rule over them and serve as the recipient of their willing and mindful conformity.

Prevalent in the "Upward Conformity" chapters is the claim that in order for the system of reward and punishment to be efficacious, the people must willingly conform to it. Only vaguely hinted at, however (perhaps only in the central and lower chapters, chapters twelve and thirteen), is another subtle claim that follows upon this one: In order for the people to conform to such a system, they must be convinced that what their superiors demand is just and correct. This latter claim is suggested in an extended section in chapter thirteen that describes how law and authority properly function from the lower levels of family leadership to the leadership of the Son of Heaven. Those below the leader conform willingly to the orders of their leader and the system of laws he promulgates precisely because they agree that such laws are just and correct:

> The Son of Heaven also issues an order to the masses of the world that states, "If [you] see anybody who is cherishing and benefiting the world, as well as anybody who is despising and robbing the world, [you] must report them [to me]." If one sees someone who is cherishing and benefiting the world and reports them, and he appears to be somebody who cherishes and benefits the world, then the superior will lay hold of him and reward him, and the masses will praise him. If one sees someone who is despising and robbing the world and reports them, and he appears to be somebody who despises and robs the world, then the superior will lay hold of him and punish him, and the masses will denounce him. In this way everyone in the world will desire to obtain the reward and praise of their superiors and avoid their denouncement and punishment. . . . The world will necessarily be in order.[73]

In this lengthy section, laws are only effectively promulgated and carried out if the people below can agree on the soundness of the Son of Heaven's judgments. Thus the people are given the right to judge the correctness of the Son of Heaven's decisions, and only their agreement with his judgments brings about a state in which they desire to perpetuate law through conformity to it.

Such claims show us that the people, and not only the advisors and ministers in official positions, provide a means of checking the basis of their ruler's authority. They do so through their agreement or disagreement with his judgments, and hence their willingness or unwillingness to conform to him. Though the people do not have the compensatory power of Heaven to punish those who do not conform to its laws, through their participation in mindful conformity to their superiors, they effectively have a means of placing a check on the power of their leader by granting or denying his laws efficacy in the world. In such a light, upward conformity becomes an ideal by which subordinates willingly endorse only those leaders and superiors who properly maintain their moral responsibility to Heaven. It is thus an ideal for leaders and superiors to preserve as much as it is an ideal by which followers and inferiors should abide.

The following passage in chapter twelve outlines why and what happens when people are unwilling to conform to their superiors. It clarifies that an individual's willingness to conform is contingent upon the presence of just and good leadership:

> Nowadays, ducal lords and great men of power conduct their government in the opposite manner. They conduct government according to [modes of] flattery and ease; the elderly fathers and brothers of their direct lineage serve as their advisors and are installed as leaders. The people know that their superior's installation of leaders goes against what is correct for orderly government, and thereupon they all form factions and secret groups, so that nobody is willing to conform upward to his superior. For this reason superiors and inferiors do not share the same judgments. If superiors and inferiors do not share the same judgments, then reward and praise are not sufficient to promote good behavior and punishments are not sufficient to halt violence.[74]

The early Mohists attribute the people's lack of cooperation with their overlords to their realization that their superiors are not conforming to the just rules of a meritocratic and good government. Thus the key to upward conformity lies in the ruler's hands; he must make sure he conforms to the just laws of Heaven. Without doing so, he will incur not only the wrath of Heaven above, but also the non-compliance and threat of revolt from below.[75]

Throughout the "Upward Conformity" chapters, authors stress the need for the conforming obedience of those below to their superiors. At the same time as they repeat the injunction to conform upward, however, they give the reader a few subtle reminders that the authority of leaders must be legitimate in the sense that the laws such leaders promulgate must be correct and their actions just. Significantly, the authors remind us that conforming obedience to superiors can only be achieved through thinking and decision-making individuals who freely accept the legitimate dictates from above and reject the obviously incorrect and illegitimate ones. Mindful conformists do not have to know better than their superiors; they simply have to be sufficiently aware of what is probably or generally right or wrong. After all, without such knowledge, they would not be able to conform in the mindful way that is expected in such a system.

Early Mohists appear to be aware of the need for checks—other than that of Heaven's wrath, which they no doubt believed strongly in—on the ruler above to make sure that he and his associates are promulgating the just and correct laws of Heaven. Although the early Mohist political system does not recommend a democratic government in which people can elect their leaders and peaceably appeal to a system to rid themselves of bad leaders, the system promoted by the Mohists allows for the idea of popular involvement in the legitimization of authority. "Those below" not only play a role in recommending those around them for advancement, punishment, and reward, they participate directly in the acceptance or denial of their overlord's just qualifications and actions. They do so by granting or denying their upward conformity to him. Consequently, their participation in a particular system of laws, and hence, the efficacy of such laws, is contingent upon a leader's just qualifications and demands. Just leaders and mindful, obedient followers are thus both necessary conditions for the efficacious execution of law and meritocracy.

The idea that people from below might somehow set checks upon the authority of leaders above sheds new light on early Mohist visions of authority and the ideal of upward conformity. It justifies the responsibility of all people to cultivate themselves and make judgments about what is right and wrong so as to conform with Heaven's will. It also reveals that conformity in early Mohist thought is a complicated ideal that in fact does not advocate the blind, unthinking conformity of any single individual or segment of society to a higher authority. Mindful conformists only conform from within a just and efficacious system of law and authority. Though not invested with political authority, such individuals are still expected to conform with caution and an eye to what is just and right, not simply to prostrate themselves to unjust leadership and demands.

Conclusion

The early Mohists of the fourth century BCE can be considered among the first to have expressed a vision for universal human behavior that takes its cues systematically and uniformly from a single higher authority. A critical part of the early Mohist strategy for promoting meritocratic and legalistic ideals consists in establishing impartial, impersonal standards of value and behavior that place all individuals in an obligatory relationship with Heaven.[76] Early Mohists establish such standards by separating the power of one's position from legitimate authority, which rests singularly in Heaven. The notion of a common authority to which everyone has access and to which everyone should conform takes humans outside of the realms of private persons and particularized interests and unifies them according to a shared system of behavior and norms. These features of early Mohist religious and political ideology reflect a belief in a highly centralized and universalized system of authority that forms the basis for their notions of human agency in the world.

The early Mohist rhetoric of universal conformity to Heaven's will places each individual in a uniform relationship to a divine system of justice and morality. Each individual possesses an equal responsibility to conform to Heavenly norms. Similarly, Heaven holds each individual accountable for his or her actions through an equal method of punishment and reward. By objectifying Heaven's responses and communications with humans, the early Mohists level the playing field so that every individual is equally obligated to conform, irrespective of his or her family background or position in society.

Despite their preponderant rhetorical emphasis on upward conformity, early Mohists are not proponents of a society of mindless followers. In fact, they believe strongly in the fundamental agency of each individual to choose his or her own destiny according to the constraints of Heaven's judiciary control. In this sense, they reveal a basic belief in individual agency qua one's freedom to fulfill one's ultimate obligations. Defined through a system of reward and punishment, this ideology of conformity or, formulated differently, this ideology of agent responsibility gives meaning to the notion of an objective, universal, and impartial system of justice among humans.

While individuals can only succeed in life if they serve as the instrument for what the Mohists refer to as "Heaven's will" (*Tian Zhi* 天志), it is nonetheless each individual's personal imperative to engage in a rational evaluation of such a will, as it is expressed and filtered through the sociopolitical hierarchy. So although the notion of conformity to both Heavenly and sociopolitical dictates ostensibly determines individual behavior, just how one interacts with such higher authorities reveals a certain measure of individual freedom of choice. Individual self-cultivation, according to the early Mohists, therefore involves a particular process by which individuals learn how to bring themselves into alignment with Heaven's will.

Also, despite their rhetoric of conformity, the early Mohists are advocates of self-cultivation as a universal goal. Throughout their writings, they mention an individual's acquisition of wisdom and morality and refer to those who attain these goods as "achieved." They promote individual learning so that one can decipher and decide on Heaven's laws, thereby enabling oneself and others to conform to Heaven's will. Early Mohists thus imagine true agents of Heaven to be conformist agents who necessarily think, act, and make decisions that derive from a studied translation of Heaven's laws in the world.

Early Mohist advocacy of the meritocratic ideal also does not support a philosophy of empty conformity. Meritocracy supports a vision of human power and agency by explicitly opening the path of self-cultivation to a universal audience. Also, because meritocracy specifies that achievement in self-cultivation should be rewarded by appointment and advancement in the political sphere, it constitutes a claim for radical social mobility wholly contingent upon one's own individual achievement or natural talents. As such, meritocracy promotes a sense of individual empowerment within a defined social structure.

Lastly, despite its universalizing tendencies, the early Mohist vision for society does not constitute an egalitarian vision of individual power and authority. Hierarchy and power differentials help dictate how Heaven's will should be mediated correctly in society. Because positions of high authority are to be commensurate with one's ability and worth, hierarchies of power can be legitimized on the basis of individual achievement rather than natural or inherited categories. Merit-based determinations of power and authority are justified through an appeal to Heavenly justice and retribution, and not through an appeal to social or cultural norms, or even to accident.

According to the political structure of authority outlined by the early Mohists, those with ability serve at the top as mediators of Heaven's laws while serving as the principal decision makers in governmental policy. Others who are not in a position of authority must resign themselves to the role of mindful conformists in relationship to their superiors' orders as well as to Heaven above. To the extent that mindful conformists do not decipher Heaven's will but make evaluations concerning its more fundamental moral aspects, they represent more passive types of conformists. Still, however, they are not mindless followers, for without knowledge of what is right and wrong, they would not be able to choose whether or not to conform in the first place.[77]

The act of choosing is therefore fundamental to the early Mohist notion of conformity. Decision-making individuals, in addition to choosing whether or not to conform with Heaven's standards, necessarily choose in a different sense: they choose the method whereby they might come to understand Heaven's will. Even their counterparts, the mindful conformists, make choices insofar as they decide whether or not to conform to a leader according to the latter's capacity for justice and righteousness. Thus, whether decision-making achieved men or mindful conformists, both types of individuals show us that conformity as a concept is not always related to the loss or denial of individual freedoms and potentials for self-expression. These two models of conformity serve as an important counterpoint to current conceptions of human freedom that do not tolerate any aspect of conformism at all. Indeed, early Mohist ideology shows us that one can speak of conformists as both decision-making and self-reflective *agents* who find freedom in a fixed and universal truth beyond the individual. The freedom they find is integral to their conformity, and their conformity detracts not in the slightest from their individual prerogative to think, decide upon, and direct the course of their lives.

The early Mohists go to great lengths to stress the importance of a single, unified source of morality for all humans: Heaven. Heaven's ultimate standards of justice therefore provide the single most important perspective by which all humans should perceive of themselves and their moral responsibilities. Mediated primarily through achieved individuals in a political hierarchy, this authority of Heaven implicates all individuals universally, and all individuals are expected to conform upwards to it. Through this type of perspective, the early Mohists set the stage—which we will see fulfilled by authors of subsequent decades—for the growth of a more cosmically directed ideal of self-cultivation, personal development, and individual empowerment that at once implicates all individuals in a shared, universal arena of higher authority and power.

CHAPTER TWO

Centralizing Control
The Politics of Bodily Conformism

Conformist ideologies were also popular in fourth-century BCE texts such as the *Laozi, Guanzi, Zhuangzi*, and even some Ru texts, uncovered from tomb excavations at Guodian, that were in circulation around the same time. In the following two chapters we examine a diversity of viewpoints on conformism that date roughly to this period, many of which depart significantly from the early Mohist conception of it. We do so in order to narrate the different stages of development in ideas about human agency that made individualistic movements of the late fourth century BCE possible. Each in their own way, these conformist viewpoints helped usher in a belief that the individual possesses direct, personal access to the power and authority of the divine cosmos itself.

Like the early Mohists, the authors of other fourth-century BCE conformist texts depersonalized the authority of the individual. They idealized the subjugation of the individual to a single, all-encompassing, impersonal source of authority. Unlike the early Mohists, however, these authors promoted a psycho-physiological type of conformism, as opposed to a conformism to principles and regulations.[1] Adopting more literal interpretations of what it means to conform to the cosmic body—the Dao of Heaven or, simply, Heaven itself—they focused on an individual's cultivation of somatic and psychological likeness. This advocacy of what I call "bodily conformism" is so pervasive in these texts that one might speculate that it was introduced into the literature through a yogic religious movement that was either popular, local, or distinctly non-Zhou in origin.[2]

In recent years, scholars have begun to focus on the relationships among the body, space, and the cosmic ideal of spiritual attainment in early China. Michael Puett has specifically outlined the development of certain traditions that rejected a view of an antagonistic relationship between humans and divinities, choosing instead to emphasize the merging of one's spirit with that of the cosmos.³ In Mark Csikszentmihalyi's account of "material virtue" in Ru traditions, we learn how ethical beliefs in certain circles became imbued with a physiological and psychological component that linked one materially with the cosmos.⁴ Mark Lewis also recently discusses the "discovery of the body in the fourth century BCE," providing a far-reaching account of the human body as a centralized, politicized space.⁵ And Nathan Sivin highlights the relationships among the state, cosmos, and body in late Warring States and early imperial China by emphasizing the resonances between macrocosmic and microcosmic spheres of the cosmos and ruler's body/state.⁶ Each scholar uses different texts to point to new and distinctive developments concerning the individual body in early Chinese history.⁷

The following account adds to these seminal accounts by stressing the historicity of a particular stance on individual agency—that of "bodily conformism"—which has not been examined in the scholarship just mentioned. By analyzing such a stance across a variety of intellectual traditions, I try to reveal larger cultural connections that might be missed in discussions of a single tradition or specific cults and practices. Like Lewis and Sivin, I show that this "bodily turn" was not limited to any single region or intellectual practice but was pervasive throughout many different circles of thought associated with the increasingly centralized courts of the day.

The writings I will examine can be grouped into two main categories: those that supported the exclusive link between a sovereign's conforming body and the cosmos, and those that encouraged the universal bodily conformism of every individual alike, irrespective of one's political position and role. The former group of texts, the topic of this chapter, bears a relationship to the needs of the centralizing state; the latter group, a topic in the next chapter, offers one response to the politicized views of individual attainment prevalent at the time. I begin now with those authors that justified a highly centralized state structure, focusing on their characterizations of the ideal relationship between the sovereign and the cosmos.

The Politics of Divine, Impersonal Authority

Texts that support a centralized vision of control through bodily conformism differ especially from the writings of the early Mohists in their views on the spatial relationships of political control.⁸ The ruler's body emerges as a centralized authority with direct control over all people.⁹ In this axial model, as opposed to the multitiered, hierarchical model espoused by the Mohists, the authority of the ruler directly affects all individuals without the mediation of an elaborate institutional framework. Cosmic authority is the prerogative of the ruler, and it is properly channeled through him and his person only.

Because of their primary focus on the figure of the ruler, such writings do not address individual power and authority much beyond the central throne. Their exclusivity conflicts directly with a belief that is implied throughout these writings—that the human body serves as a universal source of divine potential.[10] As a result, there is an underlying tension in these texts between views concerning a more universalized human relationship to cosmic authority and views concerning the ruler's role as exclusive or primary mediator of such authority. This suggests that these writings might have been taken from other, perhaps more popular, religious contexts and applied as an afterthought at court to serve the political needs of a new audience: the ruler of a centralized state. In other words, authors who gave us this particular textual legacy might have been tailoring more universal, religious concepts concerning cosmic authority to suit a ruler's desire for centralized, direct control over his people.

The *Laozi*, parts of which we now know to have been in circulation at least by the end of the fourth century BCE,[11] presents a worldview in which all humans are equally dependent on the sacred Dao of the world—a single, ineffable source of both power and authority: "The Dao is the storehouse for all things; What good people treasure and bad ones preserve."[12] This short verse drives home the point that the Dao is universal, all-encompassing, and accessible in some unspecified way to the good and bad people of the world. Just as the Mohist Heaven judges all people equally, the Dao of this passage is equally relevant to all humans.[13] In both worldviews, all humans are equally dependent on a single higher form of authority.

Similarly, the "Techniques of the Heart-mind, Upper" (Xin Shu, Shang 心術上) of the *Guanzi* also stresses the universal, all-encompassing authoritative force of the Dao.[14] This Dao, residing objectively in the cosmos, is unbounded and immanent:

> In the space between Heaven and Earth, there is nothing larger or smaller than the Dao. . . . Only the sage can obtain the empty Dao. Thus, it is said: "[The Dao] abides among us but is difficult to obtain."[15]

Although only sages can obtain its vast emptiness, the Dao here is nonetheless an all-encompassing, universal authority and power over humans. That only sages might attain it has to do with personal talent and not the inherent restrictiveness of the Dao.

In "Techniques of the Heart-mind, Upper," the authority of the Dao stands in direct relationship to the individual as a physical entity. One gains authority by physically obtaining the Dao or force of the Dao in one's person. As an authoritative force, both power and authority are merged in the Dao. One's obtainment of the Dao thus allows for total and unadulterated mediation of its powers and intent, as any form of interpretation becomes unnecessary and superfluous. In other words, cosmic authority is expressed not through principles, laws, or dictates, as in the early Mohist worldview. It is also not funneled through cultural practices such as the rites, or through teachers who act as moral exemplars.[16] Rather, the Dao can be accessed directly by individuals by means of physical cultivation of one's body.[17]

The "Inward Training" (*Nei Ye* 內業), another text found in the *Guanzi* that is associated with and predates the "Techniques of the Heart-mind, Upper," further supports a claim for the universal human relationship to the Dao:

> In general, the Dao has neither roots nor stems, neither leaves or blossoms. The myriad things depend on it to live; they depend on it to complete themselves. They call it the "Dao."[18]

Guanzi heart-mind cultivation texts and the *Laozi* here join the early Mohists in viewing humans as conformist agents with respect to a single, all-powerful, higher authority. Unlike the early Mohists, however, such idealized agency for the authors of the *Laozi* and *Guanzi* cultivation texts is structured according to a model that places the individual in direct physical relationship to the Dao. In addition, the model of the *Laozi* and *Guanzi* texts supports the shaping of the individual's body through self-cultivation, whereas the early Mohist writings only indirectly advocate individual transformation through learning and acquiring knowledge about Heaven's will.

This dependent human relationship to the universal authority of a single higher source can be found as well in Ru writings that postdate the early Mohist writings. For these Ru writers, however, the all-powerful entity is Heaven, not the Dao. Consider the case from the *Cheng zhi wen zhi* (成之聞之), better named as *Heaven Sends Down the Great Constant* (*Tian jiang da chang* 天降大常), a text from the Guodian excavations:[19]

> Heaven sends down the Great Constant to give pattern to human relationships. It tailors the propriety [that is to exist] between ruler and minister, manifests the closeness [that is to exist] between father and son, and clarifies the distinctions [that are to exist] between husband and wife. Thus,

the petty man brings disorder to Heaven's Constant, thereby going against the Great Dao, while the gentleman orders human relationships, thereby according with Heaven's *De* (power).[20]

In this text, which most likely derives from a Ru tradition of learning, "Heaven's Constant" (*tian chang* 天常) serves as the single source for all order, meaningful standards, and types of relationships among people. Heaven's Constant provides humans with eternal patterns or principles by which they might live successfully.

This passage compares nicely to certain examples taken from the *Analects* that demonstrate the power of Zhou cultural authority as a mediator of moral truths, most likely stemming from Heaven: "The Zhou based itself upon the previous two dynasties. How resplendent is its culture! I follow the Zhou."[21] Clearly, in the *Analects* there is not so much of an emphasis on the direct authority of Heaven as in this later text. While Heaven's authority is very important for Confucius, moral authority in general is dispersed through a variety of mediums, such as the rites (including the *Odes*) and human moral exemplars and their teachings.

A version of the *Wu Xing* (五行 *Five Phases*) text also found at Guodian links an individual's *De* (virtuous power) directly to Heaven:[22]

> There are five [types of] virtuous conducts. When in harmony, this is called "*De*." When the four [types of] conducts are in harmony, this is called "goodness." Goodness is the Dao of humans. *De* is the Dao of Heaven.[23]

The harmonization of the five types of virtuous conducts is the Dao of Heaven, or *De*.[24] Thus, *De* is the alignment of human action with Heaven. As in all the passages mentioned so far, the author's emphasis is on the single source of authority that all humans share inclusively by virtue of living in this world, not exclusively through one's specific culture or sociopolitical background.

As contexts for authority became less differentiated and more grounded in a single ultimate context—the Dao or Heaven—idealized human agency was construed in relationship to this context in a more unified and less particularistic way. Conformist writings of the fourth century BCE brought a discussion of the "personal" or "private" and the "impersonal" or "public" into sharp focus, sometimes even using the terms "*si*" 私 and "*gong*" 公 to render this distinction explicit.[25] They invoked this distinction by introducing a particular form of self-abnegation: the negation of selfishness and personally motivated behavior in favor of impersonal agency and the authority of the highest divine entity. A few examples demonstrate how important the concept of an impersonal, divine authority had become for these authors.

The *Laozi* proposes a basic vision of idealized kingship in which the head of a state rules through his conformity to the Dao. The social realm functions as a microcosm of the cosmos, not as a replica of the cosmos but as an integrated part with a renewed connection to it through the mediation of the sage, who happens to be the ruler. By using techniques of *wu-wei* 無為, or "non-purposive action," to liken himself to the Dao, the sage actually becomes the vessel through which the power of the Dao is channeled.[26] By this, I mean that the sage's personal attainment serves as the link that enables spontaneous, social order based on the Dao. Any discontinuity that may have existed between humans and idealized authority is remedied by the sovereign's total and encompassing instrumentality, or conforming agency, with respect to the Dao.

The term *wu-wei* in *Laozi* represents a type of idealized non-agency associated with self-abnegation and conformity to a higher power. *Wu-wei* is implicitly contrasted with certain self-determined, individual acts of will that allegedly threaten the general harmony of society:

> The Dao constantly does not act (*wu-wei*), yet there is nothing it does not serve (*wu bu wei* 無不為).[27] If dukes and kings can preserve it, then the myriad things will transform of themselves. If in transforming themselves they desire to take an initiative, I will arrest them with the Simplicity of that Without a Name. They will then have no desires. By not having desires they will be tranquil—the whole world will be secure.[28]

Here *wu-wei* is the function of both the Dao and political leaders. It epitomizes a kind of unselfishness (i.e., a state of being without desire) that preserves harmony in the world at large.[29] The positive social balance generated through *wu-wei* is overthrown when a single individual takes it upon himself to act beyond the confines of simple transformation with the Dao. Taking an initiative implies transgression because it is rooted in motivations connected specifically to the self—perhaps an insight, decision, or desire. Thus, by advocating the dissolution of "selfish" motives and initiatives, the authors of *Laozi* promote an impersonal vision of control through the generous, universal, unselfish, and authoritative Dao.

Wu-wei in the *Laozi* is similar in some significant ways to the conformity recommended by Mohist precepts. The authors in both texts desire to combat and restrain what they deem to be negative sources of power associated with individuals (*si*). They hope to deny an individual's agency to decide (early Mohists) and act (*Laozi*) based on considerations for personal profit and fulfillment, supporting only decisions or actions based on the ultimate authority of Heaven or the Dao. Fundamentally, the self-abnegation supported by both ideologies recommends not making decisions and acting from within the boundaries of "self." They wish for humans to transcend the limitations of one's own personal authority to become a conforming agent to a higher authority and make decisions in light of a larger set of principles or forces. In this light, the Laozian notion of *wu-wei*, like the early Mohist conception of *shang tong* (upward conformity), might similarly be understood as a type of human conformity to a single higher power and authority.[30]

The Guodian text introduced above, *Tian jiang da chang*, also advocates self-cultivation through the depersonalization of one's own authority in favor of that from Heaven:

> The *Great Yü* says: "I here take my abode in Heaven's heart-mind." What does this mean? This saying proclaims that I am here yet I take my abode in Heaven's heart-mind.[31]

In the passage of this text previously analyzed, Heaven serves as an ultimate, impersonal authority that relays its eternal patterns to humans as "Heaven's Constant." The author here idealizes an individual's relationship to these moral patterns. Just as the *Laozi* recommends that the sovereign employ the techniques of *wu-wei* to abide in the Dao,[32] this author speaks of the gentleman who "is here" but takes his "abode in Heaven's heart-mind." One interpretation of such rich metaphorical imagery is that the gentleman loses his own sense of identity—associated with his heart-mind—to assume the heart-mind of Heaven itself.[33] The message behind such language is clear: The gentleman should abandon self-created judgments and defer to the direct authority of Heaven.[34]

In all these texts, the specific goal of negating the delimited authority of the self in favor of the all-encompassing authority of a universal higher power differs from more general goals for humility and limited self-denial, which can be found in almost any text dating from early China. The goal of these texts is not simply to encourage individuals to assume a particular type of attitude (that of humility) in addition to many others. Rather, these texts ask that individuals give up fundamental agencies associated with the conventional self and replace them with the agency or authority of a single, higher, divine entity shared by all humans. Only by dissolving the limited agency of the self and adopting the principles or forces of Heaven or the

Dao instead might one wholly belong to a more universal cosmos and unified realm of human interaction.

Conformity and the Paradox of Impersonal Power

The writings of the fourth century BCE that we have been looking at so far share early Mohist orientations that idealize impersonal sources of authority. However, while early Mohists focus on the cognitive aspects of individual agency, many of these authors take the human body as a problem that needs to be overcome. They recommend using the body to overcome its own "body-ness" and sense of personal identity. This is because precisely at the point when one embodies a divine authority or power, one's body is considered no longer to be one's own. Consumed in a process of depersonalization, the conformist—or one might more traditionally say "mystic"—becomes not just one with the cosmos, he becomes one with the world as well, as suggested here in the *Laozi*: "The sage has no constant heart-mind [of his own]. He takes the heart-mind of the people as his heart-mind."[35]

How does the explicit prescription to negate the self relate to individual agency? Authors who embrace bodily conformism rhetorically praise impersonal sources of authority while at the same time suggesting the primacy of the body as a medium for housing and transmitting such authority.[36] Indeed, a seeming paradox arises, one that I will call the problem of the "impersonal power of the empowered person." Ideologies of bodily conformism manifest a curious trait: Their rhetoric of self-abnegation goes against what we might view as just another form of personal empowerment. After all, how can an individual really be lacking power or authority as an individual when it is precisely his or her individual body that is being empowered and given authority through conformity to a higher power? Does not the very fact of one's bodily attainment imply individual agency associated with the self, rather than conformism?

Two types of formulations found in our sources respond to these questions. The first, found in the *Guanzi* "Techniques of the Heart-mind" chapters, cedes decision-making and cognitive power to a particular individual, the achieved sage-king, in light of his subordination to the higher power of Dao. The second rhetorically denies any form of ultimate individual authority while allowing for a sage-king's deep personal participation in actions and the process of decision making. Both formulations implicitly admit to the sage-king's central position as actor and decision maker; they disagree, however, on how to speak about the powers and authorities associated with the individual. By examining each of these two examples in more depth, we gain insight into the contested nature of individual agency in relationship to the notion of cosmic conformity in early China.

In the *Guanzi* "Heart-mind" chapters, the author explicitly highlights an individual's decision-making powers in light of his or her total conformism to the Dao. As in the *Laozi*, a person's bodily health and vitality serve as the markers for such conformism. In contrast to the *Laozi*, however, which never formally condones active decision making on the part of the ruler, the *Guanzi* chapters state that those who conform to the Dao do so by transforming their bodily powers of the Dao—referred to as essences (精 *jing*)—into ordered decisions that arise from the self. The following claim for strong, self-willed leadership describes how a gentleman uses the physiological powers of the Dao so that he might himself transform and put things into order:

> That which unifies *qi* and can bring about transformations [in it] is called an essence; that which unifies worldly affairs and can bring about transformations [in them] is called knowledge. Organizing and choosing are the means by which one prioritizes affairs, and pushing change to its limits is the means by which one responds to outside things.[37] To organize and choose, yet not to get confused; to push change to its limits, yet not to become disturbed; [only] the gentleman who holds to the One [is able to do this]. By holding to the One and not losing it, he can rule over the myriad things.[38]

This statement occurs as part of a larger argument concerning the exclusively physical origins of sagely power in accordance with the Dao.[39] Such physical attainment, it is worth noting, is only possible through the personal cultivation of oneself in conformity with the cosmic Dao. Here there is little need for humans to engage in self-abnegation and denial of their own personal agencies. Cultivation of the heart-mind allows a sage-king to gain necessary access to higher powers without having to deny his own personal role in the process.

The sage-king's explicit role as decision-making agent derives from the Dao. However, it is transformed into a form of personal agency that allows for active decision making as a clearly defined "self." This is because each decision can be traced proximately to the condition of the sage-king's own heart-mind, the good order of which is responsible for producing ordered speech and policies for others to follow:

> If one's heart-mind is at peace, his state will be at peace. If one's heart-mind is well-governed, his state will be well-governed. Being well-governed is a matter of the heart-mind; being at peace is a matter of the heart-mind. With a well-governed heart-mind at the center, well-governed speech emerges from one's mouth and well-governed policies are implemented among the people.[40]

Standards and orders, which emanate from the "well-governed speech" of the sage-king, are created through a transformation from physiological processes rather than intellectual examinations of the state of affairs in the world, as was the case for the early Mohists. In other words, the authority of one's policies and orders emanate from a physiological power induced by the Dao, not from the direct verbal or intellectual authorization of the Dao. By having been transformed by the sage-king's person, such policies and orders are not entirely external to or independent of him. They constitute physical directives from the Dao that he has fundamentally absorbed, reworked, and expressed again in a different form.

Representations of a sage-king as leader and embodiment of order in the "Techniques of the Heart-mind, Lower" chapter differ noticeably from depictions of the ruler's authority in the *Laozi*. In the latter text, the boundaries of an achieved individual's agency are not distinguishable from the agency of the Dao. Social order is effected through the mysterious process of *wu-wei*, "non-purposive action," which consists in the sage-king's conformity to a Dao that does not produce active or self-consciously created decisions, but instead lets things mysteriously unfold of themselves.

Conformity in this case resembles instrumentality, in that the Dao acts through the body or person of the ruler without the ruler ever having a chance to be or act as himself. The ruler's words and actions do not arise from his own doing (*wei* 為) or even speaking, as is apparent in the following statement: "For this reason the sage abides in the affairs of *wu-wei* and carries out non-verbal teachings. The myriad things rise up, but he does not give beginning to them."[41] Here, bodily authority effected through *wu-wei* in the *Laozi* disables the sage's self in such a way that his self is no longer a self but a body without a personal identity. This corpus of the Dao, a transformed, impersonalized "self," is what leads and decides—through communication of some mysterious sort—on governmental affairs. In this scenario, one's agency does not belong to the self, as the self is but a medium or instrument of Dao.

Centralizing Control

Another passage in the *Laozi* speaks of self-abnegation, or ridding oneself of one's body or person (*shen* 身), through the ironic act of valuing it and serving the world through it:

> The reason I have great worries is that I possess a person. Once I no longer have a person, what worries will I have? Therefore, he who values serving his body over serving the world can be assigned to it.[42] And he who cherishes his person more than serving the world can be entrusted with it.[43]

This tricky and confusing passage touches on the problem of personhood, along with the problem of its materiality, as *shen* also implies "body," not merely "person."[44] Ridding oneself of one's person appears to be one solution. But how to do this is the catch. Ironically, one must value and serve it, which I believe refers to the person-centered practice of *wu-wei*.[45]

There are at least two ways in which the notion of *wu-wei* in this description implies valuing one's person. First, we know from other chapters of the text that the author advocates *wu-wei* techniques as the most effective means by which the individual can serve the world. Since the claim here is that the individual (most likely the sovereign, as the passage deals with "serving the world") does this by valuing his person, we might conclude that valuing the person is associated with *wu-wei* techniques. Second, the very fact that the author does not speak of "ruling" or "controlling" the world, but rather, "being assigned" and "entrusted" with it, lends support to the idea that what is sought is not control but *wu-wei* sovereignty. Sovereignty of this sort emphasizes the self as an effective channel for the power of the Dao.

As a channel for the Dao, the sovereign body does not disappear, nor does its value decrease. In negating one's person and body, one ironically must focus attention upon it, and not upon governance, control, or other sundry activities. This type of self-focused self-abnegation fits right into the Laozian scheme of reversal and paradox. *Wu-wei* forms of self-abnegation, previously described in terms of the negation of one's desires and agency, are cast in a different light: in terms of the emphasis placed on one's person—a localized, unique embodiment of Dao. In such a way, the *Laozi* promotes a rhetoric of self-empowered non-agency, which is effectively a form of conformism that values the self.

In a deep, structural sense, then, one might conclude that the philosophy of self-abnegation in the *Laozi* in fact supports the actualization of some sort of "self" (the scare quotes are entirely appropriate here) in communion with the impersonal power of the Dao. The self that is originally negated consists of an identity with boundaries and personal desires, and especially a type of control or agency that is associated with such a bounded individual. The "self" that re-emerges in communion with the Dao, on the other hand, is one without boundaries, personal desires, or individual agency. It is a "self" that, through the denial of its own agency, achieves a fairly limited kind of individuality that derives from focusing on the *arena of the self* in communion with the impersonal Dao. Because such a form of "individualism" is constrained by the rhetoric of no-self, I primarily refer to it here as "conformism." Nonetheless, it is important to notice that the boundaries between "individualism" and "conformism" are especially obscure in this context.

Through a comparison of the sage-king's authority in the "Techniques of the Heart-mind, Lower" chapter and his bodily power in *Laozi*, we see how the rhetoric of conformism might entail different processes and different visions of individual agency. While only the "Techniques of the Heart-mind, Lower" formally allows for true authority to be vested in the sage-king's person, the self-cultivation ideology of the *Laozi* does not deny the sage-king the power to make decisions and carry out activities. By advocating one's ultimate subordination to the Dao as a depersonalized self, the author of *Laozi* places limits on a sovereign's authority without having to deny the efficacy of his person or position in society. Indeed, the author's focus on the sovereign as the central axis through which cosmic authority might flow underscores the special power of the ruler's person and position in the world.

The physiological imagery of *wu-wei* cultivation in *Laozi* strengthens a vision of the attained sage as a person of ultimate power, not as an impersonal authority or force:

> He who embraces the pinnacle of power can be compared to a newborn baby. [A baby's power is such that] poisonous vermin do not sting it, ferocious beasts do not claw it, and birds of prey do not capture it. His bones are tender and muscles supple, but his grasp is firm. Even though he does not know about the unification of male and female forces, his penis is aroused. This is because his essence is at its peak. All day long he cries out without developing a hoarse tone. This is because his harmony is at its peak. . . . When the heart-mind controls one's material forces, we call this "forcing." When a thing becomes strong it ages, and this is called "not abiding in Dao." Not abiding in Dao brings on an early finish.[46]

Attainment of the power of the Dao can be visibly discerned through personal, physiological traits that characterize its pacifistic operations. By comparing the attained individual to a newborn child, this author identifies the type of person and body associated with such a state. The fact of the sage's rejuvenation, or reversion to the time of birth, suggests the symbolic rebirth of the individual through the process of cultivation. Interestingly, there are impersonal aspects as well, as seen in the description of the vital components of the body such as *jing* ("essences" 精) and *qi* ("material forces" 氣).[47] The attained individual is not just a person but also a harmony of bodily components, or a medley of forces in tune with the spontaneous workings of the Dao. The description is, therefore, appropriately ambivalent; the attained individual is neither individual nor Dao, just as he is both individual and Dao.

By stating that one's conformism to an impersonal Dao actually gives meaning to the sage's body and person, the author of *Laozi* reveals his awareness of how the loss of personal identity and agency at the same time corresponds to a gain in personal value and fulfillment:

> For this reason the sage places himself behind and yet and finds himself in front; externalizes his person and yet finds his person present.[48] Is this not because he has no self-interest that he is able to fulfill his self-interest?"[49]

Personal authority is redefined here through a threefold process: First, the person is divested of his or her own power and sense of self; next, he or she is reinvested with the power of an external, impersonal authority; and third, he or she thereby achieves a higher value and meaning for the self and its personal interests. In other words, one's self and person must first disappear before they can re-emerge in communion with the highest power of the cosmos—as a dual entity of "self" and the Dao.[50] This constitutes what we have been labeling the paradox of the "impersonal power of the empowered person." It is not at all a paradox, however, if we understand it as another way of depicting the "self" as it has been touched, enriched, and transformed by the powers of the divine realm.[51]

The physiological likeness of individual to the Dao and the Dao to individual attests to this duality of "selfhood."[52] When individuals embody the physiological traits of the Dao, they comport themselves in ways that are characteristic of descriptions of the Dao while still taking on human form:

> He who assists the ruler by means of the Dao does not overtake the world by force of arms. . . . He achieves his result but is not arrogant; he achieves his result but is not self-important; he achieves his result but does not brag.

He achieves his result because he cannot do otherwise; he achieves his result without force. When things are vigorous they become old—this is called "not following the Dao."[53]

Elsewhere in the book, the attributes of the Dao are described as silent, low-lying, broad, mysterious, empty, deep, and dark, among other traits.[54] By speaking of a sage-minister who is not arrogant, not self-important, does not brag, and who expresses peaceful behavior toward other kingdoms, the author suggests that the sage-minister physically conforms to the attributes of the Dao. So while this type of conformity yields decision making to an impersonal authority (the Dao), it does not completely deny one's sense of being a person with real, human traits.

The individual's proper relationship to the Dao in the *Laozi* can be distinguished from early Mohist views on the relationship between humans and Heaven. Both the *Laozi* and early Mohist writings portray the sovereign (or high minister) as a medium for divine authority. Though the early Mohists also speak of an individual's achieving wisdom and noble character in the likeness of Heaven, physiological likeness to divinity is only part of the story. For them, conformism also represents obedience to external principles, which are not so much physical forces as they are conceptual truths and standards of behavior. The author of the *Laozi*, on the other hand, explicitly argues against conformism through one's reliance on cognitive functions. This is illustrated neatly in one of the versions of *Laozi* discovered at Guodian, "proto-*Laozi* A," in which the author advocates the abandonment of wisdom and disputation, cunning and (the goal of) benefit, as well as artifice and (directed or purposive) contemplation.[55] The critique of intellectual, cognitive traits that appears in this version is most assuredly a strike against Mohist values. This is only natural, since for the author of *Laozi*, self-conscious cognition relies on an awareness of self that blocks the natural transmission of the Dao.[56]

In the society of early China, where personal power and authority seem to have been the glorified goal of many, the religious experts and intellectuals whose works we examine here turn such a goal on its head. They stress instead personal accountability in relationship to a single higher authority, thereby responding to contemporary concerns about the unchecked personal power of rulers. This suggests that some of the authors of these texts were trying to gain the ear of powerful rulers who would no doubt demand practical political payoffs for any sort of abdication of their own personal authority. By underscoring the personal rewards of abandoning the self and its own private interests, such specialists paid rhetorical lip service to the sovereign's overarching control and central position vis-à-vis his subjects while in some sense undermining his personal authority. Indeed, by advocating the ruler's use of his own body as a vessel of higher authority, these men rhetorically granted power to the ruler's person while conceding true authority to the impersonal authority of the Dao, and most likely to themselves as well.

From a political perspective, we might wish to understand the strong rhetoric of sovereign conformity found in these texts as a means of undercutting and altering the ruler's actual power and authority. Since religious experts and intellectuals were precisely the ones who claimed to speak on behalf of Heaven and the Way, and since they would have been necessary for consultation on bodily training on how to use *wu-wei* techniques or how to govern according to Heaven and/or the Dao, their writings can be seen as actually contributing to the power and authority of themselves as gatekeepers of the highest form of authority in the world. By claiming that the ruler could be all-powerful by listening to the Dao, religious experts pleased the ruler's ear while effectively giving more power to themselves.[57] In such a way, the "impersonal power of the empowered person" might be viewed as a form of flattery targeted at the ruler to make him cede control over important governmental decisions without actually knowing that he had done so.[58]

Centralized Structures of Bodily Conformism

The *Laozi, Guanzi* "Techniques of the Heart-mind" chapters, and some of the Ru texts from Guodian all support the goal of successful and orderly rule in society by focusing—though certainly not exclusively so—on the role of the ruler. Since these texts take the sovereign as a primary audience and object of discussion, they do not necessarily espouse a universal approach to individual power and authority, despite their belief in the universal powers of a single higher authority.[59] Indeed, many of these texts give pointed advice to the ruling figure according to a triadic cosmos-ruler-people relationship. In such a relationship, the ruler acts as the axial figure that mediates, accesses, and allows for cosmic powers in the social world.

The primarily centralized discussion of power in these texts is in itself revealing of important fourth-century BCE trends in political theory, practice, and social thought.[60] Indeed, if our dating is correct, it sheds light on a particular historical moment or sociopolitical culture in which rulers (perhaps in a few key locations) actively sought apologetic justifications and measures for boosting their own personal power and political control. Such writings probably not only point to representative philosophical or religious beliefs floating around at the time; they appear to be grounded as well in the political trend toward state centralization and strengthening of the ruler's position. To such an extent, they illustrate how religious and philosophical beliefs could be created, co-opted, and shaped to suit ultimately political ends.

The unification of the empire under Qin Shihuang in 221 BCE was preceded by long-term political and ideological changes, the most important of which were the adoption of centralizing policies by states throughout the multistate system. During the middle of the fourth century BCE, the state of Qin began institutionalizing a series of centralizing political reforms under the primary guidance of the Lord of Shang, or Shang Yang (d. 338 BCE).[61] The speed and extent to which these reforms or discussion of these centralizing policies spread throughout the multistate system of the late Zhou is as yet unclear. Of the texts analyzed so far in this chapter, there is not a single one for which we might convincingly demonstrate a clear a relationship to the state of Qin.[62] Yet, surprisingly many fourth-century texts, and especially those examined so far, assume a stance toward sovereign power that is reminiscent of the centralizing goals of such a state, in particular the goal of strengthening the authority of the throne. Although they each try to limit sovereign power through appeals to an ultimately higher authority, they do not fail to concede—at least rhetorically—a certain totalistic power to the throne.[63]

In the Guodian version of the Ru text, the "Zi Yi" for example, the author makes use of the familiar metaphor of the body politic to highlight the ruler's position as supreme, central figure:[64]

> The people take their ruler to be their heart-mind, and the ruler takes the people to be his body. Whatever the heart-mind likes, the body finds security in. Whatever the ruler likes, the people desire. Thus, just as the body is the means by which the heart-mind is abandoned,[65] the people are the means by which the ruler is lost.[66]

The author here likens the ruler to the heart-mind—the primary center of bodily control—and the people to the body that follows the dictates of the heart-mind. The ruler at the center of society controls the desires and security of the people, just as the heart-mind controls these things from the center of the body. And though the body and people can indeed possess the power to ruin the heart-mind and ruler, it is still these latter centers of authority that dictate the security and desires of those below.

By discussing power relationships primarily in terms of the ruler-ruled relationship, the author of the "Zi Yi" points in this passage to a single center of control.[67] Compare this with the *Analects,* where correct, influential behavior can derive from the ruler at the center, as in *Analects* 2.1, where the ruler is compared to the Pole Star, which, without leaving its place, commands the attention of everything around it.[68] But in the *Analects,* moral authority can also derive from gentlemen in other sociopolitical positions. Furthermore, moral order in society results from many sources, such as the rites and music, and exemplary writings and cultural traditions—not just from the ruler or leaders at the top center of the political hierarchy. Compared with this, the ruler-oriented focus in the "Zi Yi" is striking and undoubtedly a significant indicator of how early Ru beliefs and practices might have been applied to changing political needs.

Certain passages in the "Techniques of the Heart-mind" chapters of the *Guanzi* also strongly outline the importance of centering political control through the sovereign's heart-mind or body. The heart-mind of the sovereign serves not as a metaphor for the heart-mind of a state but as the actual, physiological seat of political control. It is in the heart-mind that the Dao comes to *reside* in the sage-king so that he may *preside* over others through his own bodily vitality and sense of center:

> When the heart-mind is still and the *qi* patterned, then the Dao can stop [there]. . . . If one cultivates the heart-mind and stills all tones, the Dao can be obtained. . . . With a settled heart-mind at the center, one's ears and eyes become acute and perspicacious, and one's four limbs become firm and solid. [The body] can be a lodge for the essences. Essences refer to the refined part of *qi*. When *qi* is directed, then life develops.[69]

Here we see how the author supports the techniques of stilling one's heart-mind and giving direction to one's *qi* so as to merge the body with the Dao, thereby bringing the Dao within.

Basing his thoughts on the "Nei Ye," the later author in "Techniques of the Heart-mind, Lower" goes on to demonstrate the tangible connection between the ruler's embodiment of the Dao and social order on a much larger scale. For example, as seen above, the state of good order in the ruler's heart-mind brings about a physiological response that allows him to lead his state actively, properly, and effectively: "If the heart-mind is in order, the state is in good order. . . . With an orderly heart-mind at the center . . . orderly policies are implemented among the people."[70]

The centering of power in the sovereign's body parallels the centralization of the state and its administration. The ruler serves as the heart-mind, or central axis, around which the people revolve. Moreover, by having control over his body, the sovereign ensures his position both as *axis mundi* to a higher power and as central sociopolitical figure functioning as the willing agent of the people.

Even the *Laozi* centers social control around the sovereign body. Although the function of the heart-mind is reversed from the texts looked at so far, insofar as it needs to be emptied and not filled with directives, the sovereign body nonetheless acts as the central locus for achieving social harmony and "control" over the bodies of other people:

> Thus, in governing, the sage empties their heart-minds, fills their bellies, and strengthens their bones. He always makes it so that the people do not know and do not desire. And he makes it so that those with knowledge do not dare to act.[71]

> Engaging in *wu-wei,*
> There is nothing that is not in order.[72]

Since the heart-mind of the sage is empty and devoid of control, he is able to use his body to bring the people over whom he rules into a state of ignorant bliss. The sovereign's techniques of *wu-wei,* or non-control, involve having the people's body mimic that of his own, so that his body serves as the central seat of bodily achievement. Though the author negates the normal functioning of the human heart-mind and defines social order in terms of non-control, he still presents the sovereign's body as the locus of power—the central axis from which all social order emanates. Indeed, as in the "Zi Yi" and *Guanzi* "Techniques of the Heart-mind" chapters, the ruler-people relationship serves as the political bedrock for the transmission of ultimate authority and power from the cosmos.

The authors of each of the texts, the "Zi Yi," the "Techniques of the Heart-mind" chapters, and *Laozi,* do not focus on the power differentials inhering in a multitiered political hierarchy, as evidenced by the early Mohists. Rather, these authors highlight the sovereign's conformism to Dao and his axial, direct relationship to the people. The "Zi Yi" and "Techniques of the Heart-mind" chapters underscore centralized political control by describing the control of the sovereign's heart-mind over his body. The "Techniques of the Heart-mind" chapters and the *Laozi* go even further by drawing an actual physiological connection between the state of the sovereign heart-mind/body and the ordered responses or bodies of his people. This tangible connection between sovereign body and people reinforces the notion that the center of the body politic is an actual physical body itself.

The People as Dependent Agents of the Sovereign and the Dao

The idea that the sovereign serves as the central axial agent of a body politic reveals how highly some authors—starting in the fourth century BCE—valued the ruler's supreme yet ultimately conformist authority in society.[73] But what about the people? What is their role in such a centralized vision of authority? Although it varies from text to text, the people appear to be dependent on the sovereign's primary cosmic agency. Let us consider the case of the *Laozi*. In that text, the people bring about social order on their own and can initiate actions themselves. However, such actions will not be connected to the Dao if the sovereign does not first allow the Dao to emanate from his person in the world.[74] Take the following example:

> I take no action (*wu-wei*) and the people transform of themselves. I love quietude and the people correct themselves. I do not engage in affairs of state (*wu shi* 無事)[75] and the people become enriched of themselves. I desire not and the people become simple of themselves.[76]

Even though the people are said to "correct themselves," implying that they author their decisions in an autonomous fashion, the phrasing of this passage clearly places the idealized agency of the people into a causal, dependent relationship with the ruler and his state of spiritual attainment. This suggests that only through the sage-king's attainment will the people have the power to act according to the Dao. Moreover, it is only the sage-king's bodily cultivation, and not one's own self-cultivation, that allows other individuals to develop each in accordance with the Dao. Thus the entire utopian vision presented in the *Laozi* is founded on the narrow stipulation that only the ruler can enable the Dao to act through the people, so that they most truly act "of themselves."[77]

In order for *wu-wei* in the *Laozi* to make sense as an effective method of political control, a particular relationship between ruler and people must exist. The people below do not engage in *wu-wei* techniques because if they did there would be little purpose in having a sage-king in the first place. For this reason, the authors of *Laozi* do not stress universal, direct access to the Dao, even though their conception of the so-of-itself (*zi ran* 自然) implies just such unmediated access. Instead, they regard the sage-king as the necessary and primary catalyst of religious efficacy in the world. This is supported by the fact that they never discuss how the common people might involve themselves in cultivation techniques, let alone in techniques such as *wu-wei* that might empower them in the same way as does the sage-king. Instead, they describe a situation in which the attainment of the common people occurs only as a result of the sage-king's personal attainment. It is thus derivative and second-order.

The term *zi* 自 used in the passage above to describe how the people and things of the world transform themselves is often translated into English as "of themselves," "of itself," etc. Throughout the text, however, it is clear that although the people might be acting as decision-making agents "of themselves," they only do so because the sage-king mediates the Dao through *wu-wei* techniques to which he alone is privy.[78] He thereby does not interfere with the Dao in the world, so as to enable it for everybody else. The term *zi* in the *Laozi*,[79] then, refers to an idealized state of acting "of oneself" that actually depends on the enabling techniques of the sage-ruler. Such an idealized state derives from what is inherent in the person, yet in the politicized writings of the *Laozi* it is latent and contingent upon the sage-king's bodily conformity to Dao.[80] In this sense, the people's self-attainment is tantamount to a kind of conformism to Dao facilitated not through their own cultivation techniques but through the catalytic process of the sage-king's *wu-wei*. The people's agency, though an agency that indeed stems from themselves, is thus contingent upon the structure of centralized kingship as presented in the text.

According to this political reading of the *Laozi*, the sovereign is the sole guardian of *wu-wei* self-cultivation, and his body is the most important instrument in the cosmic ritual of *wu-wei* conformism. Such human conformism, dependence, interdependence, and even "self-agency" recommended in the text must therefore be understood first in terms of a single ritual prerogative of the sovereign that enables the powers of the Dao to function in the world. However, though the sovereign holds primary and initial access to the Dao, the manifestation of its powers in the world is never merely limited to his person. As long as he initiates the powers of the Dao through his body, the people, thus permitted from above, act in an idealized manner "of themselves." In this way, the people are allowed to realize themselves as diverse manifestations of the creative Dao.[81]

In the Guodian version of the "Zi Yi," the author also emphasizes the ruler's pivotal role as the key agent who decides on the correct standards of behavior and judgment for the people. The ruler serves as a formal, affective model for the people by embracing certain moral virtues and dictating through his person a moral attitude for them to follow:

> Confucius says: "When the superiors like humanity, then those below will vie to be the best at being humane. Thus, in leading the people one makes his will manifest to the people. The people will then perfect their conduct for themselves in order to please the ruler at the top."[82]

Through his sense of moral taste, the ruler, who represents the heart-mind of the body politic, conveys his humanity to the people below. The people, as the metaphorical body, respond to the ruler's needs, likes, and desires by adopting the same for themselves. Thus, the vehicle through which humanity is transmitted is the sovereign. His personal moral achievements provide a formal model for society to replicate, so that moral influence inspires a type of conformity true to the literal sense of "conforming," or "agreeing in form." While the notion of conforming to the behavioral and moral model of the sage or virtuous ruler is certainly an old one that stems from the early Zhou, the metaphorical language of heart-mind/body employed by the author of the "Zi Yi" drives home the desire for a more material and physiological type of likeness or one-to-one correlation that is not emphasized in the earlier literature.[83]

The moral autonomy granted to the people by the ruler in the "Zi Yi" is derivative and based in the personal traits of the ruler and his bodily cues. For the people cannot know morality unless their ruler shows them how through his personal state of being:

> The Master says: "If the ruler feels doubt, then the people will be confused. When those below find it difficult to know [the values/decisions of the ruler], then the ruler leads ineffectively."[84]

The personal confusion of the ruler translates here into the confusion of his people and disorder in his rule. The inverse also appears to be true—that a ruler's clarity breeds clarity among his subjects:

> The Master says: "It is when he who acts as ruler can be gazed upon admiringly and understood, and when he who serves below can be categorized and put into a hierarchy,[85] that rulers do not doubt their ministers, and ministers are not confused by their rulers."[86]

The clarity of sovereign virtue finds response here in a minister's faithfulness to his lord and adherence to the duties incumbent upon his position.[87] In both of these passages, the ruler's person serves not only as the means by which the people achieve moral states of being and decision making in their own lives. The sovereign body is also a critical means for the preservation of hierarchy and social order, an important function often fulfilled by the rites in Confucius' *Analects*.

What conclusions can one draw about moral authority and the people in the "Zi Yi"? We have seen how the ruler serves as an instrument of higher authority by cultivating virtues and clarifying value distinctions for himself and others. His role as moral exemplar appears to be of paramount importance, so that his power to persuade morally lies predominantly in his person and less so in cultural goods. The people, unlike the ruler, do not possess comparable moral authority; instead, they gain moral pleasure and security by behaving identically to their ruler. Their virtues and values are therefore not keys to greater moral authority but tools given to them by their ruler that help define and create their moral actions. So while the people might be influenced to know morality and make moral decisions on their own, they are still largely dependent on the judgments transmitted to them through their ruler's person. In this text, much like in the *Laozi*, self-cultivation of the people is depicted as largely contingent upon the prior cultivation of the sovereign's person.[88]

In the "Zi Yi," as in the *Laozi*, the people below gain access to divine authority or a sense of divine morality by virtue of the sovereign's success in bodily cultivation. The people, like their sovereign, serve as instruments of a higher power, but they lack the power possessed by such a sovereign to transform and influence others. In both texts the people derive authority from their ruler rather than from any sort of self-initiated cultivation. Their personal discovery, and indeed the success of their own self-cultivation, is contingent upon the ruler's body serving as divine pivot. In light of this shared emphasis on the power and authority of the sovereign's body, we might wish to consider these diverse and seemingly unrelated texts in terms of a possible shared politico-religious orientation that idealizes the sovereign body by highlighting its pivotal access to cosmic power and authority.

One might argue that the philosophy of self-cultivation in these texts should not be read in terms of the particular relationship between ruler and ruled. Indeed, one might argue that even though texts such as the *Laozi* and the "Zi Yi" take the ruler as their primary audience, this does not mean that the authors really understood the scope of self-cultivation to be restricted in such a manner. My response is that the specific circumstances under which these texts were authored and the particular audience for whom the texts were written do make a difference, ultimately influencing the underlying way each philosophy is expressed. Since the ruler-people relationship is the primary one addressed in the text, and since the contours of such a relationship actually stipulate how divine authority is transmitted in the text, we must read these texts (at least when we wish to be historically faithful) in terms of the power relationships that give it meaning. Accordingly, the unidirectional transmission of moral knowledge and divine authority and power depicted in these texts drives home the clear hierarchical dependency of the people's cultivation on that of their sovereign—who stands not only at the center of the political hierarchy but at the center of spiritual cultivation as well.

Conclusion

The issue of a ruler's agency and control in the world was explored by many authors beginning in the fourth century BCE. In the writings just examined, authors focus on the notion that a sovereign's body must ideally conform to universal powers and authorities that derive singularly from Heaven or the Dao. They thus adopt a similar stance to the early Mohists, proclaiming that ultimate authority in society stems from a single higher source that unifies everything below it.

Also like the early Mohists, authors of texts such as the *Laozi*, the "Zi Yi," and "Techniques of the Heart-mind" chapters of the *Guanzi* all proclaim the normative dependence of humans on an all-encompassing, inclusive authority beyond the human realm. These texts all posit the existence of a universal, impersonal authority to which every human should in some way conform. Consequently, they agree on the existence of some form of common law, force, or authority that exists objectively beyond the personal sphere of individuals.

Unlike the Mohist writings, which stress upward conformity to laws, commands, and just principles, the sovereign-oriented writings examined here share in a vision for social control that focuses on the sovereign, or sage *cum* sovereign, as the single point of access to higher authority. These writings endorse the sovereign's participation in an impersonal system of authority or power while at the same time promoting his increased attention to his most personal sphere—the body—as the primary means to such ends. And because supreme authority can be housed in his body, these texts both personalize and depersonalize divine authority vis-à-vis the sovereign as an individual. They do this by underscoring the sovereign's ultimate conformism to the Dao or Heaven while at the same time acknowledging the proximate authority located in his person or body.

Such is the problem of the "impersonal power of the empowered person." In exploring it in this chapter, I highlighted two different stances on individual orientations toward decision making, leadership, and authority. One stance admitted to the authority of the sage-king's own person while the other denied it, advocating a wholly depersonalized attitude toward kingship. At base, however, both stances implicitly acknowledged the enormous authority that might be concentrated in the individual as either a body or a vessel that assumes a certain space and function, not necessarily as a person (or self) acting on his own.

Although many of the writings of this chapter make strong claims for the universality of a single type of authority and power over humans, such authority and power are not equally accessible to all. Authors reveal a need to legitimize the central authority and power of the throne and its direct control over the people. As fundamentally political as well as religious or philosophical in scope, these texts assert the privileged role of the sovereign body as mediator or activator of divine authority in the world. The mediation of higher authority is not accessible via the bodily cultivation of just anyone; it is stipulated by the power structure inherent in a sociopolitical structure with the ruler at the center and the people in direct relationship to the ruler. In such a centralized structure, the sovereign serves as the critical axis of cosmic authority who might ensure its supremacy, efficacy, and beneficent influence over all other beings.

Given the undoubtedly different traditions of thought espoused by these various texts on sovereign conformism, such similarities in political orientations should not be cast aside as mere coincidence. I would like to suggest that the shared focus in these texts on sovereign authority over the people constitutes an explicit appeal to centralizing aspirations and policies of the day. The goals of such policies were consistent with the goals of state reform promulgated in Qin since the time of Shang Yang.[89] This interpretation, which posits a fourth century BCE or later dating for many of these texts, contends that centralizing tendencies took on many different guises. It suggests that men of different religious and intellectual traditions sought ways both to limit sovereign authority by making it conform to divine power at the same time as they tried to aggrandize the throne—at least rhetorically—by granting it divine authority vis-à-vis the people.

The autocratic undertones of these writings suggest that the specific audience was to be rulers and the ruling elite of any given state, and that authors needed both to appeal to the aspirations of such men and to make their beliefs competitive with centralizing policies which were most vigorously being brought to fruition in the state of Qin. Their particular emphasis on the centralized, universal power of the throne demonstrates one way in which intellectuals and religious specialists were responding through their writings to the demands of an increasingly centralized political climate.

We should consider the political focus of these texts in light of Aihe Wang's thesis that various political groups arose during the Warring States period to "deprive the hereditary ruler of monopolized divine authority and to disperse such authority among themselves in order to increase their own power."[90] While such a thesis might have merit for an earlier date between the Shang and Spring and Autumn periods, the claim that hereditary rulers ever monopolized divine authority during the Warring States periods is not at all self-evident.[91] What the texts examined so far indicate, on the contrary, is that certain intellectuals were compelled to re-establish the exclusive, divine authority of the sovereign as his very own privilege. Certainly, these thinkers did make room for their own authority as advisors or, most importantly, as arbiters of knowledge concerning access to the divine world. But they did so by appealing to the privileged position of the sovereign as the vehicle through which divine authority should be mediated in the world. This suggests that authority might have already been dispersed and that many authors dealt with this dispersal by attempting to appeal to sovereign fantasies of possessing a strict monopoly on divine authority.

CHAPTER THREE

Decentralizing Control and Naturalizing Cosmic Agency
Bodily Conformism and Individualism

In the textual record we also find ideologies dating to the fourth century BCE that went beyond the sovereign to address bodily conformism at a more universal level. Zhuangzi in particular spoke of spiritual attainment in terms of the relatively decentralized power of the Dao that might obtain in each individual, and not merely in leaders of the state. While he still stressed each individual's conformity to or communion with the single higher authority, Zhuangzi nonetheless addressed bodily agency in terms of an individual's personal and unique link to the cosmos. This approach to human agency, which viewed self-cultivation in terms of a universal and directly accessible ideal of attaining cosmic agency, was but one step removed from the full-fledged empowerment of the individual—or "individualism"—that developed some time in the fourth century BCE as well. Indeed, Zhuangzi's unique interpretation of human agency provides us with the final, necessary link between ideologies of bodily conformism and individualistic views on agency in early China.

The other fourth-century BCE writings we examine in this chapter shifted the locus of cosmic power and authority from *outside or separate from* the self and person to *inside or intrinsic to* the self and person. Through the concept of *xing* 性, human nature—a concept that became dominant as early as fourth-century BCE debates on the self—such texts began to naturalize idealized, often divine, agency as an inherent part of the self, rather than as something apart or distinct from it.[1] They therefore moved away from the goal of conformism to an external power—or, conformism to an authority not intrinsically associated with agencies of the self.[2] Instead, they supported a type of conformism to the inherent powers and authorities of the individual itself—which we dub "individualism" in this book.[3]

Freedom and Zhuangzi's Conformism as "Transcendent Individualism"

Zhuangzi's "Inner Chapters"—or the first seven chapters of the *Zhuangzi*—describe a transformation of individuals in spiritual terms, taking the Dao of Heaven as the means by which individuals might negate and transcend their selves to attain cosmic authority and idealized interactions in the world. Like the writings on sovereign conformism already examined, Zhuangzi advocates "conformism" to the Dao, insofar as he proposes that individuals lose their own sense of identity to join with a dynamic and ever-changing higher power.[4] Significantly, however, Zhuangzi does not privilege bodily cultivation of the sovereign head. For him, individual relationship to the Dao is characterized not by dependence on political institutions or the central figure of the sovereign, but by direct, individual access to it through one's own person. Because his thought lavishes attention on the individual person while at the same time endorsing the transcendence of "self," the problem of the "impersonal power of the empowered person" also seems to apply here.[5]

The "Inner Chapters," generally datable to the later part of the fourth century BCE, present many varying descriptions of conformism with the impersonal Dao. One such depiction highlights the loss of one's sense of self (*ji* 己), especially as it relates to one's identity and sense of agency. Zhuangzi expresses this perhaps best in an unlikely conversation between Confucius and the latter's best disciple, Yan Hui:

> Confucius said, "Unify your will. Do not listen with your ears but listen with your heart-mind. Do not listen with your heart-mind but listen with your *qi* (material-force). [Normal] listening stops at the ears, and the heart-mind's capacity extends only to making a tally [of what has been heard]. As for *qi*, by being empty it awaits outside things. Only the Dao can collect in its emptiness. 'Fasting the heart-mind' is [attaining] emptiness." Yan Hui replied, "Before I had begun to obtain the assignment,[6] I perceived of myself as a reality. After obtaining the assignment, there hadn't begun to be a Hui. Might this be called emptiness?" Confucius replied, "That's it."[7]

Zhuangzi illustrates here the connection between losing the self and attaining the Dao. The operations of the heart-mind and other bodily functions help contribute to a sense of self. One loses this sense precisely by rendering bodily functions, especially that of the heart-mind, inoperative through the act of "fasting." Thus, though the self is a critical *factor* in one's unification with the Dao, the underlying goal is to strip the self of its role as *actor*, or self-conscious agent, in the world.

Yan Hui's response to Confucius reveals that he has arrived at a state of awesome realization: The boundaries of Yan Hui as an identity cease to exist in his own perception. Quite unlike the familiar Cartesian axiom of "I think, therefore I am," Yan Hui's existence might be described as "Perceiving, 'I' no longer am," in which the "I" represents a conception of the self that is dissolved through its union with the Dao. In the attained state of selflessness, there is no distinguishable subject that perceives because perception is no longer bounded by the self. Since the former Hui ceases to exist as such, any kind of agency he previously might have possessed will also not be his own. "Hui" must now rely on the agency of the Dao to act.[8] As instrument for the Dao, "Hui" transcends himself and conforms to its impersonal powers.[9]

Zhuangzi's use of the phrase "fasting the heart-mind" clearly denies each individual his or her mechanism for control.[10] Edward Slingerland notes that this "starving" of the heart-mind purges "it of the accumulated deposits of *shifei* distinctions that constitute language and conventional conceptions of righteousness, in order to create a clearing of tenuousness in which the Way will gather."[11] His analysis of the metaphor of a container or vessel helps shed light on what I have been calling a "conformist" stance that necessitates the collection of external agency within the receptacle of the body. Indeed, there seems to be a certain material component associated with the heart-mind, so that he who fasts it allows for the emptying of *qi* (material-force) in the body. Being stripped of its operational fuel, the body no longer has anything by which to guide itself.[12] It then becomes possible for the force of Dao, playfully but accurately suggested in this passage as an "agent, envoy, or assignment" (*shi* 使), to collect there and replace it as the motivational agent in the body. In our own terms, one's personal agency is replaced by the impersonal agency of the Dao.

Notably, the expression of this impersonal agency is not the same for every individual. The very fact that each individual still persists in a particular, individualized form and within a particular, unique environment means that the impersonal agency of the Dao takes on a different form in any given context. Whenever Zhuangzi depicts the "True Person" of the Dao (one of several names for an idealized being in the text), such a being assumes a different type of power and role in society.[13] This is important because conformity with the Dao does not mean that every individual transforms himself or herself according to a uniform ideal; rather, it means that every conforming perspective of the Dao manifests itself differently in the world.[14]

For Zhuangzi, the problem of self is more epistemological and ontological than political, suggesting that his deep engagement with the concept

Decentralizing Control and Naturalizing Cosmic Agency

really does implicate individuals on a universal scale. At the beginning of the text, Zhuangzi introduces the problem of self in terms of the limitations of perspective and the forces that constrain rather than free a person from dependencies in the world. Consider the following lengthy passage, in which Zhuangzi promotes the ideal of ultimate freedom from the confines of personal perspective and individual agency:

> Thus those whose knowledge enables them to succeed in an official position, whose behavior is appropriate for overseeing a village, or whose virtue is suitable for a ruler and proof for an entire country, also view themselves in such a manner [as though there were nothing better].
>
> Song Rongzi simply smiled at them. What is more, he was neither encouraged when the world held him up for praise nor discouraged when the world held him up for blame. He had a firm grasp of the division between inner and outer, made distinctions based on the boundaries between honor and disgrace, and that was all. Although worldly affairs did not trouble him, he still had areas in which he was uncultivated.
>
> Now Liezi, he traveled with the wind as his chariot, floating beautifully along and not returning for fifteen days. He was not troubled by the attainment of blessings. By this, even though he avoided having to walk, there was still something that he relied on. As for one who rides on the truth of Heaven and Earth and takes the transformations of the Six *Qi* as his chariot in roaming around in infinity, what does he have to rely on? Thus it is said, "The perfected man has no self, the spiritual man has no merit, the sage has no name."[15]

Why do Song Rongzi and Liezi fall short of Zhuangzi's ultimate ideal? Song Rongzi distances himself from the troubles and pitfalls of worldly affairs, such as flattery and blame, honor and disgrace, as well as the competition to gain a name. His detachment, states Zhuangzi, is praiseworthy in many respects, for he does not allow such external forces to propel him into action. But he has still not attained ultimate achievement. Comparing this to the example of Yan Hui above, we might infer that it is because Song still has a strong sense of self. He has not gotten beyond using his heart-mind to make evaluative distinctions about himself and his actions.

Liezi, on the other hand, exhibits a great lack of his own physical agency. He gives himself over for fifteen days to the vagaries of wind travel. While such physical freedom strongly implies mental freedom from inhibiting perspectives, Liezi must still rely on something—in this case, the wind—to embark on his spiritual journeys. But the Dao, unlike concrete, bounded entities such as the wind, is limitless. To exchange one's personal agency for that of another bounded entity is good, because one has succeeded in transcending the self. However, it is still not as good as exchanging one's personal agency for the unbounded nothingness of the Dao. Since both Liezi and Song Rongzi avail themselves of some kind of bounded agency, neither has fully accomplished the state of absolute freedom that Zhuangzi holds most dear.[16]

Zhuangzi ends this passage by extolling the sage/spiritual/perfected man who relies on boundless and decentralized truths of the cosmos—or "nothing" at all.[17] The agency of such a person has been dissolved into the power of the cosmos, an unending cycle of transformations that abides by its own laws and truths. By letting oneself go with the flow of cosmic power, each person transforms his or her self into a conscious (but not self-conscious) manifestation of the Dao. There is no residue of one's self-identity in the world.

In this striking formulation of freedom and autonomy, the sage is autonomous with respect to his immediate environment, and even his own mental and physical forms. Yet this type of freedom also ironically makes such an individual—now more aptly called a selfless-individual, or phenomenon of the Dao—utterly dependent on the powers of the cosmos. Mocking the sense of self-righteousness and importance that often accompanies a creature's entrenchment in one perspective, Zhuangzi describes an impersonal ideal that obviates the necessity of having a perspective or personal agency at all.[18]

In the "Inner Chapters" attained states come in at least two distinct flavors. One state, that of "fasting the heart-mind," consists in emptying one's heart-mind and losing one's sense of identity in order to conform to the Dao.[19] In such a state, one loses the capability to discern distinctions and boundaries as intellectually meaningful. Instead, one transcends the distinctions so as to realize the oneness of everything. The second state, as in the example just discussed, is that of the "ever-changing, selfless perspective," in which an achieved individual perceives boundaries but is not attached to them as a self. The individual thus complies with the ever-changing conditions and terms of the things he or she encounters.[20] Both of these images are consistent with losing oneself to gain the perspectives and operational modes of an impersonal Dao.[21] The latter image, however, gives us deeper insight into the workings of Zhuangzi's Dao. Rather than act uniformly throughout the world according to predictable, standardized principles, this Dao proceeds by allowing the multitude of things to transform of themselves.[22] Each transcended individual object thus takes part

Decentralizing Control and Naturalizing Cosmic Agency 59

in a unique process of infinite transformation. To such an extent, the conforming individual achieves a freedom from his or her own worldly identity to wander leisurely, and infinitely, according to a process of individualized transformation. The famous reference to leisurely wandering (*xiao yao you* 逍遙遊) in the title of chapter one appears to represent this type of transcendent freedom.[23]

Such ideals for individual freedom are expressed in a variety of ways in the text. Chapter four of *Zhuangzi*, "Current Times in the Human World," presents many parables that fetishize all that is useless, a category which especially includes crippled and deformed human beings.[24] There we find the story of Carpenter Shi, who encounters a sacred oak tree of unusable wood, which presents us with the paradox of useful uselessness: "An apprentice asks [Carpenter Shi], 'If it inclines to being useless, then what is it doing as a sacred site?'"[25] Carpenter Shi responds that the holiness of the tree is merely a pretext for its preservation, and, further, that what the sacred oak "preserves is different from the [norms of the] multitudes."[26] Here, *wu yong* (無用), or "non-instrumentality," does not mean uselessness in any absolute sense. At the same time as it points to conventional uselessness, it underscores a sacred, transhuman usefulness in relationship to the cosmos.[27] Indeed, the statement that "nobody knows the uses of the useless" at the end of the chapter suggests that true instrumentality exists and that it can only be understood by those "selfless individuals" who are no longer driven by the norms and self-bound agencies of the human world.[28]

Significantly, many of the anecdotes Zhuangzi uses to exemplify non-instrumentality take commoners who are disconnected from politics to be protagonists and aspiring sages. The famous Cook Ding story in chapter three captures Zhuangzi's vision of non-instrumentality in the non-political realm. In it, Cook Ding attributes his success at carving an ox not to a desire to produce results or benefit society but to the spiritual and aesthetic pursuit of "relying on the patterns of Heaven":

> Just now, I used my spirit to encounter and not my eyes to see. My faculty of knowing shut down and my spirit desired to act. Relying on the patterns of Heaven and striking along the great seams, I channeled my way through the great cavities, every movement following upon the one before it. I never [interfered] with the ligaments and tendons, not to mention the bones![29]

The fact that Cook Ding is a commoner not involved in the useful pursuit of politics clearly demonstrates that conformism with the Dao is not limited to the work of sovereigns and top ministers of state. Moreover, that a commoner like Cook Ding might be able to achieve the highest possible state of cultivation also reveals that it is within the capability of even a commoner to enlist the agency of Heaven (otherwise referred to in the text as the "Dao") in the world.

Zhuangzi's use of cripples, freaks, disadvantaged people, and commoners as examples of individuals who achieve the highest form of spiritual power suggests the universality of cosmic potential for humans, and indeed, all creatures alike. Paul Kjellberg proposes that Zhuangzi's "cast of misfits and outcasts" is "paradigmatically uncertain," suggesting that this "cast" appears to raise questions in the reader rather than provide solutions.[30] In a later article, Kjellberg expounds on this idea to show that with regard to cripples, "the defects may be natural" and "can put their possessors in a better position to continue to lead natural lives by distancing them from society's restrictive norms."[31] Such interpretations certainly have merit. I would add that Zhuangzi's use of such figures underscores the importance of transcending one's humanness. According to Zhuangzi, there is little basis for rejecting or excluding anyone or anything from aspiring to become an attained being, since the latter goal in itself is to find one's unique relationship or union with the Heavenly Dao. The following passage, which celebrates the attained individual as a unique, "non-human" specimen of Heaven, reflects how Zhuangzi engages the notion of transcending the limits of what is human:

> Gong Wenxuan caught sight of the Commander of the Right, and, in astonishment, exclaimed: "What man is this that he should have such deformed legs![32] Is he of Heaven or man?
>
> "He is of Heaven, and not man. When Heaven gives life it makes things singular, but human appearances have duplicates. This is how I know that he is of Heaven, and not man."[33]

The Heavenly specimen in question cannot be considered human because it departs from the human form. Though it defies any category of identification, it conforms to the infinitely diverse patterns of Heaven's transformations. This entity is therefore not an individual human, but an "individual" in a most sublime, transcendent sense: conforming to Heaven's diversity, not humankind's uniformity. Thus, Zhuangzi's "selfless conformism" might be understood as a conformism grounded in the individuating effects of Heaven's agency, which bestows diversity and uniqueness upon its beings.

Zhuangzi appears to idealize abnormality so as to highlight the cultivated "individual": an entity in which human form, function (instrumentality), and identity cease to define one's existence and control one's behavior. The process of true attainment is open to anyone, even freaks and abnormal beings, precisely because such a process denies our fundamental differences in relationship to a single higher power. It celebrates instead the unique manifestation of everything as differentiated agencies of the Dao.[34]

Zhuangzi's use of commoners as achieved individuals also supports the idea of self-cultivation as a universal norm. It emphasizes the potential value in any life activity, including the most mundane chores and socially debased lines of work. Critics might claim that Zhuangzi includes commoners in his ideal not to stress equal opportunity with respect to self-cultivation, but to show salary-seeking and position-grubbing *shi* how to find satisfaction in mundane activities. According to such a claim, Zhuangzi's use of commoners would function as a pedagogical tool. After all, if the Dao can be found in mundane pursuits such as butchering, feeding the pigs, and cooking, why would one need to bother exclusively with politics?[35]

I do not find this explanation satisfactory, however, because Zhuangzi consistently depicts attained commoners, and not unemployed members of the *shi* class, in their various roles. If he had wished to limit his ideal to the *shi* class, he might only have depicted the *shi* in their pursuits outside the political realm. But this is not the case.[36] Thus, Zhuangzi uses commoners to attest not only to the universality of the Dao in everyday affairs but to its universal accessibility regardless of social class and occupation as well.[37]

Zhuangzi not only proposes a universal conception of conformism with the Dao, but a non-political one as well. In the "Inner Chapters," Zhuangzi does not think of idealized action in terms of *wu-wei*, "non-purposive action" (無為), *wu-shi*, "non-engagement in affairs" (無事), or in terms of any of the key political concepts of human agency used in the *Laozi*. Rather than invoke such concepts, Zhuangzi advocates losing one's sense of self and the agency associated with a self-willed heart-mind, irrespective of one's political position.[38] Importantly, in the *Laozi* sagely sovereigns are specifically involved (more precisely, *not* involved) in self-cultivation techniques that allow for the Dao to manifest itself in the world. In *Zhuangzi*, on the other hand, everybody—not just the sovereign—possesses a self and a heart-mind that can be overcome, and everyone can initiate the workings of the Dao for one's self. Thus, Zhuangzi's prescription for bodily cultivation more consistently invokes a language of universal relevance than the political language used in the *Laozi*.

Zhuangzi's emphasis on the irrelevance of politics in self-cultivation demonstrates to a certain extent the importance of political appointment as a norm in his society. That Zhuangzi specifically elucidates the irrelevance of politics can perhaps be best seen through the concept of "non-instrumentality," or "non-utility" (*wu yong* 無用). Through this concept, which arguably complements the concept of non-purposive action in *Laozi*,[39] Zhuangzi seeks a more complete escape from the language of political control and utility that likely prevailed in elite circles at the time. Therefore, in claiming that Zhuangzi's thought is non-political, I do not mean to say that Zhuangzi's ideals were utterly disconnected from the political realm. In fact, by stressing the irrelevance of politics in particular and by denying its value in life, Zhuangzi essentially demonstrates his connection to politics—or, at least, his connection to the issue of what Yuri Pines calls the "imperative of political service."[40]

On a more spiritual and conceptual level, the notion of non-instrumentality stresses a negation of efficacy in the world, which suggests the utter rejection of controlling outcomes by having an influence or effect on them. Along these lines, it also negates the practical uses of objects and individuals. Thus, Zhuangzi's use of the term "non-instrumentality" verifies his rejection of having purposes, goals, and uses for things in the world. This fundamental rejection of human control can be understood in terms of one's freedom from any worldly constraint, whether social or political or of any kind. It can thus be viewed as a type of conformism to the manifold processes inherent in the Dao.

To what extent does this make Zhuangzi's thought "individualistic"? This question is important because we will soon make use of the term "individualism" to describe an intellectual orientation that possesses much in common with Zhuangzi's thought. On the one hand, Zhuangzi does not explicitly attribute the processes of the Dao to powers inherent in an individual's body or spirit. Rather, he describes such processes as though they were immanent in the act of overcoming one's self and body. We might therefore say the agency of Dao with which one conforms consists in individualized processes related not to the self but to the transcendent "self." And the freedom that obtains is a freedom of the inspired or transcendent individual. This makes Zhuangzi's thought indeed individualistic, but individualistic in a special, deeply interconnected way, that is, as the transcendent individual relates to the whole of the cosmos. Humans become individuals not by virtue of being unique in and of themselves, but by virtue of being unique as an individualized manifestation of the workings of Dao.

In our glimpse of Zhuangzi's visions for self-attainment—or, to be precise, the attainment of a transcendent "no-self"—we have seen that he shares a belief with many other fourth-century BCE authors in the conformity of the individual agent with the normative powers and authorities of the cosmos (either dubbed as "Heaven" or "Dao"). Where Zhuangzi differs from a typically conformist stance is in his notion of the individualized processes of the Dao, which blur the boundaries between conformity and individualism. We have addressed such a problem by referring to Zhuangzi's ideal in terms of a transcendent self that is at once conformist and individualistic. Indeed, Zhuangzi's thought sheds light on the ways conformist ideologies might intersect with individualistic ones—by insisting on the transfusion of divine agencies into the unique physical boundaries of the self.

By focusing on the goal of transcending the self and achieving direct, physico-spiritual connection with the Dao, Zhuangzi makes individual attainment theoretically accessible to all individuals irrespective of sociopolitical position and the hierarchical mediation of power and authority. Zhuangzi's use of cripples, freaks, and commoners further suggests the broad, universal scope of Dao cultivation. Nonetheless, we cannot go so far as to say that Zhuangzi's thought does not at all concern the realm of politics. While it defines an ideal as distinct from such a realm, the very fact that it tries to make such a distinction attests to the importance of politics at the time, and to Zhuangzi's awareness of the perceived value of pursuing a political career.[41] In this sense, one might say that Zhuangzi's spiritual stance constitutes one type of reaction to contemporary concerns about the importance of the state in an individual's life.

The Rise of Individualism in Early China

Also during the fourth century BCE, theories on human nature develop in direct correlation to an increased focus on the individual body and its relationship to the divine realm.[42] With the rise of an explicit discourse on human nature, early Chinese thinkers for the first time begin discussing individual relationship to the spiritual cosmos in terms of a universally innate human agency, and not in terms of universal conformism, either as mediated by sociopolitical instruments and sovereigns, or as dictated by the loss of "self." They call into question the idea that individuals should serve as mediators and conformists of higher powers apart from the self, and they introduce new metaphors that depict humans as cultivators of their own inherent agencies. Formulations on acquisition and procurement give way to articulations of one's inherent means of fulfillment, of inborn potentials, personal endowments, and individual empowerment.

While the human body served as the primary locus for the attainment of idealized authority in many texts previously examined, the fact remains that this agency was not "of the self" and, furthermore, that it was acquired by somehow shedding some aspect of the self. In the individualistic approach I now introduce, the body is not merely a *medium* of authority—it is an individualized *source* of it. What follows generally describes a new way of imagining the powers of the self vis-à-vis the external world, marking a new orientation and attitude toward divine authority, cosmic power, and other idealized sources of agency.

Naturalizing Cosmic Power: Individualism in Mencian Thought

> There is a great deal of difference between an innate law and a law of nature; between something imprinted on our minds in their very original, and something that we, being ignorant of, may attain to the knowledge of, by the use and due application of our natural faculties.[43]

Unlike the form of innate power described above by John Locke, some authors of the fourth century BCE in China saw a continuity between cosmic or natural laws and the innate powers of each individual. Nonetheless, Locke's claims that the two types of laws can be distinguished in some sense from the other holds true even for the early Chinese case. The figure whose writings provide us with one of the earliest and most complete representations of early Chinese individualism was Mencius. In his writings on human nature, Mencius appealed to the innate moral agencies of the individual. By naturalizing moral motivation, Mencius revealed a new orientation toward human agency, one that saw the individual body as a universal source—as opposed to a medium—of cosmic authority and natural patterns.[44] His writings helped form the beginning of a new spirit of debate that emphasized individual agency as a critical factor in self-cultivation and/or political control.[45]

Mencius' formulations on *xing* respond directly to contemporary theories held by his purported opponent in debate, Gaozi.[46] In *Mencius* 2A2 Mencius praises Gaozi for surpassing him in the art of "not moving one's heart-mind" 不動心, yet he is sharply critical of the latter's views on individual relationship to morality. Elsewhere in the text (throughout chapter six), Mencius refutes Gaozi's claims as a means of presenting his own beliefs in a polemical fashion. This polemic, one that concerns the internality or externality of moral motivation, is couched in larger questions of how to locate the sources of moral motivation and characterize the idealized relationship between humans and ethical behavior.[47]

The metaphor of an individual's organic and inherent potential for moral development pervades Mencius' writing on *xing*. The vegetative metaphor

Decentralizing Control and Naturalizing Cosmic Agency

of *xing* as something akin to a "moral seed" reflects an implicit assumption that moral motivation stems from within an individual (*nei* 內) and that it is not acquired through conformity to an external standard (*wai* 外) or source of authority and power.[48] The counterpart to this metaphor, one that provides Mencius with a potent rhetorical weapon against Gaozi's position, is the metaphor of violent attack from the outside, as well as artificial manipulation of the *xing*, featured in the following passage:

> Gaozi states: "*Xing* is like the willow tree. Righteousness is like cups and bowls. To have human nature engage in benevolence and righteousness is like making cups and bowls out of the willow tree."
>
> Mencius replies: "Is it that you follow along with the nature of the willow in making cups and bowls out of it? Or must you violate the willow before you can make it into cups and bowls? If you must violate the willow tree before you can make it into cups and bowls, then this means that you must violate man before you can make him moral. Your statements necessarily lead the people of the world to view morality as disastrous!"[49]

At stake is the continuity of morality with our innate tendencies. Do we as humans possess instinctive knowledge of morality and motivation for moral behavior, or do such goods have nothing to do with our natural state of being?

Gaozi compares *xing* to the raw materials endowed upon us at birth. The act of making cups and saucers out of what was once the raw material of the willow tree constitutes an act of great cultural achievement. By likening aspects of morality to cultural achievement or tradition, Gaozi locates morality in what is created by humans and not intrinsic to human nature. Mencius, on the other hand, addresses the issue in terms of internal and external forces working upon humans. He associates inherent natures with a state of being whole and well, and external actions with violence and destruction. Significantly, for Mencius moral motivation belongs to the realm of our inherent or internal natures.

Mencius' language of destruction and violation amplifies the negative effects of viewing morality as external to human nature. An individual places his or her very humanity in jeopardy by seeking moral guidance exclusively through external forces. Such extreme language challenges conformist positions on moral agency and supports a quite new outlook on human agency, one that seeks the sources of human power and authority in our innate constitutions.

The internal-external debate on sources of moral agency and authority is further elaborated in *Mencius* 2A2. There, Gaozi denies the connection of human *xing* to morality by declaring the absolute necessity of study and discipline through tradition and culture. Unlike Mencius, he advocates the total subordination of the human heart-mind (the seat of a person's controlling mechanism, the will, *zhi* 志) to *yan* 言, or what might be translated in the passage as "sayings," or "teachings." Gaozi's view of moral cultivation differentiates between internal and external locations of moral knowledge and authority, strongly affirming the separation or autonomy of the individual from such goods: "Gaozi says: 'Do not seek in your heart-mind what you have not obtained through sayings. Do not seek in your *qi* what you have not obtained in your heart-mind.'"[50]

For Gaozi, sayings, associated with teachers who transmit learning, serve as legitimate sources of morality. He points out that there is a proper source for morality, proper stages in which it is mediated, and proper directions in which it should take seat in the human body. The process of moral internalization to which he alludes is one in which objectified moral principles are clearly transmitted from an external source into the self.

Mencius' response to this claim confirms that the internal-external debate at hand revolves around concrete sites or sources of morality, signified by the term "rightness" (*yi* 義):[51]

> "I dare to ask how it is that you surpass Gaozi [in not moving your heart-mind]?" Mencius responded: "I know the sayings, and I am good at nourishing my nimbus-like *qi*."[52] "I dare to ask what you mean by nimbus-like *qi*." Mencius responded, "Ah, it is hard to describe. Such a *qi* is of utmost grandness and firmness. When one nourishes it directly without harming it, then it permeates the stretches between Heaven and Earth. Such a *qi* is congruent with rightness and the Way. Without it, one deteriorates. This is [a process whereby one] concentrates that by which rightness is produced. It is not [a process whereby] one accepts rightness after it assails from without. When one's behavior does not settle well with the heart-mind, then one deteriorates. This is why I say that Gaozi, in designating it as something external, does not know rightness."[53]

Mencius shows here that morality exists materially in time and space, growing from within one's body through the cultivation of one's own nimbus-like *qi*. In other words, the motivation for moral behavior exists within each individual as a force that affirms both life and morality—a force that every individual can nourish physically on his or her own. This underscores the interior and materialistic origins of universal morality and moral motivation in the human body.[54]

Decentralizing Control and Naturalizing Cosmic Agency

In *Mencius* 6A2, a famous passage on the nature of water, we see how Mencius emphasizes the inherent agency that humans possess for moral behavior. His description of this agency is congruent with his discussion on the materialistic force of *qi* that impels us to know what is good and to do it too:

> Gaozi states: "Human nature is like whirling water.
> Dredge a canal on its east side, and it will flow eastward; dredge one on its west side, and it will flow westward. Human nature having no preference for what is good or not is like water having no preference for east or west."
> Mencius states: "Although indeed water does not have a preference for flowing east or west, can one say that it has no preference for flowing up or down? Human nature moving toward the good is like water flowing downward. Just as there is no man who does not possess goodness in him, there is no water that does not flow downward."[55]

Mencius declares that just as the flow of water naturally tends downward, man's *xing* naturally moves toward goodness. *Xing* is defined here by its function, by how it naturally propels man toward morality. Furthermore, such a function is universal, implying that every person possesses not only the potential to be good but also the moral agency that compels one toward the good.

Reinforcing the dichotomy between internal and external moral agency, Mencius depicts the latter as an impediment to the natural development of *xing*:

> Now, as is the case with water, by splashing it, it can be made to shoot up over the top of one's head,[56] and by stirring and conducting it, it can be made to travel up a mountain. How can this be said to be the nature of water, though? It does so because *environmental forces cause it* to do so. That humans can be made to behave immorally is because their natures are also like this. [italics mine][57]

Environmental forces (*shi* 勢),[58] or forces external to the self, may cause a human to act in ways that defy the intrinsic tendencies of *xing*, just as water can be made to move in directions other than downwards. This is a case of external forces overriding the power of *xing*, the internal force of human nature. The fact that morality is associated with forces as well as materiality makes it necessary for us to think about Mencian claims on *xing* in terms of innate moral agency and not just moral qualities or potentials.

By depicting Gaozi's views through a vocabulary of obstruction, violence, and destruction, Mencius vividly describes his support for a belief in an individual's internal sources of moral control. He considers all immoral behavior to stem from a *xing* that has been tampered with or obstructed through external forces: "That humans can be made to behave immorally is because their natures are also like this [i.e., can be misled and forced from without]."[59] Human nature, then, can be either fulfilled or obstructed. It can be directed by two main kinds of forces—its own intrinsic moral agency, or extrinsic, potentially obstructive forces.

Mencius' claims go even further to integrate moral motivation with life processes associated with the human body. As A. C. Graham points out, in early Chinese there is an etymological connection between the terms "life" (*sheng* 生) and "human nature" (*xing* 性)—a connection at times so close that scholars sometimes permit the substitution of the term *sheng* for *xing*.[60] Mencius takes advantage of this linguistic connection to collapse the distinction between the two, thereby naturalizing moral agency as that which is intrinsic to basic life processes. To him, moral motivation, rooted in human nature, is inextricably tied to the agency that fills our very lives with health and vitality.[61]

In *Mencius* 6A3, Gaozi raises the question of the semantic equality between *xing* and life, claiming, "What we [receive from] life is called '*xing*.'"[62] Here, Mencius cleverly brings Gaozi to admit implicitly that that claim is tantamount to the claim that "the nature of a dog is just like the nature of a cow, which is just like human nature."[63] Since such a statement defies common sense, the reader is supposed to conclude that Mencius has cornered Gaozi and exposed his faulty reasoning about the meaning of *xing*.[64] To Mencius, *xing* cannot possibly refer to "life" or "life forces" exclusively, for such a meaning would not distinguish the *xing* of humans from that of other creatures. Rather, it must encompass that which makes humans different from others: our inclinations toward moral behavior. Thus, we learn that Mencius views *xing* not as life processes or vital forces universal to all living creatures but as vital forces that are uniquely human.[65]

Throughout chapter 6A, Mencius outlines his version of the uniquely human life forces of *xing*.[66] In 6A6, for example, Mencius highlights the four attributes of the human heart-mind, which he links to human nature, and relates them to the four Ru virtues of humaneness (*ren* 仁), rightness (*yi* 義), one's sense of propriety (*li* 禮), and knowledge (*zhi* 智).[67] In 6A8, he again claims that moral characteristics define the human heart-mind, referring to it as "the heart-mind of humaneness and rightness."[68] He then claims that such a heart-mind is fundamentally characteristic of human nature (*xing*) just as the vegetation atop a mountain is fundamentally characteristic of the nature (*xing*) of a mountain.[69] These examples, considered together, reveal that Mencius identifies morality with the inherent life forces and bodily processes of humans, such as those of the pumping and thinking heart-mind. Morality is as natural to humans as it is for them to use their heart-mind to think, feel, and pump blood throughout the body.

Mencius' use of the imagery of death and destruction to indicate the misuse of human nature attests to the fundamental connection he posits between moral motivation and life. For example, in passage 2A2, Mencius tells us of the man from Song who tries to aid in the growth of his rice plants by pulling on them. As a result of this kind of unnatural interference (a kind of *shi*), all the sprouts of rice wither and die.[70] Death is thus one possible outcome when one interferes with the natural life potential of *xing*. The correct method of moral cultivation is characterized as "not moving one's heart-mind," or stilling it so that the power and brilliance of one's moral *xing* can usher forth. This corresponds to nourishing life by tending to one's natural morality and moral agency, and vice versa. Doing harm through neglect or interference impairs both, just as the cultivation of one (morality) implicates the cultivation of the other (life).[71]

Aside from external forces, there are other threats to our cultivation of moral life—threats from within. For example, wayward forms of *qi* have the potential to misdirect *xing*: "When one's will [function of the heart-mind] is one,[72] it moves one's *qi*. When one's *qi* is one, it moves the will. Now, one falls and rushes because of *qi*, and so [it] actually moves the heart-mind."[73] From this we learn that competing agencies in the body will try to lead humans in one direction or the next. At the same time, there exists a natural, correct balance of bodily powers that one can and should obtain. Mencius envisions this natural balance as one in which the heart-mind and the *qi* abide in a dominant-subordinate but nonetheless mutually defining process. He suggests that maintaining this type of physiological balance in the body—achieved in part through the practice of "not moving one's heart-mind"—has repercussions for one's state of moral achievement and awareness.

For Gaozi, vitality and morality are distinct, so that the acquisition of the latter, and not the development of one's *xing*, is what distinguishes humans from other living beings.[74] In contrast to this, Mencius insists on the organic connection between a Heavenly endowed, natural state of living (not just being) and an achieved state of moral attainment. For Mencius, each individual person is his or her own moral agent by virtue of living properly and healthfully as a human being. By locating the seeds of morality in *xing*, one's Heavenly endowed agency for human life, Mencius demonstrates that cultivating oneself morally is tantamount to attaining the proper measures for the basic vital functions of human beings.[75] Mencius therefore not only naturalizes individual moral agency by making it a universally inherent trait. He proposes a radical physiological claim that connects proper moral cultivation to proper cultivation of one's inherent life forces.[76]

The general emergence of a discourse on universal sources of cosmic authority and power culminates with Mencius in a radical claim that locates such authority and power specifically within each individual. The internal-external dichotomy outlined in Mencius' writings is especially conducive to what Edward Slingerland refers to as metaphors of possession and containment, providing a suitable means of explaining difficult concepts such as moral agency and potential in terms of space, material, and location.[77] By arguing that all humans innately possess a material force that impels one toward morality, Mencius' claims are ethical as well as physiological and psychological. His writings thus represent some of the first Ru attempts to explicitly embrace and expound on the psycho-physiological sources of morality in the individual body.

Accompanying this conceptual breakthrough to individualized sources of idealized power and authority is a discourse that sharply distinguishes between individual and environmental sources of control. Metaphors of interiority take the place of idealizations of human conformism, and even loss of self. They support an individual's own agency and promote the proper, natural, and even vital development of an individual's body in and of itself. As we have just seen, Mencius' claims on *xing* alter the boundaries of individual moral agency and potential by showing that humans need not conform to what is outside of them in order to reach their highest goals; rather, they need but focus on cultivating and developing what is already inside.

Yang Zhu: An Early Individualist?

One cannot speak of a history of individualistic movements in early China without at least coming to terms with what we know about Yang Zhu (Yangzi 楊朱 / 楊子) and his legacy. The figure of Yang Zhu, an "egoist" or "individualist" who lived sometime during the fourth century BCE, loomed large in the mind of his contemporary, Mencius, and he was still considered to be relevant by thinkers from the second century BCE who wrote the *Huainanzi*.[78] Though there is no solid evidence that anything he may have authored has been transmitted through the ages, we can still gain insight into his views from descriptions and condemnations of his teachings by Mencius and other writers of a slightly later period, the Han.

Many scholars now believe that Yang Zhu's teachings are represented in anonymous treatises found in eclectic volumes such as the *Guanzi*, *Lüshi chunqiu*, and *Zhuangzi*.[79] For example, Fung Yu-lan speaks of the absorption of Yang Zhu's thought into some ideological strains running through the "Daoist" writings of *Laozi* and *Zhuangzi*, while A. C. Graham attributes whole chapters and sections of the *Zhuangzi* and *Lüshi chunqiu* to Yangist authors.[80] While these evaluations are certainly reasonable, they are not based on direct, textual statements linking Yang Zhu the man with such teachings or writings.[81] Since Fung and Graham's claims about actual Yangist texts are based on speculation rather than evidence, I will refrain from discussing such writings here in association with the Yangist point of view. Note also that by referring to this perspective as "Yangist," I am not claiming the existence of a school of thought in early China by that name. I am merely acknowledging the existence of a particular point of view—explicitly attributed to the figure of Yang Zhu in a few early textual references—that might be referred to hermeneutically as such.

Other more skeptical scholars, such as Qian Mu, have mentioned the possibility that Yang Zhu was but a marginal figure during the Warring States period whom Mencius uses to belittle the Mohists and who serves as a neat ideological foil to their doctrines.[82] However, many of Qian Mu's claims are based on the assumption that, since we do not have an extended early record of the large impact of Yang Zhu on his Warring States contemporaries, then he must not have been important at all.[83] Such a claim is, of course, also an assumption, since it is entirely possible that Yang Zhu's name and work fell into oblivion by the middle of the Han Dynasty even though he might have had a significant or even a locally significant influence prior to that time. Given that there is very little evidence for or against the notion that Yang Zhu bequeathed an important intellectual legacy on early Chinese thought, I will try to evaluate what little evidence we have in terms of the type of viewpoint Yang Zhu might have espoused. I will limit myself to direct characterizations of Yang Zhu and his intellectual legacy derived from writings from the Warring States and early Han periods.

Yang Zhu, like Mencius, appears to have viewed the self and human body as an important resource for universal, objective forms of authority through *xing*.[84] There are only three texts from the Warring States period and early Han that speak directly of Yang Zhu's views on the self. The earliest source is the *Mencius*. In one critical remark, Mencius compares the followers of Yang Zhu and Mo Di to runaway pigs who need to be brought back to the sty.[85] In two other passages, Mencius provides more substantial comments about his doctrines: "The words of Yang Zhu and Mo Di fill the world. If the teachings of the world do not follow Yang [Zhu], then they follow Mo [Di]. Mr. Yang advocates egoism (*wei wo* 為我), which is tantamount to denying one's ruler. Mr. Mo advocates universal caring, which is tantamount to denying one's father. To deny one's father or ruler is to be like birds and beasts."[86] Again, Mencius compares Yangist and Mohist doctrines to the dirty world of the birds and beasts. But he offers more concrete criticism by equating the egoism of Yang Zhu with a fundamental lack of respect for government, on the one hand, and the universalism of Mo Di with a fundamental lack of respect for the father figure, on the other. But what is this Yangist doctrine of "egoism"?[87]

Mencius 7A26 gives a possible answer, although certainly not an entirely fair or accurate one: "Yangzi supports egoism. Even if he were to benefit the world by pulling out a single hair, he would not do it. Mozi advocates universal caring. If by exerting himself from the crown of his head to the heels of his feet he might benefit the world, he would do it.[88] Zi Mo held to the middle. Holding to the middle is closer to it [being right]."[89] The caricatures of the self-satisfied Yangist and the self-mortifying Mohist are indeed humorous and almost too perfect in the contrast they provide, giving the reader reason to suspect that they might not actually accord with the self-identified ideals of either side. The caricature suggests that Yangzi's so-called egoism is founded on a principle of preserving one's self or body over and above anything else.

A look at a passage from the *Lüshi chunqiu* supports the claim that Yang Zhu valued the self (*ji* 己) over and above other things: "Lao Dan esteemed softness, Confucius benevolence, Mo Di universalism, Guanyin purity, Liezi emptiness, Tian Pian evenness, Yang Zhu the self, Sun Bin strategic force, Wang Liao going first, Ni Liang going last."[90] From the transmitted record, we have knowledge of the primary values of Lao Dan, Confucius, and Mo Di, and what the author here says about all of them appears to be verifiable and on target. Thus, from this passage, we might reasonably assume that one of the most significant values for Yang Zhu was self (*wo* 我) according to the *Mencius,* and self (*ji*) according to the *Lüshi chunqiu*. But just what sense or aspect of the self Yang Zhu supported, and the extent to which he valued this aspect over and above other, outside objects, appears to be in question.

The ambiguity in our sources concerning which sense of self Yang Zhu valued is further confused in the description of his teachings found in the *Huainanzi*: "Keeping one's nature whole, preserving one's genuineness, and not letting things tire one's form (body)—these Yangzi advocated but Mencius denounced."[91] In this example, the "self" to be valued consists in *xing*, the body, and "genuineness" (*zhen* 真)—a vague concept that seems to refer to a spiritual ideal, inherent or original to the individual.[92] If this description is even remotely accurate, then Yang Zhu idealized certain aspects of the self that help define its essence, whether material, spiritual, or both.[93] By insisting on a sharp separation between that which is internal or associated with the person on the one hand, and the "things" (*wu* 物) that might tire it on the other, the Yang Zhu depicted in this passage joins Mencius in basing his ideals on a fundamental inner/outer distinction. However, his recommendation that one keep the self and its aspects free of outside contamination would constitute an even more extreme form of individualism than what we have encountered with Mencius.

In the passages from the *Lüshi chunqiu* and *Huainanzi*, we glimpse a view of Yangist beliefs that are perhaps more descriptive and less biased than those found in Mencius' account. In neither of these later texts is there any sense that Yang Zhu advocated "selfishness," understood in terms of a self that actively seeks profit from certain situations. At most, one might claim that such beliefs belie a form of passive "selfishness" that does harm to the world through lack of attention and care for it. But such a claim is only valid from the perspective of someone who places value in the individual's responsibility to contribute to the social good—as Mencius does. In the absence of such social standards, the charge of "selfishness" becomes empty, and one might just as easily refer to Yang Zhu's thought as a consecration of the essence of being human, or more precisely, of possessing a "self." Similarly, in the absence of any knowledge about the social ideals of Yang Zhu, or whether he presented his perspective on any form of idealized society, it is unfair to criticize his teachings as advocating an egoism typified by selfishness, rather than, say, an egoism understood as personal salvation.[94]

In the interest of using what we do know about the intellectual contexts of the fourth century BCE to think through Yang Zhu's beliefs, I put forth the following hypothesis. Like Zhuangzi, Yang Zhu (as characterized by later texts that attribute a certain, relatively consistent perspective to his beliefs) seems to have supported the preservation of some essential and vital spirit that is ultimately related to the human body and its wholeness. Unlike Zhuangzi, who wished to deny one's awareness of the boundaries of the self and its materiality, Yang Zhu appears to have glorified the existence of these and called for the preservation of a strict separation between what is inside and belonging to the sphere of the self and what is outside and belonging to the sphere of things. Thus the main distinction between Zhuangzi and Yang Zhu, I suggest, lies in the fact that Yang Zhu valued the self as a material body that is spiritual and perhaps even sacred precisely because of its essential materiality and life-producing qualities. Zhuangzi, on the other hand, did not directly embrace the cult of bodily vitality. He wished for individuals to transcend their bodies and their materiality so as to embrace what he sometimes referred to as the spirit (*shen* 神) of the Dao, which should be understood in terms of an ethereal type of vitality.

Given the description of Yang Zhu's thought in the *Huainanzi*, in particular his emphasis on preserving genuineness and *xing* as ends in themselves, it seems fair to call him an individualistic egoist rather than an apologist for selfish egoism.[95] After all, there is no convincing evidence that Yang Zhu promoted selfishness in the sense that he inspired individuals to seek self-profit through the exploitation of public resources or goods. Moreover, if we disregard Mencius' clearly biased critiques, there is no clear indication that Yang Zhu tacitly condoned harming or destroying society through his ideals. Rather, most of the reliable evidence points to the fact that Yang Zhu redefined what it meant to value the self (*wo* 我, ji 己) in terms of one's personal, material-spiritual salvation. If we can trust the characterizations of these later sources, then Yang Zhu was perhaps one of the first thinkers, like Mencius, to see *xing* and the self as a primary source of idealized individual agency and meaning.

Conclusion

The *Zhuangzi*, which focuses on individual attainment irrespective of politics, underscores an individual's direct access to an idealized, cultivated state of being. According to its conformist stance, the entire human body—and not exclusively the sovereign body—serves as the direct medium of higher authority and power. Every individual regardless of sociopolitical position, gender, and health has the same potential instrumentality and direct connection to the Dao. Viewing the individual body itself as a unique locus for idealized power, Zhuangzi argued for a more decentralized body politic, insofar as each individual could become his or her own center of control. Zhuangzi thus helped pave the road for a new mode of thinking about individual agency that theoretically addressed the commoner and artisan in the same manner as the sovereign and state official. No longer was the political sphere or sociopolitical hierarchy a necessary mediator of universalized authority in the world; all individuals might theoretically gain access to the higher powers and ideals of the cosmos by virtue of their own personal cultivation.

The theoretical gap between propounding the privileged power of a single sovereign body and proclaiming the direct agency of every individual is significant. The latter claim suggests that there was an audience of people in early China not necessarily involved in governing or in giving political advice to rulers who found it beneficial or necessary to cultivate themselves and distinguish themselves from the political realm in certain ways. It also suggests that there was room for theorizing about individual ideals, social organization, and life distinct from—but nonetheless connected to—the realm of politics.

It is but a small leap from this decentralized, individual-oriented understanding of conformism to an approach that explicitly attaches cosmic agency to the self through the concept of human nature. In our discussion of Mencius and Yang Zhu, we saw how these authors identified the body as the source—and not merely the instrument—for cosmic authorities and agencies. Such an approach to human agency marks the development of what I call a new, individualistic orientation that locates inherent agencies within the human body. This individualistic orientation is characterized by the idealization of unconscious, automatic, natural agencies of the body that, if preserved or properly nourished, bring about health, vitality, the requisite conditions for individual salvation, moral achievement, and even social order—depending on a given author's predilections.

Our discussion of Mencian and Yangist claims on *xing* demonstrates a growing belief in the efficacy and power associated with the individual body. It also shows that there were different ways of idealizing *xing*. Because our knowledge of Mencius is more complete, we can appreciate more fully how Mencius' claim for universal moral agency might represent a critical moment in the history of views on the self and its powers. By arguing precisely for the positive, innate power of every individual to cultivate morality, Mencius appears to have shifted current debates from the acquisition of external power and authority through conformism to the proper cultivation of what each individual possesses within himself or herself. Mencius not only naturalized cosmic agency in the self; he went one step further to identify moral agency with innate vital agency, marking the beginning of a long-term cultural trend that links the cosmic powers and processes of life with the goals for moral and/or spiritual cultivation.[96]

We cannot be certain whether thinkers like Yang Zhu also linked *xing* to cosmic power. However, it is highly likely that Yang Zhu served as a well-known spokesperson for individualistic movements that emphasized the value, meaning, and dignity in nourishing the self and body (or certain aspects of it) for the sake of larger religious goals. Yang Zhu perhaps represents the earliest example of an unadulterated individualism that sacralized the material body and self, holding its preservation in highest esteem. Rather than view Yang Zhu from the narrow social perspective of the *Mencius,* which condemns him as an advocate of selfish egoism, we should consider other possible interpretations, taken from cues in later (Qin and Han), seemingly more neutral descriptions of Yang Zhu's philosophy. Such sources clearly suggest that Yang Zhu proposed a coherent stance that glorified certain innate agencies of the individual.

Traditional scholarly accounts of individualism rarely apply such a term to early Chinese thought, and when they do, they do so only sparingly, to such figures as Yang Zhu and later third- to second-century BCE writers who allegedly promoted bodily selfishness and private over public life.[97] Individualism, as I have introduced it in this chapter, was a broad orientation that shared a deep spiritual relationship to the goal of bodily conformism—also prevalent in texts of the same period. Individualistic authors, rather than idealizing one's conformity to an external source of authority or power, naturalized cosmic or divine sources of authority in the world by locating them within the human body itself, thereby making the self in and of itself a source of idealized authority.

CHAPTER FOUR

Two Prongs of the Debate
Bodily Agencies vs. Claims for
Institutional Controls

Starting from about the third century BCE, authors ubiquitously grounded their proposed programs for education, self-cultivation, and legal and political reform in arguments concerning the natural biological conditions of humankind. Hardly a thinker existed who did not have some opinion concerning the relationship between innate, universal human functions such as *xing* and the goals of either self-cultivation or social order and control. Intriguingly, unlike the approaches found in earlier writings such as the core chapters of the Mohists and fourth-century BCE conformist texts—which allocated great powers to external sources of authority of all kinds—authors of this later period almost unanimously agreed that innate agencies act as highly deterministic forces in one's life. Two distinct stances emerged: the individualistic belief that innate agencies are powerful in a positive way and should be followed or developed to their full capacity; and the belief that innate agencies are powerful in a negative way and should be suppressed, restrained, or otherwise blocked by institutionalized safeguards and measures of control. These two stances can be viewed as offshoots of earlier debates—explored in the previous chapter—that rendered explicit a psycho-physiology of human control.

Individualism understood in terms of the positive powers attributed to *xing* and other bodily agencies must therefore be distinguished from other, more negative beliefs about the self. Individualistic authors exhorted individuals to preserve or develop in an organic fashion the positive aspects of their selves, so that such individuals might prevail in the face of external threats or negative influences. While individualistic authors seized upon aspects of the self that highlight human dignity, bodily power, and cosmic meaning and authority, other authors remained suspicious of innate human agencies. These skeptics focused on the need to curb negative agencies of the self to prevent selfishness and social chaos, which they saw as ensuing from them. Thus, the debate about Yang Zhu's status as an individualist or selfish egoist, outlined in chapter three, is not merely of interest to us today. Condemnation of selfishness had its roots in Warring States contexts as one side of a two-pronged discussion about the highly deterministic powers located within or associated with the self.

The Deterministic Powers of Bodily Agencies

Some writers of the third to second centuries BCE attempted to integrate all humans into a seamless and interconnected web of cosmic powers. They joined Mencius and Yang Zhu in using the notion of *xing* to argue for a person's inalienable claims on bodily power and authority within this dynamic system. Like Mencius, their views concerning innate bodily authorities manifested a broadened perspective on who can legitimately exert agency in the sociopolitical sphere. Unlike Mencius and perhaps more like Yang Zhu, many of these other thinkers presented *xing* in amoral terms, as an individual's physico-spiritual access to idealized cosmic order. They pointed to *xing* and sometimes other agencies inherent in the human body as the means by which an individual might personally fulfill his or her role in a cosmic order.

Health and vitality constitute areas of critical concern for individualistic movements in the third and second centuries BCE.[1] While many of the claims on health and vitality reveal an undeniable link to themes and concepts found in the *Laozi* as well as the "Heart" chapters of *Guanzi*, they also demonstrate important discontinuities. Most significantly, they differentiate themselves from such conformist approaches by propounding a belief in one's internal, innate sources of cosmic authority and power. This difference is critical to what seems to have become—by the third century BCE—a widespread belief in the individual body as a legitimate source of cosmic authority and agency. Below we will examine some individualistic perspectives that view bodily agencies as the sole or primary source and power for human attainment in the world.

Utopian Order through Bodily Equilibrium

A. C. Graham and Liu Xiaogan have grouped certain writings from the "Outer" and "Miscellaneous" chapters of the *Zhuangzi* according to what they believe are internally consistent perspectives that differ from those of the rest of the book. Graham speculates that one perspective, noted for its distinct flavor of social criticism, derives from an author who might be labeled the "Primitivist."[2] Liu slices up the text along somewhat similar lines and relegates such a perspective to what he dubs the "Anti-sovereign School" (*wu jun* 無君).[3] In the following analysis, I accept the premise that much of the writing in several of the chapters under question is sufficiently distinct from most other portions of the text to warrant considering it as a distinct authorial perspective.[4] I follow Graham's label of "Primitivist" not to designate any particular school of thought that existed at the time, but as a hermeneutical tool for clarifying the core tenets of a certain intellectual orientation that is expressed by a certain author (or authors) in the received text.[5]

Primitivist writing can be characterized not only by its unique emphasis on the sacred powers of *xing* but also by its nostalgia for an idyllic period of the remote past in which humans lived harmoniously and in touch with their most pristine roots—notably, without a ruler to guide them.[6] It thus presents an individualistic agenda attached to an overarching sociopolitical ideal. By recommending that each individual place all of his or her faith in the powers of *xing*, the Primitivist suggests that one can rid oneself of impulses responsible for the creation of culture and social norms.[7] This results in the reversion not just of the individual back to his or her most basic nature, but a reversion of society as well back to an era of primitive political structures and human interactions.[8]

Earlier, we saw how Mencius criticized Gaozi's position on morality, saying that his words necessarily would lead "the people of the world to view morality as disastrous!"[9] Mencius feared that Gaozi's externalistic approach would give skeptics grounds to denounce ethical precepts altogether as exterior violations of the self. In retrospect, we can see that Mencius' critique was not entirely unrealistic, since the Primitivist position in fact makes use of the very line of logic Mencius feared most. Indeed, the Primitivist denounces morality as an external overlay and an unnecessary pollution of *xing*. He utterly rejects the trappings of culture and civilization, and dismisses certain modes of behavior as artificial and alien to one's natural endowment.

Both Graham and Liu stress the extreme, anti–status quo position expressed through the Primitivist writing. Graham goes as far as to present the Primitivist as rejecting "the whole of moral and aesthetic culture,"[10] which, Graham claims, is apparent in the author's critique of the traditional ethical or spiritual masters: Confucius, Zeng Can, Shi You, Yang Zhu, and Mo Di.[11] In addition to this list of thinkers, the Primitivist criticizes those who "establish power (德) from an outside source."[12] He also criticizes famous cultural figures of the past who symbolize the ultimate human achievement in music, crafts, and visual art respectively: Master

Kuang, Artisan Chui, and Li Zhu.[13] Such critiques illustrate the Primitivist's deep rejection of external sources of authority and power over human life. Adding to Graham's insights, I suggest that these go beyond the realm of morality and aesthetics to include the rejection of all varieties of actions not stemming from one's *xing* within (including, and perhaps especially, the realm of politics). Following in a Laozian vein, but using the language of *xing* in addition to that of *wu-wei*, the Primitivist considers rational human knowledge and technologies to be prime examples of things that do not stem from *xing* and accord with the cosmic Dao.

For the Primitivist, *xing* is best characterized as that which is inherent or endowed in a thing prior to and distinct from any contamination of human culture. To demonstrate the areas over which *xing* has control, the author draws on examples from the animal world, such as the short legs of a duck and the long legs of a crane.[14] Here, *xing* is not limited to the human world. It is the general term for an endowment and force that determines a constant, natural order, enabling all things to "live without knowing why."[15] In other words, *xing* automatically determines life, without creatures having to understand why it does so, and without creatures having to do anything about it. Since the obtainment of *xing* obviates the need for knowledge and willful action, the notion of "one's active obtainment of *xing*" becomes paradoxical.[16] Perhaps aware of such a paradox, and in an attempt to reduce one's level of self-conscious or purposive activity, the Primitivist author recommends the more passive activities of not "losing" (損) or preserving one's *xing* rather than cultivating it.[17]

According to the Primitivist, the allotment of *xing* in humans is neither good nor bad, but right and powerful, insofar as it is used synonymously with the word "*De*."[18] Indeed, the power of *xing* is valuable not for ethical reasons but because it derives from cosmic processes, of which humans are a critical part. Because of its connection to the cosmos, *xing* allows one's behavior and perception to be truly keen or right, because it brings the self into proper alignment with workings of the cosmos.[19] *Xing* thus serves as the body's representative of cosmic operations.

Given this characterization, we might ask what lies outside the domain of *xing*. The following passage illustrates how the Primitivist distinguishes knowledge from *xing*, the latter of which is based in cosmic operations:

> When there is too much knowledge of bows, crossbows, bird-snares, stringed arrows, and triggered traps, then birds are disordered above. . . . We disturb what is appropriate for the sun and moon above, dissipate the essences of the mountains and rivers below, and interrupt the cycles of the

four seasons in between. There is not a single insect creeping on the ground or flitting in the air that does not lose its *xing*.[20] How completely those who desire knowledge have disordered the world! Since as far back as the Three Dynasties this has been the case; they neglect the plain people and take delight in toadying sycophants, abandon tranquility and *wu-wei* and take pleasure in clamoring ideas. All such clamor has thrown the world in disorder![21]

Here the author pits two aspects of being human against each other: having knowledge—which is artificial and hence harmful—and possessing a *xing*. According to a zero-sum calculation, the obtainment of one brings about the loss of the other, so that an individual's preservation of *xing* is tantamount to the relinquishing of his or her knowledge.

Relinquishing knowledge not only helps preserve the self; it helps bring cosmic order to the natural world as well. Human physiological states characterized by tranquility and preserved through *wu-wei* render an individual capable of both fitting into and continuing the orderly cycles of the cosmos.[22] By contributing to widespread cosmic order through their own personal preservation, individuals participate in a social ideal through individualistic means. Such a stance recommends an internal politics of *xing* over a politics of human knowledge, technology, and social institutions.

Other examples demonstrate the Primitivist's reliance on the body as an agent for worldly order. In addressing the sovereign's problem of governing the world, the Primitivist adopts a somewhat Laozian solution, which suggests viewing active governance as an afterthought, and instead finding "comfort [or safety] in the conditions of one's *xing* [nature] and *ming* [Heaven's Mandate, or destiny]" and engaging in *wu-wei*.[23] He restates the Laozian ideal: "For this reason when one values using one's body in governing the world, he can be entrusted with the world. When one cherishes using one's body in governing the world, he can be assigned it."[24] In his nonchalant attitude toward politics, the Primitivist nonetheless demonstrates the salutary political effects of his method.[25] Far from recommending an anarchist state, the Primitivist supports the traditional monarchy, intimating that a sovereign's bodily agency, not sociopolitical power, is the necessary criterion for good rulership. His recommendations for individual agency through the preservation of *xing* do not push for a meritocratic platform of social mobility but for the increased agency of all individuals, including that of the sovereign, within a depoliticized sphere of action.

The chapter "Horse Hooves" demonstrates that cosmic control does not lie exclusively, or even primarily, in the ruler's hands. Taking this position to the extreme, the author at one point describes a utopian past in which all people of the period shared in their power (*De* 德) and were guided by a constant *xing*.[26] In such an era, there was no distinction between "gentleman" and "small man," and people lived in harmony with animals, that is, without desires and without knowledge.[27] There is no mention of a sovereign here, precisely because there is no room for making a distinction such as "sovereign" in the first place. Such a political stance is slightly different from the one we have just described.[28] It fully accepts the universal and equally valid powers of *xing* so that there is no need for a ruler. *Xing* in this passage denotes the simple agency of every human to fulfill and harmonize with one's cosmic and social environment. Because of its non-institutional nature, *xing* effaces political position and the political state, substituting such hierarchies with the harmony of the cosmos.

In their total rejection of artifice and external sources of knowledge, these Primitivist authors take a stand in what has become an explicit debate over internal and external sources of idealized authority and power.[29] By rejecting the necessity of social structures, institutions, knowledge, technologies, and cultural practices in favor of a cosmic or natural law and power that is accessible through the human body, proponents of this ideology share a basic, individualistic point of view. Such a view assumes that ultimate value lies in what humans possess innately and in what is accessible to every individual. For the Primitivist, this internal, innate, and universal human agency to interact ideally in the world derives from *xing*, which is ultimately a part of the natural cycles of the cosmic Dao.

This brings us back to the issue of internal vs. external methods of controlling life, so central to the Primitivist's worldview. For the Primitivist, individuals who have fulfilled their innate potentials for cosmic agency, thereby bringing themselves in touch with the cosmic equilibrium of *xing*, do not conform to any external standard. Behavior that is right is defined as "employing the character of one's *xing* and *ming* (Heaven's Mandate, or destiny) and that is all,"[30] because cosmic authority and power are already encoded and endowed within. Even the acuteness of one's senses, such as keen hearing and seeing (*cong* 聰 and *ming* 明) occurs of itself and is grounded in what is spontaneous and unimpeded within the individual.[31]

The Primitivist cleverly uses metaphors of possession and theft to suggest that standards for true perception and engagement with the world are internally possessed:

> As for seeing another without "seeing of oneself" (*zi jian* 自見), or possessing something without "possessing of oneself" (*zi de* 自得), this is possessing the possession of others without possessing it of oneself.[32]

In this scenario, individuals are admonished to function in a manner complicit with their own internal standards, or "of themselves" (*zi* 自)—as they truly are according to *xing*. This idealized vision of internal human agency is characterized by a spontaneous mode of interacting with the world and thereby creating a true sense of reality. When one neglects this mode of engagement, everything one takes in from the outside remains superficially obtained, or belonging to another, external source.

The underlying metaphor of theft, or "possessing the possessions of others," gains meaning when the author juxtaposes the behavior of Robber Zhi with that of the esteemed and ancient hermit, Bo Yi. "They both similarly acted excessively and in a biased manner,"[33] he states, after articulating their faults as "arriving where others [expect one to] arrive and not arriving of one's own [accord]."[34] Thus, excessive and biased behavior results from one's being disconnected from one's own inherent possessions and basing behavior on external standards of expectation and gain. Both the robber and the moral recluse commit themselves to behavior that is externally motivated, and, therefore, according to the metaphor of theft, they violate and do damage to their own natural possessions.

The imagery of violation and damage is apparent in the Primitivist's discussion of what one does to *xing*. He speaks of "losing *xing*" and "pairing it off," as though it were possible to separate oneself from this intrinsic aspect of life. In the examples of ducks with short legs and cranes with long necks, the author shows us how this is possible:

> Though a duck's legs are short, if you lengthen them it will be miserable; though a crane's legs are long, chopping them off will bring grief. Thus, if the *xing* of a thing makes it long, it is not to be cut off. If the *xing* of a thing makes it short, then one must not lengthen it.[35]

The act of cutting off or lengthening the legs of ducks and cranes is a violation of *xing* because one actively moves to negate what is inherently right for it.[36] The loss or "pairing off" of a body part is a concrete loss that symbolizes the loss of *xing* through cultural manipulation. Although one does not literally lose *xing*, one loses grasp of its vital power through outside interference, and thus becomes damaged in a manner similar to that of a duck with long legs and a crane without them.

In summary, the Primitivist focuses on the notion of "mutilating life and losing *xing*" (殘生損性) in order to launch an attack against prevailing claims for laws, traditions, and authorities that are not based in the cultivation of one's own cosmic powers.[37] By employing the metaphor of theft to illuminate polarities between what is external and alien or internal and inalienable to a given object, he pits knowledge and culture against one's personal vitality and innate powers. The Primitivist naturalizes what is ideal by locating it in the cosmic capacity and authority of an individual's *xing*.

In favoring the individual preservation of cosmic authority and power as a means to social order, the Primitivist rationalizes a political vision not entirely unlike that of the *Laozi*. The main difference, however, lies in his naturalized and more universally accessible conception of individual power. Since he does not prioritize the exclusive role of the ruler as cosmic conduit, the Primitivist presents a utopian vision that speaks to every individual's direct relationship to cosmic power. This difference points to a noteworthy distinction between theocratic conceptualizations of cosmic authority and power, as expressed in the *Laozi*, and biocratic ones, as expressed in the Primitivist ideal. Below we turn our attention to an example of theocratic individualism from the third century BCE to demonstrate that not all forms of individualism were promoted universally.

Imperial Power through Vitality and Health

The following writings from the *Lüshi chunqiu* (or *Mr. Lü's Spring and Autumn Annals*) of 239 BCE, like the Primitivist ones just examined, also demonstrate the trend to idealize the inherent power of the body.[38] Although they address more exclusively the interests of the sovereign,[39] thereby resembling the sovereign-oriented writings discussed in chapter two, they clearly advocate a type of human agency that has universal implications if applied outside of the sovereign's sphere.[40] This set of writings also agrees with some other third-century BCE writings on human agency in the relationship it draws between vital processes inherent in human life and idealized conditions in the social and natural worlds.

A. C. Graham identifies five chapters in the *Lüshi chunqiu* as representative of a latter-day Yangist school, which he names the "Nurture of Life" chapters.[41] While it is far from clear whether these five chapters are Yangist or not, their message is particularly individualistic, and so they are worthy of analysis here. Much like the *Laozi* and *Guanzi* writings already examined, these chapters directly address issues concerning a ruler's health and vitality, linking cultivation of the sovereign body with the betterment of society and the world. Yet they present different methods of achieving such

Two Prongs of the Debate

a goal. At the core of this difference is a vision of sovereign power in *Lüshi chunqiu* that presents the ruler, by virtue of his personal agency, as full arbitrator of his and his people's destiny.

As mentioned previously, the terms "*sheng*" (life 生) and "*xing*" 性 held a very close linguistic relationship that authors of the day sometimes exploited in their writings on human nature.[42] A. C. Graham analyzes the usage of the two terms in the *Lüshi chunqiu* chapters "Taking Life as One's Basis" and "Favoring the Self" (both chapters classified under Yangist "Nurture of Life" writings). He shows that "*xing*" in these chapters does not refer "to life in general or particular lives," as does the term "*sheng*," but "to the course of life proper to man, in particular, to health and longevity."[43] Graham thus marks a semantic distinction that places *xing* in these passages into a subcategory of the general topic of "life," particularly concerned with aspects of vitality, and referring to a course of development.

Graham's general association between "*xing*" and life and his more specific claim for "*xing*" as "course of life" in these chapters are insightful, and they help explain what appears to be a link between *xing* and health in the text. For example, the act of "making Heaven whole" is the Son of Heaven's way of "nourishing all that Heaven gives birth to and not disturbing it."[44] Here, "making Heaven whole" refers specifically to preserving one's own vitality as endowed to one by Heaven through *xing*, a kind of cosmic code responsible for the materialistic flourishing of life.[45] The text further supports the notion of an automatic course for *xing*, seen in the comparison of the sovereign's *xing* with clear water that has not been muddied by disturbances.[46] This image of *xing* conveys its innate potential for clarity and its vulnerability to external interference. By tampering with the ultimately spontaneous, automatic processes of *xing*, we "stir up the mud," so to speak, thereby impairing our very potential for health and life.

As in the *Laozi*, the "Nurture of Life" chapters demonstrate that with health comes a powerful capacity to govern the world without forethought and conscious effort:

> When what is Heavenly about him [the Son of Heaven] is whole, then his spirit is harmonious, his eyes, ears, nose, and mouth are sharp, and his 360 nodes all run smoothly. This type of person does not need to say a thing for others to have faith in him; he does not need to plan ahead in order to do what is appropriate; and he does not need to think in order to obtain.[47]

Here, the Son of Heaven achieves a kind of spiritual sagacity and sensory perspicuity that enables him to know without thinking and to legitimize his control through the faith of others.[48] Through cultivation of his *xing*, the Son of Heaven manifests effortless and spontaneous harmony with the outside world and those over whom he rules. Thus the preservation of *xing* in this passage implies much more than "the proper course of life," as Graham would have us understand it. It reaches beyond the Son of Heaven's proper course of life to include his proper relationship to society and the state.

In the above passage, the sage ruler's preoccupation with self-cultivation involves using his body as an instrument for personal health as well as the establishment of his legitimate control over the world. But the text refers to control of a certain type. As long as the Son of Heaven wields the cosmic power of health within him by paying attention to a certain *modus vivendi*, his body will harmonize itself in the world so that no further effort is needed to control it. Thus, by harmonizing with the world in a vital, biological way, the Son of Heaven might establish his authority as leader without having to actively control the world. The result of this type of non-control (some might identify this concept with *wu-wei*) is overall social harmony. We see this as well in "Taking Life as One's Basis," where the author demonstrates how the attainment of social harmony is necessarily a part of the Son of Heaven's "vital interests," that is, his proper course of life. Effort well spent for the Son of Heaven is effort that cultivates his health and enlists the cosmic agency of his body to govern the world. If such an effort is not put forth, the administration will fall into disarray and the state will be lost.[49]

Implicit in these claims is an understanding that the Son of Heaven, who occupies the pinnacle of the politico-cosmic structure, serves as the primary source for cosmic authority and power. For the Son of Heaven, then, *xing* serves as a sociopolitical mechanism as well as an individual endowment, and allows for the ordering of the entire body politic, including the body of the ruler himself. As in the writings on sovereign conformity analyzed in chapter two, the "Nurture of Life" chapters stress the primary importance of a ruler's engagement with his person in order to achieve administrative control. The only difference is that in this particular case, the conception of *wu-wei*, so vaguely defined in the *Laozi*, is more clearly translated into a bodily regime that emphasizes the purification of the *xing*. Moreover, since every human possesses a *xing*, the social implications for everybody's own personal self-cultivation are necessarily broader than those in the sovereign conformity texts above.

Authors of the "Nurture of Life" chapters establish human authority and power not in tradition, history, or knowledge, but in the cosmic operations inherent in one's own body and epitomized in the body of the Son of Heaven. They thereby establish a visceral, innate connection between human agency and cosmic agency. Because these chapters focus so exclusively on the bodily cultivation of the Son of Heaven, it is difficult to argue that they are truly any more individualistic than the fourth-century BCE texts on sovereign conformity discussed in chapter two. However, their usage of the notion of *xing* as the pivotal element in bodily cultivation is new, and it points directly to the universalizing discourse on *xing* that in some circles did render self-cultivation implicitly open to all. Perhaps the very fact that authors chose to bolster the position of the Son of Heaven in this manner attests to the popularity of individualistic discourses at the time.

Negative Powers of the Self and Claims for Institutional Controls

Having discussed thinkers who emphasize the importance of harnessing innate bodily agencies through self-cultivation, we can now turn to the other side of the emerging debate over the intrinsic powers of the self. The writings of two third-century BCE thinkers, Xunzi and Han Feizi, illustrate how key writers of the period might also fully embrace the notion of the highly determining power of innate or intrinsic human agencies. In contrast to the individualistic approach described above, however, these thinkers emphasize the primarily negative, selfish aspects of such agencies to rally for institutionalized methods of control in society.

In supporting the use of more external sources of control and influence, these third-century BCE authors are similar to the Mohists. Yet they can be distinguished from the Mohists—who in their writings imply that human nature is extremely malleable—by virtue of their firm beliefs in the innate, albeit negative, powers of the self.[50] To Xunzi and Han Feizi, *xing* is powerful and deterministic, not weak and indeterminate. By insisting on the detrimental, selfish forces of *xing*, these authors justify their opposition to the cultivation of one's personal agencies as a viable means of social control. They are thus inextricably involved in debates on the power and authority of *xing* in human life and society, and their advocacy for institutionalized methods of control can be understood in terms of their opposition to individualistic trends and a discursive emphasis on private sources of authority that existed at the time.[51]

Base but Malleable Natures in the Xunzi

In the chapter "Against the Twelve Masters," Xunzi positions himself starkly against many of his predecessors and contemporaries. In particular, he pointedly critiques the teachings of Mencius and Zi Si, grouping them together as proponents of "the Five Phases" and lambasting them for possessing theories that are "utter abominations that do not adhere to correct standards of categorization."[52] In regarding these figures as impostors trying to pass off their own nonsensical ideas as the Master's (Confucius') own true words, Xunzi implicitly claims that he himself is knowledgeable of the traditions of the sage-kings Yao and Yu on the one hand, and the traditions of the sages Confucius and Zi Gong on the other.[53] But did Xunzi really have more in common with these esteemed forebears than he did with Mencius and Zi Si? This analysis of Xunzi's writings will show that his claims for personal cultivation and cosmic connection through ritual education and strong external guidance, though institutionalist in orientation, are deeply connected to a discourse on human agency that differs considerably from that of his forebears and their contemporaries, like the early Mohists. Indeed, Xunzi's views can be considered to be one kind of reaction to contemporary beliefs in the innate agencies of the individual, placing him squarely in the midst of later Warring States debates on the topic.

Like the early Mohists, Xunzi legitimizes moral self-cultivation by subscribing to the view that humans are malleable creatures of potential:

> Thus it is said, "The person of *ren* (humanity) likes to proclaim and demonstrate this to other people." . . . If Kings Tang and Wu were present, then the whole world would follow them and become ordered; if Kings Jie and Zhou were present, then the whole world would follow them and become disordered. This being the case, does this not show that human states of mind (*qing*, dispositions 情) are inherently malleable [literally, can inherently be like this or that]?[54]

This passage characterizes the people of the world as incredibly impressionable and protean, as they take their cues from kings, who serve as models of significant, influential power—whether good or bad.

Unlike the early Mohists, however, Xunzi readily and explicitly acknowledges the deterministic power of universal human nature, or *xing*. Humans share in certain fundamental bodily needs and desires for what is beneficial for themselves, and such desires determine many aspects of their behaviors:

> There are universals among humans. When hungry, desiring to eat; when cold, desiring warmth; when tired, desiring rest; liking benefit and disliking harm—these desires are all present when one is born. They are not what people wait to possess. Even Yu and Jie were similar in these [aspects].[55]

This depiction of shared, innate inclinations at first glance appears to contradict Xunzi's belief that human nature is so malleable. Either human behavior is largely shaped by one's innate tendencies, or it is influenced by environmental determinants. How might Xunzi justify his claims concerning human malleability and the potential for change on the one hand, and the determining power of *xing* on the other?[56]

Admittedly, espousing the two beliefs is not necessarily a contradiction. Depending on the extent to which *xing* is deterministic, one can legitimately posit a claim for a certain degree of human malleability. But Xunzi's terminology perhaps begs the question. When discussing *xing*, Xunzi speaks of it as base, fundamentally unchanging, and deterministic. Notably, Xunzi also describes the "inherent" (*gu* 固) quality of human malleability not in terms of *xing* but in terms of an individual's *qing* (dispositions, emotions). *Qing*, associated with the human heart-mind, might well be open to change, though the *xing* is not.[57] By distinguishing between inherent natures and human potential through the concepts of *xing* and *qing* respectively, Xunzi shows that humans can change by training aspects of their heart-minds, which are more open-ended and less determined by universal, debased tendencies of *xing*. Therefore, it is because Xunzi subscribes to a subtle account of the self—one with contradictory tendencies and potentials—that he is able to embrace both views of human malleability and the determinism of human nature.[58]

It should therefore come as no surprise that Xunzi thinks that while human nature is fundamentally base and guides us toward low and unsavory goals, there nonetheless exist an elite few who are able to transcend their baseness to become sages:

> If a Yao or Yu, then one constantly [meets with] security and glory; if a Jie or Zhi, then one constantly [meets with] danger and shame. If a Yao or Yu, then one constantly [meets with] expediency and ease; if a craftsman, farmer, or merchant, then one constantly [meets with] obstruction and toil. Now, why is it that there are many who are the latter [types of people] and engage in the latter [types of activities], while there are only a few who are the former [types of people] and engage in the former [types of activities]? I say that it is because of the baseness [of human nature].[59]

This passage demonstrates many things, but foremost it shows that some humans are able to engage certain potentials—presumably by using their heart-minds effectively. By doing so, they move beyond their base natures, while the rest lag behind under its influences. Xunzi is therefore able to respond to the question of how humans can progress beyond their base natures in the first place, given the powerfully deterministic character of their *xing*.

Because Xunzi views the self as possessing multiple, competing agencies—some of which hold ultimate sway over human actions when we do not concertedly attempt to overcome them—he not surprisingly endorses a type of moral self-cultivation that relies heavily on the guidance of external authorities. Such external authorities aid individuals in overcoming the base and selfish aspects of *xing* so as to cultivate the *qing* in a constructive manner:

> Yao and Yu were not born perfect. They started by altering what was inherent in them and matured with refined behavior. Only after this process was completed were they perfected. At birth, a human is inherently a petty man. Without a teacher and without laws, then he will see only profit![60]

This statement shows us how Xunzi utilizes the discourse on inherent natures and their determining powers to justify and support his vision of human attainment. Since humans are fundamentally base in their natures, they must alter themselves through external guidance to move forward. This is even the case for Yao and Yu, the great ancient sages among humankind.

The passage above mentions the importance of having external guides (teachers and laws) to help one alter one's originally petty nature and move beyond the baseline of self-interest and profit.[61] By prioritizing the act of acquiring rather than innately possessing, and by emphasizing the role of teachers and laws, Xunzi underscores human reliance on cultural traditions and institutions in the self-cultivation process. That he recommends reaching well beyond the self for the purpose of improving the self is characteristic of Xunzi's formulations on moral cultivation and is reminiscent of Confucius' orientations on the value of culture in individual development.

Unlike Confucius (as depicted in the *Analects*), Xunzi is distinctly self-conscious of the boundaries of the self and its powers, as he frames his writings in response to questions about human nature and the nature of human potential. His position on moral cultivation is constructed to refute claims, such as those found in the *Mencius*, for innate universal moral agency in humans. He does not follow the lead of the *Analects*, which takes for granted the necessity of cultural forms on the assumption that human potential is fundamentally protean in nature.[62] Rather, Xunzi bases his arguments for the necessity of external controls, forms, and influences on an assertion that human nature acts as a powerful, non-moral determinant in one's desires

Two Prongs of the Debate   91

and actions. This betrays his deep involvement in a later Warring States discourse on the deterministic powers of *xing*.

Xunzi's deep-seated involvement with the issue of shaping and altering, not idealizing, innate human agencies attests to his commitment to an externalistic approach to individual authority in society. Notably, Xunzi distinguishes between his conceptions of human nature, which he claims is both powerful and base, and the malleable self, associated not strictly with human nature but with its dispositions toward external forces and authorities. To him, moral cultivation must consist primarily of seeking out external sources of authority such as teachers, laws, and ritual, etc., for guidance. But does he draw a connection between the base natures of humans and the external authorities one must invoke in the self-cultivation process?

Although Xunzi states that human nature is base, he explicitly shows that humans have the potential to change themselves. While in one statement he claims that humans need external authorities ("Without a teacher and without laws, then one will see only profit!"), his descriptions of the ancient sage-kings Yao and Yu suggest that these great men of the past relied on their own work and judgment to reach an attained state and create standards of authority that might guide others in their own processes of moral cultivation. Xunzi is explicit about the fact that Yao and Yu were born with the same natures as everyone else ("Yao and Yu were not born perfect") and that they had to change themselves to become sages ("They started by altering what was inherent in them and matured with refined behavior").[63] The question then arises as to how exactly Yao and Yu achieved sagehood. Did they make use of internal capacities, or did they discover external authorities in society and the cosmos that they could use to transcend their own natures?

A famous passage in the text responds to this question in clear and explicit terms. Xunzi alerts his readers to his central notion of *wei* 偽, "human effort," which he takes as the critical process by which humans transform themselves from base, animal-like beings to sophisticates of culture and morality:[64]

> An interrogator poses the following question: If human nature is evil, then how did the rites and justice come about? To this I reply: The rites and justice are both generated by the sage's human effort (*wei*); they do not originally stem from human nature. When a potter molds clay to make a vessel, the vessel is the product of his human effort and not originally from human nature. . . . The sage piles up his thoughts and ideas, trains through

human effort and precedent, and thereby produces the rites and justice and sets forth laws and regulations. As a result, rites, justice, laws, and regulations are generated by the sage's human effort; they do not originally stem from human nature.[65]

Human nature, according to Xunzi, does not inherently serve as a force that helps create principles of ritual authority and justice. Yet the agency required for the creation of these cultural practices and norms still lies in humans themselves and not in any higher power beyond them. This agency, attributed to the process of human effort, constitutes a positive potential for humans. Distinguishable from what is inherently universal to *xing*, this potential is fulfilled only through the work of certain individuals.[66]

Xunzi thus believes that ultimate authority in society is created by humans through their own concerted effort, not adopted from powers externally higher than humans themselves. This fact demonstrates the degree to which idealized sources of authority have by Xunzi's time become associated with the potentials or characteristics of individuals themselves. Indeed, it is an individual's agency that creates idealized institutional forms and cultural precepts, not his or her conformity to external agencies of the cosmos. By proclaiming external authority as derivative of human agency rather than as derivative of Heaven and the cosmos, Xunzi acknowledges the fundamentally individual sources of idealized authority in the world.

This passage also reveals an important Xunzian distinction between human nature and idealized human agency. Whereas Mencius locates idealized human agency in human nature itself, Xunzi asserts that there is nothing ideal about it. Human effort, not *xing*, is responsible for the creation of ritual or objective authority. Thus, idealized forms of human agency do not directly stem from *xing*.[67] Yet to the extent that human effort is generated by the individual, it constitutes a potential that all humans might fulfill.[68]

In the chapter "Zheng Ming" 政名 ("Rectification of Names"), Xunzi demonstrates that the processes of human effort derive from the functioning of the conscious heart-mind (both its innate and acquired aspects): "When the heart-mind contemplates and one's capability translates this into movement, this is called human effort [i.e., the agency of natural thought]. When an action is completed after one's ideas have accumulated and one's capabilities are trained, this is called human effort [i.e., the agency of acquired thought]."[69] Here it is clear that the functions that constitute human effort are inherent in all individuals. Yet for Xunzi, only the sage has fully used his efforts to acquire the necessary ability to know and decide on morality.[70] He does this by piling up his "thoughts and ideas, training through human effort and precedent" to produce "the rites, justice . . . laws, and regulations."[71]

Given the universality of human effort, why do only a few people achieve sagehood while the others remain far behind? Significantly, Xunzi does not presuppose that one's engagement of human effort is universal, necessary, or equal. In fact, it appears that although the function of human effort is universal to all humans, an individual's proper commitment to it is not. Differentiation might occur for many reasons, environmental or natural. Given Xunzi's emphasis on external authorities that guide individuals in self-cultivation, however, he seems to consider the environment to be a leading factor in shaping one's level of moral commitment.

Unlike Mencius, Xunzi does not speak in terms of a naturalized moral agency, in the sense that such an agency might, under the right circumstances, automatically guide one toward moral behavior.[72] Instead, he differentiates between the agency or functions inherent in thought processes and the morality that is a product of the accumulation of these thought processes. This distinction Xunzi draws between actual moral cultivation of the self and the universal human ability to think and learn is critical. It allows him to make use of a broader discourse on innate human capacities so as to deny a necessary link between such capacities and moral behavior, goals, and norms. Rather than undermine or refute the notion of powerful, innate agencies in humans, Xunzi affirms their existence and works them into his main arguments for the necessity of external authorities, controls, and guides in society. He thus participates in the widespread debate of his day on innate sources of human power and authority.

Politics of Might and Legal Authority in the Han Feizi

Han Feizi (d. 233 BCE) and the authors of the text attributed to him, the *Han Feizi* (~235 BCE), advance their claims about the proper methods of statecraft on the basis of a belief in the universally negative aspects of human nature.[73] The *Han Feizi* thus participates in some general assumptions about human agency prevalent at the time: that it exists universally in humans, that it serves as a powerful determining force over human life, and that it often drives humans to act in similar ways. Largely influenced by political theorists such as Xunzi, Shen Buhai, Shen Dao, and Shang Yang, Han Feizi advocates the use of external and institutional controls over individuals. But, interestingly, his appeals to such methods of control are grounded in certain basic assumptions concerning the deterministic influences of innate human psychological tendencies over life. Insofar as other, earlier supporters of institutional control, such as the early Mohists and Shang Yang, were not apt to consider the issue of human nature as relevant to their idealized programs for state order and control, the fact that Han Feizi's ideals are rooted in certain basic beliefs about the power of human nature is striking and worthy of analysis.

In what follows, we examine the issue of Han Feizi's political thought, focusing on an overlooked facet of the author's eminently pragmatic, institutional approach: his implicit views on human nature and agency. So while we will elide much of Han Feizi's numerous political theories, we highlight a fundamental, implicit orientation that informs his entire approach to political philosophy. The fact that Han Feizi unconsciously absorbed such an orientation on human agency demonstrates that not even he—an eminently practical and realistic political thinker—was immune to the effects of discourses on human nature and its powers so prevalent in his day.[74]

As seen so far, since the onset of early Mohist visions of universal law, thinkers began constructing theories on universalized forms of power and authority, relating humans to them in a variety of ways. The thought represented in the text of *Han Feizi* reveals certain commonalities with early Mohist rule by universal law. But it differs with respect to configurations of human power. In advocating institutional standards of control, Han Feizi is apprehensive that human potential and power might transgress the bounds of official, state-sanctioned channels of authority. As we will see, this apprehensiveness corresponds to an underlying lack of faith in the existence and efficacy of universal, positive human potentials in helping bring about social order. So while Han Feizi disagrees with his contemporaries over the specific nature and value of innate human agency, he is actually similar to them, and not to the early Mohists, in appealing to it as a justification for his proposed methods of control.

Han Feizi believes that human behavior is shaped by deterministic, negative human agencies. Because of such a belief, he supports a model of control that compensates and rectifies rather than cultivates and develops. By insisting on the potency of negative human agencies rather than positive, idealized ones, Han Feizi establishes a basis for advancing arguments about the necessity and reliability of external, objective controls over humans. One critical aspect of his claim is that he sees human nature as something immutable and powerfully determining in human life:

> Nowadays, if there were one who went around telling people "I will make you wise and long-lived," the people of the world would think him mad. Now, wisdom is determined by [one's] nature, and long life by [one's] destiny. They are not what people can learn from others. To take what is

impossible for people and try to persuade others [that it is possible] is what the world would call "mad." . . . Likewise, to try to teach people to be humane and just is the same as saying you can make them wise and long-lived. A ruler who has proper standards will not accept such an idea.[75]

The basic logic of this passage is revealing. It suggests that since humans are fundamentally not malleable, and since most are neither wise nor moral, strict and punitive measures are needed to maintain social order. Intriguingly, Han Feizi's claims concerning *xing* in this passage do not refer to universal qualities inherent in humans (human nature) but to individual traits endowed upon a person at birth (one's individual nature). Despite this different usage of *xing*, Han Feizi nonetheless implies that innate human nature is unchangeable. To have individuals acquire certain traits not present in their *xing* is thus "mad" because it goes against their unchangeable natures.

The belief that *xing* is differentiated among individuals yet also universally unchangeable can be seen in other sections of the *Han Feizi*: "It is because of the dispositions and *xing* of humans that the worthy are few and the unworthy many."[76] Han Feizi asserts here that humans are by nature differentiated in such a way that there are few worthy and many unworthy individuals. *Xing* in this passage stipulates a general truth about the differentiation and the frequency of certain fixed traits in human beings. Similarly, the following comment demonstrates the consistently determining force of one's individual *xing* in one's life:[77] "People's *xing* have constancy. Crooked [people] become crooked, and straight [people] become straight."[78] Although individual natures are indeed differentiated, they are each fixed and not responsive to processes of education and cultivation that try to change them. In other words, one's endowment very much defines one's self.

The early Mohists, who spoke of a universal inherent agency to make choices about morality and one's behavior, did not allocate much power to human nature as a determining force in one's life. In fact, their claim for individual responsibility to choose one's actions and help determine the outcomes in one's life stands fundamentally in contradiction to Han Feizi's implicit claim for a highly deterministic power of *xing*. While many interpretations of Mohist thought emphasize its reliance on the logic of coercive power,[79] one should recognize that the Mohists also fundamentally believed that one can easily transform the self. For them, humans are extremely malleable creatures who are almost exclusively influenced by their outside environments, despite their inherent powers to choose their own course of behavior.

This belief is most apparent in the "Xiu Shen" (修身 "Refining One's Person") and "Suo Ran" (所染 "That By Which One Dyes") chapters of *Mozi*. These two chapters are generally considered to be later than the core chapters of the text, so it is perhaps fair to say that we are dealing with later Mohist thought.[80] In "Suo Ran," the author shows that environments influence humans just as dyes change the color of cloth: "That which enters is transformed, and the coloring itself is also transformed . . . . [This principle of influence] applies not only to the dyeing of silk. States also have influential forces. Shun was influenced by Xu You and Bo Yang, Yu was influenced by Gao Yao and Bo Yi."[81] Here, the underlying presumption is that people actually have very little control when it comes to changing themselves through their own personal devices; environments are extremely powerful and influential factors that shape the trajectory of humans. Yet humans can still choose the appropriate kinds of environments in which they wish to live.[82] This malleable vision of the self serves as an underlying rationale for the efficacy of external law in society. Because of this malleability, humans need proper environmental standards to guide them (such as a strong moral authority in a ruling position). Moreover, their malleability allows them to conform easily to these laws, so that they might adopt them wholly when such laws are in place.

This line of reasoning is far removed from the one in *Han Feizi*, which argues for the use of laws on the grounds that it is the only way that individuals can be effectively controlled against the power of their own self-determining agencies. Since Han Feizi thinks of the self as basically not malleable, he does not think one can alter one's character (self-cultivate) or even choose to practice individual responsibility if one is not so inclined in the first place. As a result, he believes the state should correctly apply external, coercive laws upon individuals. His belief in the powerfully determining negative forces of innate natures renders necessary his support of coercive laws that do not attempt to alter the self fundamentally, but rather to affect the level of chaos and order in society.

In accordance with his belief in an unchangeable individual nature, Han Feizi posits a stark distinction between inborn traits and that which one acquires more objectively from one's environment. He speaks of an individual's acquired abilities and powers as objective, external aids that do not and cannot fundamentally change the self. When transformation does occur, it does so in the external realm beyond the self, with the help of external tools, as seen in the metaphor of "state cosmetics" put forth in the following passage:

Two Prongs of the Debate

> For this reason, admiring the beauty of a lovely woman like Mao Qiang or Xi Shi does not improve your own face. If you apply base, powders, and black liner, however, you may make yourself twice as attractive as you were to begin with. [Similarly,] talking about the humanity and justice of the former kings does not make your own state more orderly. But if you make your laws and regulations clear and your rewards and punishments certain, it is like applying base, powders, and black liner to the state. Thus the enlightened ruler takes seriously such aids [to rule] and neglects singing praises [to the former kings]. Therefore, he does not follow the way of humanity and justice.[83]

This passage gives us a clear example of how Han Feizi lacks faith in the power of positive human potentials. It demonstrates instead his belief in external methods of correcting behavior and thereby inducing social transformation. It also sheds light on his basic premise that one's inborn traits are unchangeable, that *xing* is not malleable, and that the latter possesses a high degree of deterministic power over human life.[84]

In this repudiation of traditional moral standards as a means of running a state, Han Feizi discloses much about his perceptions of innate human qualities and an individual's abilities to change himself or herself. One's beauty, which Han Feizi presumes here to be unquestionably inborn, can only be improved through the use of cosmetics, external objects or techniques that one can acquire and apply to oneself for the better. In like fashion, a ruler, not being able to fundamentally alter the extent of his own moral nature, must rely on the external aids of regulations and laws to strengthen his authority and create order in his state. The metaphor of state cosmetics drives home the point that human natures, and hence the natures of leading officials and the way they govern a state, cannot effectively be transformed except through additives and alterations applied externally. Furthermore, such additives are useful in transforming behaviors and governing a state effectively, whereas empty admiration of human nature and sagely morality—like admiring the beautiful faces of Mao Qiang and Xi Shi—is of no help at all.

Though Han Feizi does not usually address the topic of *xing* explicitly, it is nonetheless a concept that critically affects the way he orients himself toward policymaking and political theory. Han Feizi's implicit vision of human nature, as presented at various points throughout the text, is certainly negative insofar as it denies the serious possibility of self-improvement. For Han Feizi, very few people are endowed with innate capacities for goodness and wisdom. Most people are actually endowed with negative innate agencies that need correction through punitive means. They are ignorant and immoral. They are weak and disorderly.[85] And most of all, they are self-interested.[86] Moreover, since human nature is not malleable, people without an external means of help will necessarily remain in such states, thereby contributing to the disorder of society.[87] Indeed, Han Feizi's predominantly negative stance toward innate human agency, along with the fact that such agency constitutes a deterministic and unchanging force in one's life, provide him solid grounds for supporting the necessity of external controls in society.

Throughout his writings, Han Feizi rallies for institutional controls at many levels, always justifying them through his belief that innate human agencies exist primarily as powerful negative forces that determine behavior. But on what basis can Han Feizi insist that institutional controls are the only effective means of controlling negative human agencies? What are his specific arguments for the necessity of external, institutional controls rather than personal or bodily forms of authority in society and life?

Han Feizi appeals to two different claims. First, he argues vehemently against virtue ethics by openly denying the efficacy of positive individual virtues such as *De* (virtue, power) and *ai* (愛 love, caring, affection) extolled by rival thinkers of the day. According to Han Feizi, positive virtues are both too rarely embodied by people and too weak to change society and effect order in the first place. It is therefore futile to base one's political decisions and systems of government on them. Second, Han Feizi insists on the efficacy of institutional controls by proclaiming the sheer power that incentives and disincentives, as well as positions of authority, have over the human psyche. Han Feizi's claims for the weakness of positive virtues and the strength of incentives and positions of authority go hand in hand to support his recommendations for overcoming the negative aspects of innate human agency in society.

Han Feizi's renunciation of the efficacy of using positive virtues as a means to effect social order resounds throughout his book. He openly criticizes methods that encourage leaders to personally embrace a compassionate attitude toward the people, epitomized through the term *ai*, a term historically associated with the Mohists and even with the Ru.[88] In "Eight Claims," Han Feizi analogizes the relationship between mother and son to that between ruler and state. He states, "The nature (*xing*) of [the relationship between] mother and son is [that of] love."[89] However, "If a mother cannot even preserve her home through love, then how is a ruler supposed to be able to maintain his state through love?"[90] As Han Feizi states clearly in the passage, a mother's love is of no use when it comes to controlling her son and bringing order to the household.[91] Han Feizi then asks how a ruler, who is trying to bring order to many more people than merely a son, is supposed to make use of the same ineffectual method of ruling his state. By positing a sharp disjunction between the positive, natural dispositions of humans (*xing*) and effective methods of rule, Han Feizi directly refutes rival claims that posit the continuity between the two.

Han Feizi also argues for the necessity of institutional controls by declaring their power to overcome the negative agencies that shape human behavior. In "Measures of the Heart," he states, "Now, it is the people's nature (*xing*) to rejoice in disorder and not view the law as applicable to themselves. This is why the enlightened sovereign rules his state by clarifying rewards to encourage the people's merit and invoking strict punishments so that the people might view the law as applicable to themselves."[92] Han Feizi argues here that perverse natures among the people can effectively be combated with methods of rewards and punishments. Such a claim actually endorses military might, since, as Han Feizi continues, the correct use of rewards and punishments is rooted in the use of military might and prohibitions.[93] It also demonstrates that certain aspects of human nature, such as our ability to be motivated out of fear, can be controlled through the appropriate institutional controls. So even though the negative agencies of humans are powerful, in the end they will succumb to incentives and disincentives backed by force that exploit human fears.

A passage in "The Five Vermin" similarly appeals to the ways in which human psychology, and effectively human nature, can be best harnessed through external methods of control. It relates a story of a bad, uneducable son, claiming, "People inherently [grow] proud with affection (*ai*), yet they obey might (*wei* 威)."[94] This particular statement leads us into a multilayered argument for the necessary use of might as a means of overcoming bad natures among humans. First, there exist positive forms of behavior, nurturing elements associated with human benevolence such as affection, which one might try to enlist to help transform human behavior for the better. Second, such forms of behavior are ineffectual with respect to the goal of controlling people. Last, a much more effective way to control people is to induce the fear of punishment through one's might. This is because it is natural for humans to respond to strong-armed methods of control, and not nurturing methods, which only exacerbate an already bad situation. Thus, according to Han Feizi's psychology, people are naturally obedient when they fear a negative consequence.

In "On Problematizing Authority" (*shi* 勢), Han Feizi provides more insight into why institutional controls are the only effective means of ordering society. In this fabricated philosophical debate Han Feizi uses the voice of his intellectual forebear, Shen Dao, along with two other voices (one contrary to Shen Dao's and the next contrary to the contrary position), to debate the issue of external vs. internal sources of power and authority, or institutional vs. bodily forms of control. In the debate, Shenzi (Shen Dao) introduces his case for the importance of *shi* (external authority, influential environmental conditions, or the power of one's political position) as the only effective means of control:[95] "Flying dragons ride the clouds and soaring serpents travel the fog. When clouds and fog have cleared, however, dragons and snakes are no different than earthworms and ants, for they have lost that by which they were kept buoyant."[96] Shenzi goes on to show that this law of nature has an analogous counterpart in the social world: "Yao as an ordinary man was not even able to put three people in order, yet Jie as the Son of Heaven could throw the whole world into disorder. Because of this we know that one can rely on the *shi*, and that virtue and knowledge are not worthy of admiration."[97]

The debate continues, as a critic of Shenzi's claim—quite possibly in the voice of someone influenced by Ru or Mohist beliefs—counters by saying that *shi* in itself does not bring about a well-ordered world. In order to achieve the latter, one needs a virtuous and knowledgeable leader.[98] Finally, Han Feizi ends the debate with a rebuttal providing a defense of Shenzi and critique of the power of personal morality and knowledge. In this rebuttal, Han Feizi shows that *shi* does not merely point to external authority alone, but to its power to promulgate laws and exert might so that orders are carried out.[99] Defined as such, *shi* represents a tool of authority that should be wielded in conjunction with the laws so that objective social order can prevail.

Interestingly, in this passage Han Feizi does not attempt to argue that personal virtues and knowledge are not at all effective in ruling a state. Rather, he merely claims that *shi* is more effective as a long-term plan. It is not practical, he argues, to get rulers to govern through virtue and personal achievement alone because one would have "to wait for the worthy [man] to order the world," which, according to his argument, rarely occurs in human history.[100] Thus, Han Feizi's belief that worthiness in humans is rare, and that one cannot gain it if it is not there from the beginning, plays a critical role in his advocacy for the institution of strong external controls in society.[101]

From this excerpt we learn that *shi* for Han Feizi does not correlate to the absolute, unbridled, and arbitrary power of position. It is simply one aspect of the effective use of objective laws, standardized systems for promotion and demotion, and military might associated with one's position. Moreover, unlike personal virtue and knowledge, the use of *shi* is user-friendly and universally accommodating. That is, *shi* can be used effectively to rule by anyone—especially the average ruler—and not just by those rulers who are born virtuous and wise.[102] It is therefore a much more reliable and practical method of ruling a state.[103]

In this section we have seen that Han Feizi's views contrast sharply with many individualistic perspectives formulated around the same time. However, though the content of Han Feizi's claim is the opposite of these other perspectives, he is actually quite similar to them in approach. Like his opponents, Han Feizi participates in an intellectual culture that readily acknowledges the efficacy of human nature and its strongly deterministic power over life and behavior.[104] Such an approach appears to be new to third-century discussions of the human psycho-physiology of control, a subsection of which took inborn agencies and the concept of *xing* as its primary area of concern. As we have seen so far, this emphasis on the inherent powers of individuals and human beings was not present in the writings of the early Mohists, and only appears in its developing stages in other texts previously examined.[105]

Conclusion

Debates about *xing* dating from the third and second centuries BCE generally presented two basic orientations on human agency: "internal," individualistic orientations, which placed faith in universal processes of bodily cultivation, promoting the development or preservation of *xing* or other personal, cosmic agencies as a means to individual attainment and authority; and "external" orientations, which advocated institutional methods of control and discouraged individual reliance on the powers of *xing* as a primary means of achieving personal and social ideals. While the former orientation proclaimed the existence of positive, innate agencies in need of cultivation and/or preservation, the latter orientation insisted on the existence and power of negative innate agencies that must be fiercely combated through institutional and social means. Unlike conformist ideologies, these later orientations shared the fundamental belief that all humans are innately endowed with certain agencies that have the potential to affect their behavior greatly.

Individualistic authors of the period shifted the center of power and authority in the world to the individual. They tailored their claims regarding an individual's access to idealized authority to their own political agendas, whether such agendas involved sometimes stripping politics, and thus the throne, entirely of its authority or increasing the power of the throne through an emphasis on the sovereign's centralized bodily control. The former agenda, implicit in one of the Primitivist author's views on society and government, did not advocate social mobility as much as it advocated the dispersed allocation of control among individuals. According to such a view, idealized social order arises out of the particularized control of individuals who each participate in a unified cosmic sphere of control. The power of the throne is thereby diminished with respect to the power of cosmic individuals interacting in harmony with one another. This type of writing reflects a belief that individuals of all sorts might be able to achieve a measure of idealized control in society by virtue of their innate connections to the cosmos. Its anti-imperialistic stance claims that individual agency is autonomous and depoliticized—and a possibility for all.

In the "Nurture of Life" chapters of the *Lüshi chunqiu*, the power of the throne is exalted through the ideal of the ruler as ultimate cosmic authority. This writing appeals directly to the central sovereign's aspirations for more autocratic rule by privileging the sovereign's innate claims to cosmic authority over that of anyone else. Yet unlike the writings on sovereign conformism analyzed previously, the primary emphasis of these writings switched to the sovereign body as source—and not instrument—of cosmic authority. Furthermore, the authors of these writings proclaimed the innate powers of the sovereign body as the primary means of state and cosmic control, thereby differentiating their views from many other contemporary ideologies that supported imperial rule by institutions and laws.

Certainly, the varied agendas of the later, third- and second-century BCE individualists reveal how different political and social norms were being proposed at the time. They attest to how completely unrelated authors used ideals concerning the individual cosmic body as justifications for very different types of personal and social control. This shared perspective on innate, individual power appears to have been generational—a product of the times—and therefore a function of historical development rather than coincidence.

On the other side of the debate, there were authors of the third and second centuries BCE who explicitly condemned such overreliance on the powers of the self. Two important authors, Xunzi and Han Feizi, supported the active restraint, suppression, and avoidance of what they deemed to be negative, innate agencies associated with the self. To these thinkers, the individual was the locus for a complex interaction of dynamic and often selfish forces. They regarded with apprehension the very components of the self that were deemed auspicious by others. This apprehension and suspicion constituted the basis for their externalist or institutionalist approach to self-cultivation and state order.

Xunzi's and Han Feizi's advocacy for institutional and/or cultural methods of achieving social order was tightly linked to their attitudes toward human nature and the negative and positive agencies associated with the self. In Xunzi's writings, which are not as radically opposed to the powers of the self as are Han Feizi's writings, we saw how he rejected the guidance of *xing* while encouraging individuals to develop powers of learning and the studied acquisition of virtue and merit. By locating negative agencies of the self in one's *xing* and positive agencies that enable self-transformation in one's potential for human effort, Xunzi provides his readers with a nuanced account of the self and its potentials that ultimately deprives individualism of its primary grounding in the cosmic self. Instead, Xunzi endorses the development of a stark distinction between self and nature, or cosmos, encouraging individuals to engage in an educational process that relies heavily on external cultural and institutional forms of guidance. Such external guides are intended to lead humans away from the determining forces of their innate natures toward a higher form of achievement that is not directly derivative of *xing*.

Han Feizi especially associated humans with a variety of negative agencies that must be overcome. For him, the key to social control lay in using external and institutional methods for ordering oneself and the people. Han Feizi justified such measures by proclaiming their exclusive powers to suppress, regulate, overcome, and exploit these negative human powers. By arguing for the exclusive efficacy of institutional controls in dealing with our unchangeable, innate agencies, Han Feizi devalued the use of personal powers or characteristics such as caring and virtue. In such a way, Han Feizi distanced himself from virtue ethics and ideologies that supported authority derived from personal or bodily sources.

Late Warring States proponents of both internal and external approaches to authority and agency differed from earlier, non-individualistic thinkers in their basic assumptions about human nature. In earlier texts, some authors neither took human nature to be a central concept of debate nor considered it a powerful determinant in life.[106] The authors in this chapter, on the other hand, assumed that innate agencies might largely determine human behavior. In their discussions on such agencies, in particular the agency of *xing*, they revealed a heightened awareness of and willingness to discuss various components of the self, its powers, and the relationship of such powers to the natural cosmos. This suggests that at the dawn of the first Chinese empire, discourses on both individualism and institutional controls were but two possible responses to a more widespread interest in the psychophysiology of human agency and control.

CHAPTER FIVE

Servants of the Self and Empire
Institutionally Controlled Individualism at the Dawn of a New Era

Having distinguished between individualistic writings that more fully idealize one's natural, internal sources of authority and writings that idealize institutional, external controls in society, we now proceed to examine writings from the third through second centuries BCE that at once idealize both types of control.[1] By adapting the demands of individualistic trends to those of the centralizing state or to Ru ritual norms, many writers of the third and second centuries BCE promoted individual agency and achievement while also providing a mechanism of external control over individual agency. Below, we examine writings that present syncretic mixtures of individualism and institutionalism. We will see that for certain authors interested in the building of an effective, centralized bureaucracy, there was a way of accommodating notions of individualism in education and administrative control.

The writings analyzed in this chapter differ from early individualistic writings in two main ways. First, without having to argue explicitly about it, these authors assumed that universal human endowments serve as a source of power and authority over life. Second, they built upon this assumption to argue for the necessity of external controls in conjunction with, not instead of, the development and fulfillment of innate human endowments. Also, unlike some certain third-century thinkers such as Xunzi and Han Feizi, who viewed most human agencies as negative, these authors maintained a more neutral or even positive view of what every individual possesses within. Consequently, they did not aim to negate, heavily compensate, or correct these agencies by means of external controls such as ritual, objective laws, and standardized bureaucratic procedures; instead, they considered the use of external, institutional controls a means of properly developing, expressing, and outfitting what is already inherent within each individual.

Below, I explore strands of later Ru and Zhuangzian writings that support both bodily and institutional types of controls in new and contrapuntal ways. These writings, namely the *Zhong yong* ("Centering on the Commonplace") and passages from certain later chapters of the *Zhuangzi*, assume that the inherent agency of humans is highly deterministic yet not entirely positive when taken on its own. Each text thus demonstrates the necessity of using both internal and external sources of power and authority to attain one's ideals. Each text also reflects the varied ways in which authors wished to incorporate individualistic conceptions of power and authority into the state system in early imperial times.

Teachings and Innate Moral Potentials in the *Zhong yong*

The *Zhong yong* of the *Book of Rites* (*Li ji*) is a Ru text that accommodates claims on both internal and external controls over humans.[2] Although the dating of the *Zhong yong* is uncertain, its arguments on the powers of the self in society contrast with those found in the *Mencius* and *Xunzi* in ways that suggest a similar context of debate. For example, unlike Xunzi and similar to Mencius, the author of *Zhong yong* makes an overarching claim for the innate moral potential of every human on the basis of *xing*. Unlike Mencius, however, this author does not go so far as to argue for an innate moral agency that propels humans toward the moral path.[3] While Mencius also supports the development of *xing* through various external tools such as the rites, the author of *Zhong yong* differs from him by defining *xing* explicitly as a positive, yet incomplete, moral potential. For the author of *Zhong yong*, one must necessarily rely on various factors, including one's innate capabilities, one's education (*jiao* 教, instruction), and one's effort in order to realize one's *xing* successfully. In a syncretic vein, he views the fulfillment of *xing* to be predicated upon a constant interaction between internal agencies and external moral guidelines.

Like many writings examined so far, the *Zhong yong* promotes the cultivation of a type of human agency that is similar or related to Heaven's agency.[4] This can be seen in the following passage: "That which fulfills is the Dao of Heaven. That which fulfills it [the Dao of Heaven?] is the Dao of humans."[5] The term *cheng* (誠 "to fulfill"), sometimes translated in its noun form as "sincerity" or "creativity," refers here to both Heavenly and human actions.[6] The author differentiates between the processes of Heaven and the processes necessary for humans, but he does so by using the same term, *cheng*, to refer to both. And because the processes of Heaven are fulfilled through humans, the author implies not only congruence between the two but their mutual interdependence as well. According to the text's logic, the "Dao of humans" is congruent with cosmic processes while also being unique as an extension or necessary addition to such processes.

This belief in a uniquely human yet cosmically connected Dao carries important implications. In the following passage, we see how the Dao (presumably the human variety) is distinct from and not necessarily a part of *xing*, which has direct connections to Heaven, or the cosmos: "What is commanded by Heaven is called '*xing*.' What directs human nature is called the 'Dao,' and what cultivates the Dao is called 'instruction.'"[7]

This passage, which makes up the opening segment of the *Zhong yong*, shows that instruction, *jiao*, not *xing* in an of itself, is what allows humans to cultivate the Dao and properly direct their personal growth as moral and cosmically connected beings. Whereas *jiao* refers to instructions that provide one with standards of authority external to the self, *xing* refers to the innate and cosmic connection one has with the commands 命 of Heaven.

Throughout the text, education (*jiao*) and human nature (*xing*) are described as complementary, so that external (*jiao*) and internal (*xing*) authorities are each assigned clear yet connected roles. In the following section, we see that the process of moral cultivation includes the input of both internal and external agencies:[8]

> [To go] from fulfilling to being clear, we call this "[deriving from] *xing*." [To go] from clarifying to being fulfilled, we call this "[deriving from] instruction." If one is fulfilled, then one is clear. If one is clear, then one is fulfilled.[9]

Describing two different but congruent processes of moral development, that of "fulfilling" (*cheng*), which derives from human nature, and that of "clarifying" (*ming* 明), which derives from instruction, the author of *Zhong yong* asserts the bidirectional possibilities for self-cultivation. The movement from inner realization to the clarification of values, referred to as "*zi cheng ming*" 自誠明, "[to go] from fulfilling to being clear," describes a mode of creating moral knowledge through inherent moral insight. The counter movement, referred to as "*zi ming cheng*" 自明誠, "[to go] from clarifying to being fulfilled," starts with knowing or learning values from external sources of instruction and proceeds to the process of internalizing such values as they accord with moral insights inherent within. The commensurability of the two processes is suggested by the statement that being fulfilled corresponds to being clear, and vice versa, showing that both goals are attained through either process.

From the beginning of the text we learn that instruction helps distinguish the human Dao from the Dao of our *xing*, dictated by what Heaven commands. In the quote above, we learn that our *xing*, when properly cultivated, can also lead us to the same goal as that achieved through instruction. But what does it mean to cultivate one's *xing* properly? How does one move from fulfilling (*cheng*) to clarification (*ming*) without faltering or messing up? Another quote from the text provides a response: "The virtue of *xing* lies in matching internal and external Daos."[10] This states that *xing* is best utilized when a person felicitously mixes his or her natural, or innate, intuitions and insights about morality together with teachings passed down through Ru tradition. The process of harmoniously combining the insights and teachings—or "matching" them—helps develop *xing*. Thus, in using *xing* properly one must not rely exclusively on its powers; one must avail oneself of both internal and external inputs of authority, guidance, and control.

By equalizing the authority of internal and external sources and methods of control, the author of *Zhong yong* demonstrates that the fulfillment of our *xing* is continuous and compatible with the human Dao. In other words, he demonstrates that moral instruction is naturally congruent with and necessary for the development of powers and authorities associated with the self: "Only [he who] is fulfilled to the utmost (*zhi cheng* 至誠) is able to exhaust his *xing*."[11] Externally guided self-cultivation (characterized by the process of "fulfilling oneself to the utmost") is therefore wholly compatible with the natural development of *xing*.

The fact that only he who utilizes external guides will properly make use of, or "exhaust," his *xing* reveals some important points about this power of the individual. First, the full use of *xing* must occur not just naturally of itself, but in conjunction with the use of external guides. Second, and related to the previous claim, the proper use of one's *xing* is not a universal given for all individuals. Unlike Mencius, this author does not argue for the innate agency of *xing* to impel all individuals toward morality (barring those whose environments impede or do not properly promote its proper development). Rather, the statement above suggests that *xing* is merely a moral potential that finds its proper expression through external guides. Only certain individuals achieve moral perfection, thereby exhausting their *xing*, not because they were pushed along the natural course of *xing* to do so, but because they effectively used external guides to locate and develop its implicit potentials. A thoroughgoing back-and-forth between internal potentials and external guides is critical to this conception of the fulfillment of *xing*.

According to the text, an individual's correct personal fulfillment, or insight (*zhi cheng*), is never incompatible with good instruction (*jiao*). Nor is instruction incompatible with how one fulfills oneself from within. Indeed, the process of self-transformation is grounded in the notion that internal authorities and potentials should be properly fitted with external dictates and expectations, and vice versa, if either internal or external authorities are to accord with the Dao. This means that self-cultivation according to the Dao necessarily involves the adjustment of external authorities with internal ones so that neither prevails and neither is denied a voice. Interestingly, this view integrates claims for internal sources of moral agency—like those of the *Mencius*—with claims for the idealization of external sources of control over moral behavior—like those in *Xunzi*.

The *Zhong yong* presents a syncretic approach to the problem of internal and external sources of authority and power. It does so by reconciling claims about the moral potential of *xing* with claims about the value and necessity of moral exemplars, rituals, and textual education. Like the *Mencius*, the *Zhong yong* builds on a claim that *xing* possesses actual moral potential, and does not—as someone like Xunzi might argue—just consist of certain component parts (emotions, desires, etc.) that might be shaped in moral ways.[12] It also joins texts such as the *Xunzi* in acknowledging the innate powers of *xing* while still insisting that such a nature must be shaped by external inputs.[13] But whereas Xunzi explicitly denies the moral potential of *xing*, the author of *Zhong yong* accepts such potential as the basis on which a process of learning through external authorities should occur.

Institutional Controls through Bodily Wholeness in the *Zhuangzi*

In chapter four we discussed the Primitivist's vision of bodily cultivation and his idealistic proposals for humans to return to a state of complete oneness with their own innate, cosmic natures. Another seemingly discrete perspective found in some of the later chapters of the *Zhuangzi* presents a vision of cultivation that is more syncretic in its approach than that of the Primitivist, but nonetheless incorporates much of its faith in the power of innate human agency. The so-called "Heaven Chapters" (chapters twelve through fourteen) of the "Outer Chapters" combine a Laozian vocabulary of stillness and tranquility with a belief in a characteristically Zhuangzian "spirituality" ("numinosity," *shen* 神), which represents a divine connection with the Dao of Heaven and Earth.[14] However, in a vein quite unlike that of either the *Laozi* or *Zhuangzi*, the author(s) of the perspectives that dominate these chapters—whom I, following A. C. Graham, conveniently refer to as the "Syncretist"—also takes pains to incorporate external forms of institutional control into the bodily cultivation of the Dao.[15] He (or they, but I use "he" as shorthand) advocates the use of bureaucratic regulations and institutions as necessary counterparts to internal agencies and controls. Ultimately, such an approach demonstrates how individualistic ideals for bodily cultivation could be blended and altered to fit the needs of a changing political and social environment—in particular, one in which centralizing measures and the state's ability to organize and control a large bureaucratic apparatus had become a paramount challenge.[16]

Universally Innate Human Agency: "Refined Numinosity"

In writings analyzed in chapter two that focus on the cultivation of the sovereign body, the sage serves as the primary cosmic link between the Dao of Heaven and the people of the world. The Syncretist author gives the sovereign the same status as that allotted in the writings in chapter two. Unlike those earlier writings, however, he presupposes that the august thearch (*di* 帝)—a clearly imperial title for the supreme sovereign of the land—possesses his own Dao within:

> The Dao of Heaven revolves without obstruction, and so the myriad things mature. The Dao of the august thearch moves forth without obstruction, and so all under Heaven returns to him. The Dao of the sage moves forth without obstruction, and so all within the bounds of the great seas submit to him.[17]

Here, the Syncretist draws a parallel between the cosmic Dao of Heaven and the idealized Dao of the august thearch. He speaks of the latter Dao as emanating from the thearch's person without obstruction, in the same manner as the Dao of Heaven revolves around Heaven. The language in this passage invokes the familiar imagery of emanation, as though one were to possess an ideal from within, found in the Primitivist's descriptions of the Dao in humans. It does not speak of "obtaining" (*de* 得) something borrowed from outside his body, for the Dao is the thearch's own personalized Dao.

Similar to the Primitivist viewpoint, the Syncretist posits the existence of inherent agencies in all individuals—indeed, all cosmic beings—that connect each with the spirits of Heaven and Earth. Instead of locating innate power in one's *xing*, however, this author points to a vital and spiritual force of a different kind: refined numinosity (*jing shen* 精神) immanent in both the human body and cosmos.[18] Refined numinosity represents the primary aspect of the body that should be cultivated.[19] But cultivation *per se* is not the correct goal. Just as the Primitivist idealizes the act of returning to one's original nature, the Syncretist extols the process of quieting one's refined numinosity so as to guide it back to its original (*ben* 本) state of clarity. He thus claims: "Emptiness and stillness, tranquility and mildness, serenity and peacefulness, and *wu-wei* are the root of the myriad things."[20] By connecting refined numinosity with stillness and stillness with the root of all things, the Syncretist author suggests that refined numinosity is innate to and immanent in every myriad creature of the world. He also implies that the process of stilling oneself leads one back to an original state in which refined numinosity is at its peak.

Refined numinosity thus takes on the same function as the Primitivist's *xing*: an original attribute of humans that endows one with and ensures one's connection to cosmic agency and potential. Indeed, the individual's idealized relationship with the Dao is unmediated and direct, since in the forging of such a relationship he or she merely moves to repossess and activate an inherent cosmic force within. As is true of many post–fourth-century BCE writings, humans cultivate themselves not to conform to an external Dao but to uncover its authorities and divine agencies within, thereby helping complete cosmic functioning and serve on their own as a vital nexus of cosmic agency in the world.

Bodily Cultivation and Active Rulership

The Syncretist joins the authors of *Laozi* in advocating *wu-wei*, or a type of spiritual process that denies such capacities as knowledge and the human will their agencies and authority over the body. Yet instead of advocating a type of *wu-wei* that functions mysteriously to bring order to the world and help the ruler achieve spiritual attainment, this author shows how *wu-wei* applies to the realms of decision making and the fulfillment of responsibilities incumbent upon a ruler. By making *wu-wei* explicitly a part of the *act* of governing, the Syncretist strips this concept of its mystique, rendering it into a psycho-spiritual exercise that aids in the activities of ruling a state:

> With restfulness comes emptiness, out of which emerges fullness and the organization of what is full. The state of being empty induces stillness; stillness brings on movement, and such a state brings on obtainment. Stillness progresses to *wu-wei*, after which one becomes reliant in taking on affairs. *Wu-wei* becomes contentment, and he who is content is impervious to all worry and anxiety, so that he has a long life. Emptiness and stillness, tranquility and mildness, serenity and peacefulness, and *wu-wei* are the root of the myriad things.[21]

In this passage, the Syncretist explicitly promotes movement as a necessary consequence of refined stillness, thereby underscoring the fact that orderly methods of control arise from those passive elements of the sage-king's cosmic body that have induced his activity. The notion that *wu-wei* brings about activity that is defined according to the parameters of one's official duties appears to go against the basic premise of *wu-wei* in the *Laozi*, in which *wu-wei* denies a ruler's standard way of being involved in affairs. By insisting that activity, fulfillment, and contentment are necessary states of being that result from *wu-wei*, stillness, and tranquility, the Syncretist defines *wu-wei* as merely one critical step in a cyclical process of psycho-physiological development. *Wu-wei*, far from being an unfathomable approach to life that functions mysteriously in the world, induces activity, procedure, and a set progression of bodily states.

The differences between the *Laozi*'s presentation of *wu-wei* and the Syncretist's presentation can be linked to the Syncretist's implied cosmology, which posits, in addition to the singular and encompassing supremacy of the Dao in all things, an unequal but complementary relationship between Heaven and Earth. Active movement is allowed in the process of self-cultivation because it concurs with the *yang* force, associated with Heaven. Stillness, on the other hand, concurs with the *yin* force, associated with Earth. Because Heaven and Earth are complementary, both the sage-king's movement and stillness attest to his inner state of achievement—identified here as his "unified heart-mind":

> Thus, it is said: "His movement is from Heaven; his stillness is from Earth. He fixes his unified heart-mind, and so rules the world in an orderly fashion. His corporeal numen causes him no harm; his ethereal numen does not tire.[22] He fixes his unified heart-mind and the myriad things submit," meaning that he avails himself of the state of emptiness and stillness, extending it over the realm of Heaven and Earth, and joining in communication with the myriad things. Such we label "Heavenly music making." Heavenly music making is the sage's heart-mind used to rear the world.[23]

Though it is clear that the psycho-physiological "state of emptiness and stillness" still constitutes a primary state of achievement, the application of such a state in the world of things, called "Heavenly music making," calls forth both the activity of Heaven and the stillness of Earth as integral to the act of ruling the world. Indeed, it is the harmonizing of the attributes of both Heaven and Earth in the human body that constitute individual attainment, and not merely the loss of one's self-agency, as implied by *wu-wei* in the *Laozi*.

Another important twist to the notion of *wu-wei* in the Syncretist's writings is that it is to be carried out from within an institutional structure of dictates, laws, and official duties. According to this view, an individual's involvement in *wu-wei* does not help him mystically establish social order; he must still actively carry out his official duties ("become reliant in taking on affairs") according to the institutional constraints granted him. Only in such a way will he be able to help create order in the realm. The author thus mixes *wu-wei* with external controls such as the responsibilities incumbent in one's position, or "affairs," to arrive at a syncretic solution to idealized forms of personal authority and institutional control.

Wu-wei *and* You-wei: *Differentiated Spheres of Agency and Social Control*

In what seems to be another vein of the Syncretist's writings, the particular roles of ruler and minister are associated each with two major types of human agencies: *wu-wei* ("lacking activity") and *you-wei* (有為 "possessing activity").[24] The following discussion will demonstrate how the Syncretist combines the goal of cultivating one's inherent cosmic agency with the goal of controlling oneself and society through institutional methods to arrive at an idealized vision of society and official state practices. Central to his syncretic vision is the notion that certain ideals are only appropriate for certain roles; in other words, goals for the individual are to be apportioned according to one's particular role in the political hierarchy. They are therefore not to be understood as universal goals for every individual.

A passage in the "Tian Dao" (Heaven's Dao) chapter of the *Zhuangzi* suggests that many different types of people actually engage in *wu-wei* types of bodily cultivation, and for a variety of social ends. This appears to suggest that *wu-wei* cultivation is universally accessible to all and that it has diverse and positive effects in the world:

> Enlightened to this, Yao faced south as ruler, and Shun faced north as his minister. Maintaining this on high is the power of the emperor and Sons of Heaven; taking this on in a lesser position is the Dao of the dark sages and untitled kings. Those who retire from society and wander with it leisurely are the men of the rivers and seas, mountains and forests. Those who interact in society and brush over the age with it achieve great deeds and an illustrious name, and all under Heaven is united. When still, they are sagely; when active, kingly. With *wu-wei,* they are exalted, and although simple and unadorned, nobody in the world can compete with their beauty.[25]

Wu-wei, along with other goals of self-cultivation such as tranquility, define universal spiritual states achievable by all human bodies. Hermits and men of illustrious reputation alike can enjoy the beauty and efficacy of these states, for they can be applied in society and affect the world in many ways.

Slightly later in the same chapter, however, the author depicts a contrasting viewpoint on *wu-wei* and its idealized scope. He alludes to problems in sovereign control arising from the universally accessible practice of *wu-wei* in the realm of politics:[26]

> If the superior [i.e., the imperial king] commits to *wu-wei,* and his inferiors follow suit, this is having those below share in the same power as the ruler above. When those below share the same power as the ruler above, they do not fulfill their proper ministerial roles. If those below engage in *you-wei,* and the ruler on high also engages in it, this is having the ruler on high share the same Dao as those below. When he above shares the same Dao as those below, he does not fulfill his proper role as ruler. The ruler on high must commit to *wu-wei* and make use of all under Heaven. Likewise, those below must engage in *you-wei* and take action for the use of all under Heaven. This is a principle that does not change.[27]

Here the author more systematically distinguishes between the agencies of Heaven and Earth fit for a ruler and the agencies of the bureaucratic sphere fit for ministers and those below the ruler. Thus, when elaborating on *wu-wei* in the political sphere, the Syncretist indicates that although everyone can engage in *wu-wei* techniques, not just anybody should do so in an official capacity. To him, *wu-wei* is a spiritual agency fit only for the imperial king, and it should be paired with the subordinate power of *you-wei,* "possessing activity," fit for ministers below. By circumscribing *wu-wei* in this manner, this author transforms it into an exclusive prerogative of the sovereign. At the same time, he poses a different solution to the problem of how a ruler who governs by virtue of *wu-wei* might still lead effectively and have his orders carried out. Rather than having the ruler harmonize both stillness with activity in his body, he proposes that the ruler focus on inactivity while ministers and officials who should not "share the same Dao" as the ruler above engage in activity.[28]

Previously, we saw how a Syncretist author in the *Zhuangzi* discussed the ruler's self-cultivation of *wu-wei* in terms of its creation of movement as well as reliance in government affairs. Stillness engendered movement, so that a single individual might enter a phase of *wu-wei* yet promptly emerge prepared for activity and the capacity to carry out affairs of state. Now, however, on the claim that the Dao of Heaven and Earth belongs exclusively to the ruler, the author—possibly, but not necessarily, different from the previous author whose statements we just examined—argues that real government activity should be taken up on the part of ministers in accordance with the *you-wei* type of agency befitting them. But how can *wu-wei* imply movement if movement and government activity belong to the domain of *you-wei*?

Rather than view *you-wei* as an outright denial of a ruler's agency, we might consider it to be entirely congruent with the *wu-wei* agencies deemed appropriate for him. That is, a ruler's agency of *wu-wei*, representative of the operations of both Heaven and Earth, can take on both active and passive forms. A minister's agency of *you-wei*, however, is singularly active. On this interpretation, *you-wei* consists in the power to prosecute one's tasks in conformity with assignments from above, and nothing more. Whereas the agency of *wu-wei* is all-encompassing, the agency of *you-wei* is not.

By distinguishing between *wu-wei* and *you-wei*, the Syncretist sets up a system whereby the administration of government affairs is carried out by ministers functioning in a manner corresponding to the workings and functionality of the Earth. The imperial king, who rules instead by the agency of the Dao, or Heaven and Earth together, does not micromanage the government and execute its affairs so much as he allows them to be carried out effectively by those beneath him:

> Therefore, as for those of old who ruled over the world, though their knowledge fell over the entire realm of Heaven and Earth, they did not do their own strategizing. Though their discernment could chisel out the myriad things, they did not do their own persuading. Though their capabilities were enough to exhaust all within the great seas, they did not carry out affairs on their own. Heaven does not produce yet the myriad things transform; Earth does not make things grow yet the myriad things are nurtured; the imperial king commits to *wu-wei* yet the deeds of the world are accomplished.[29]

The imperial king is to avoid strategizing, persuading, and carrying out affairs. Such "deeds of the world," as this author phrases it, need to be accomplished. But they are the jobs of ministers, who exclusively make use of the agency of Earth. Thus, while the imperial king provides the overall power and authority to carry out affairs, the actual execution of governmental matters is left to the ministers below.

Characteristic of the interdependence of Heaven and Earth in the world, the power of *wu-wei* in this scenario depends on the execution of *you-wei*, just as the power of *you-wei* depends on the authority of *wu-wei*. A plant metaphor describes well the symbiotic relationship of higher and lower agencies implicated in such terms: "The root lies in what is at the top; branches lie in what is below. The essentials are in the sovereign, while the details are in the ministers."[30] Just as a plant relies primarily on its roots but also on the branches that carry sustenance up from the roots to the many areas of a plant, an ordered empire relies primarily on the imperial king but also on its ministers who fulfill his fundamental and all-encompassing authority.

Because of their different positions in the world, both imperial king and minister must focus on different goals of cultivation, goals which, when combined, translate into a unified goal for society. These different goals are mutually dependent upon each other for their success. Thus the power of *wu-wei* as a tool for ultimate power and authority is diminished as compared to its power in the *Laozi*. *Wu-wei*, the power of the sovereign's body, depends here on a counterpart, *you-wei*, for its full effectiveness in the world. Only through such a counterpart can the authority of the imperial king and the efficacy of his *wu-wei* be ensured.

The Syncretist author in such a way grounds political role differentiation in patterns and operations inherent in a fundamentally hierarchical cosmos, and ultimately, Dao—of which kings and ministers are necessarily a part. The different powers of *wu-wei* and *you-wei* represent the bureaucratization of spiritual authority and power perceived to be inherent in the cosmos:

> What is exalted or lowly, first or last are given in the movements of Heaven and Earth; that is why the sage takes them as his models. That Heaven is exalted and Earth deemed lowly is in accordance with the positions of the divine and luminous. That spring and summer come first and then autumn and winter is in accordance with the progressions of the four seasons. . . . If Heaven and Earth, in all their numinosity, exist as hierarchies of the exalted, lowly, first, and last, then how much more this must be true for the Dao of man! . . . If one expounds on a Dao but negates its hierarchies, then he negates his Dao. How can he who negates his Dao while expounding on it take hold of the Dao?[31]

The Syncretist's Dao here is the Dao of an unequal natural world, born of the interaction between a superior Heaven and an inferior Earth. So although all humans might be equally endowed with innate cosmic agency within, the cosmic hierarchy dictates the differentiated ways humans should make use of their innate cosmic agencies. It stipulates that one's political position—upper or lower—should correspond to an appropriate cosmic agency—*wu-wei* or *you-wei*.

This view of natural hierarchies provides the Syncretist author with a rationale for accepting external methods of control as a necessary supplement to the cultivation of bodily agency on the part of a ruler and his ministers. The author uses a rhetoric of "root and extremities" (*ben mo* 本末) not only to describe the position of ruler in relationship to minister, but also to refer to the organic, hierarchical relationship between bodily cultivation on the one hand and the use of institutional, external methods of control on the other.[32] By proposing that both internal and external methods are necessary, if only in proper relationship to each other, the Syncretist provides an interesting accommodation to the two dichotomized approaches of bodily cultivation and obedience to institutional procedure and law.

The following passage outlines the acceptable institutional methods a minister might employ in his *you-wei* efforts at carrying out vital government tasks:

> The operations of the three armies and five weapon units are the branches of power. Rewards and punishments, benefit and harm, and the instigation of the five punishments are the branches of education. Systems of rites and laws, measures and numbers, forms and names, and comparison and detail are the branches of orderly government. The pitches of bells and drums and the appearance of feathers and flags are the branches of music. Public crying and weeping sessions, hempen chest clothes and mourning hats, and the gradations of ceremonial clothing for funerals—these are the branches of mourning.[33]

Here is a clear example of how the Syncretist author incorporates methods of traditional administration into his overarching beliefs in the cultivation of the sovereign body. The methods and institutions of government, explicitly connected to the role of ministers, all have to do with traditional forms of control that are not typically linked to Laozian or even Zhuangzian self-cultivation techniques. External, institutional controls such as rewards and punishments, the armed services, and the rites are all presented as viable methods for carrying out the necessary details of government.

Given that *you-wei* is linked to institutional methods of control, does this mean that it is not at all associated with cultivation of the self? The answer, I believe, is no. Just as *wu-wei* is a technique of the self used by

Servants of the Self and Empire 117

the ruler to govern effectively, *you-wei* is also a technique of the self used by ministers to carry out official duties. Take the following passage, which shows how the above-stated methods of government are correlated with dynamic, *you-wei* movements in the minister's body: "These five branches [i.e., power, education, orderly government, music, and ritual] rely on the circulation of refined numinosity in the body, as well as the movements of the techniques of the heart-mind,[34] before they can be pursued."[35] While the imperial king engages in *wu-wei* and stills his refined numinosity, preparing himself for movement, the minister engages in *you-wei* and ensures the proper circulation and movement of his refined numinosity. This proper circulation and movement allows him to carry out tasks successfully according to the institutions and regulations mentioned above. Thus, an individual controls the innate agencies of his body differently to bring about *wu-wei* and *you-wei* states that are necessary for fulfilling different responsibilities of government.

You-wei, unlike *wu-wei*, is modeled on the movement of the Earth rather than the stillness of Heaven. Involving the movement of one's refined numinosity, it can appropriately be applied to help a minister carry out his active duties in government. *You-wei* thus provides a minister with a personal, spiritual way of carrying out official duties and institutional controls. Only when fueled by the proper methods of *you-wei* do such controls become efficacious and useful methods by which ministers might assist in governing a state.

While external controls that clarify administrative roles, remunerations, punishments, and rewards form a part of the natural cosmic hierarchy of control and are crucial to successful governance, they are still inferior to the ruler's bodily cultivation of the Dao and the minister's cultivation of *you-wei*, or Earthlike agency. Indeed, the Syncretist ranks such external methods a mere fifth and ninth in a nine-level scale of political efficacy:

> When the men of old expounded the Great Dao, it was only at the fifth stage that forms and names could be brought up, and only at the ninth stage that rewards and punishments could be spoken of. To expound on forms and names too hastily is not to know their basis. To expound on reward and punishment too hastily is not to know their beginning. Those men whose words invert the Dao, whose explanations go against the Dao, are to be governed by men; how can they govern others? To expound on reward and punishment too hastily—this is to know the tools of good government; it is not knowing the Dao of good government. He can be employed for the world but is inadequate to be the employer of it. He is what we call a

"dialectician"—a person of one frame of reference.³⁶ Systems of rites and laws, measures and numbers, forms and names, and comparison and detail did exist for the ancients. It is what those below used in serving him above, not what he above used in rearing those below.³⁷

Distinguishing between the Dao and tools of good government, the Syncretist emphasizes that tools must be employed by humans and must not serve as the employers of them. By equating external controls with tools that require an underlying agent to put them to use, the author underscores their secondary position as instruments rather than primary agents of control. To him, the cultivation of an agent's cosmic power and connection remains the first step to good government.

I have shown how the Syncretist author argues for the implementation of a variety of different methods—both external and internal—to bring order to an empire. He justifies the use of institutional methods by claiming that they are actually controlled at a higher level through the dynamic agency of the minister's body, *you-wei,* as well as through the tranquil, passive, and active agency of the imperial king's body, *wu-wei.* Accorded a status secondary to that of one's internal state and cosmic connection, external controls are incorporated into a picture of a hierarchical cosmos, one in which individuals assume differentiated roles in society and cultivate themselves differently depending on their role in the cosmic hierarchy.

Significantly, the discussion of cultivating one's refined numinosity through *wu-wei* and *you-wei* concerns rulers and their ministers, and few people beyond this restricted sphere of political involvement. The author's lack of interest in promoting more universal cultivation of these agencies suggests that this text might have been written for a specific audience at court, and that it might have arisen from within an environment in which the state was becoming increasingly bureaucratized.³⁸ This environment, one that seems to resemble that of the early imperial state, is not individualistic; it does not openly support universal cultivation of the inherent cosmic Dao within.³⁹ In many ways this writing resembles the sovereign-oriented writings of the fourth century BCE, even though it speaks explicitly of innate agencies (as refined numinosity) and includes the bodily cultivation of ministers and their subsequent need for employing active methods of external control. The general orientation of this syncretic text appears to cater to the needs of a centralizing regime, perhaps during the Qin or Han empires, in which institutional controls, and not just the religious power or authority of the ruler, constituted a clear and undeniable means to the stability of the state.

Conclusion

The two writings examined in this chapter have given us a glimpse of syncretic accommodations of both external and internal methods of control. They differ from each other according to authorial predilections; one espouses primarily Ru goals while the other advocates a Laozian and Zhuangzian faith in one's ultimate connection to the spiritual forces of the cosmos. Despite such differences, all the writings reveal how authors attempted to temper the innate powers allotted to individuals by incorporating external controls in some fashion. The author of the *Zhong yong* is interested both in external and internal guides for moral behavior, and in his writings he rallies for the equal efficacy of both. He differs from Xunzi by arguing, much like Mencius, for the inherent moral potential of *xing*. But because this author does not think that all humans have the same capacity to make proper use of their *xing*, he is able to make a case for the necessity of instruction—the external counterpart to *xing* that helps individuals utilize their *xing* to fulfill the Dao. The *Zhong yong* thus accommodates claims for the value and importance of external as well as internal controls over behavior. Proper external controls are not superfluous; they complete a natural process of moral development that would not necessarily be completed of its own or without their aid.

The *Zhong yong* reveals much about the development of a discourse on universally innate human powers starting from the fourth century BCE. Like Mencius and unlike Xunzi, the author of *Zhong yong* asserts that *xing* possesses a component of moral potentiality. He departs from Mencius' extreme claim for the moral agency of *xing* by implying that only certain individuals actually have the ability to fulfill their moral potentials, or what I have translated as "to exhaust one's *xing*." But because the author of *Zhong yong* distinguishes *xing* itself from one's agency or capacity to cultivate the self properly (in this respect like Xunzi), he is able to stipulate reasons why humans need to rely on external controls (instructions and teachings) in the process of moral cultivation. The author's emphasis on both fulfilling *xing* and taking strict heed of teachings reflects an awareness with the dialectic on internal vs. external authorities, which appears in writings of the later Warring States era.

Lastly, in the Syncretist passages from the "Outer Chapters" of *Zhuangzi*, we saw a philosophy that incorporated standard institutional methods of control into a regime of individualized cultivation of the body—in particular for the imperial king and his ministers. The "individual-oriented institutionalism" described by the Syncretist deems external controls to be necessary, just as the branches of a tree are necessary to its root and to the whole tree. They are, however, still an inferior aspect of social control. The Syncretist author incorporates many lesser methods of social control into his larger vision of the Dao that is innate to every individual. He evaluates methods of control according to a cosmic hierarchy upon which human behavior and the cultivation of *wu-wei* and *you-wei* techniques are to be based. His writings thus provide a unitary yet variegated method of acknowledging both internal and external controls in the process of attaining social order. This method supports an individualistic ideal without abandoning the more hard-nosed, practical techniques of governance—some amount of which would have been expected in political circles of the early imperial regimes.

Through these syncretic accounts of how individuals might avail themselves of external controls while also maintaining access to their own innate sources of cosmic or moral authority and power, we see how authors came to accommodate the claims of both individualists and institutionalists into their own religious, moral, and political syntheses. While the reasons for such accommodations are not fully known, and while we cannot be sure of the provenance or dating of these writings, we can speculate that they arose as one type of response to the discourse on the psycho-physiology of human control that had swept through intellectual circles since the late fourth century BCE.

The Syncretist's account, in particular, hints at its potential origins in the context of the early imperial court. The author's politico-spiritual ideals of *wu-wei* and *you-wei* do not promote ways in which all individuals might tap into their innate powers of cosmic agency. Rather, they outline religious and procedural ways in which high-level court officials might better carry out their duties in the service of the state. In such a text, individual cosmic agency is not glorified as a potential agency of everyone. Rather, it exists as a means by which an elite few might become more efficacious in the art of rulership. What we had previously understood to be a form of individualism, as encountered in some writings of the later Warring States period, seems to have been transformed in this text to serve an exclusively imperial purpose. This demonstrates how ideas about the powers of innate bodily agencies—once introduced into the discursive culture of early China—could be tempered and altered to suit the particular social and political needs of the day, but could not be erased entirely from the intellectual tradition.

CHAPTER SIX

Conclusion

> I suggest there are conceptual resources in Chinese philosophy that promote a wider, more inclusive perspective and that encourages [sic] its readers to think of the self in terms of its interdependencies and relationships.
> —Karyn Lai, "Understanding Change"[1]

In an environment of increasing social mobility and political centralization, intellectuals from the fifth through the third centuries BCE put forth competing conceptions of human agency, each of which presented a different view of the sources of authority and power that underlie an individual agent's actions. This book draws connections between the growth of a universalistic conception of the self in relationship to Heaven's—or cosmic—authority and power. Such a universalized conception of the self was epitomized in an elaborate discussion concerning *xing* (human nature), which spawned the growth of a relational form of individualism in early China. It also shows how an integrated conception of the self and cosmos brought into being a discussion about internal vs. external sources of authority in self-cultivation and in political theory. This latter concern and manner of dichotomizing agency and control can be found in a variety of late Warring States writings, which include claims for one extreme over the other, as well as syncretic positions that accommodate the powers of both types of authorities.

The form of individualism that emerged from the context of these discussions involved not so much the radical autonomy of the self as the innate power of the individual to fulfill his or her own proper relationships with the cosmos. In other words, it involved viewing the individual body and self as the primary source of cosmic authority in the world. This type of individualism, moreover, did not necessarily develop into widespread individualistic movements in later times, although it did remain a part of the core intellectual traditions in East Asia for more than two thousand years.[2] Instead of developing directly into more extreme individualistic movements, some individualistic ideals became incorporated as early as the Qin and Han periods into a hierarchical system of authority supported by the newly formed imperial state. At this time of empire building, authors incorporated individualistic ideals into their vision of how the centralized state should function, and in particular how a ruler should cultivate himself as head of state. By the early imperial period, other individualistic ideals became incorporated into comprehensive theories about sagely cultivation that included the guidance of cultural and institutional traditions as well as cosmic determinations stemming from within the individual body.

The early Mohists of the fourth century BCE advocated the equal relationship of all individuals to Heaven's standards and system of justice. Such a belief attempted to unite all humans uniformly with a single source of divine authority. By promoting man's upward conformity to Heaven's standards, early Mohists universalized human responsibilities and obligations, thus unifying individuals in terms of similar goals and behavioral norms. At the same time, the early Mohist rhetoric of upward conformity spoke to the fundamental power of each individual to take responsibility for his or her own actions, and it spoke as well to the more universal potential of humans to achieve some level of moral character and wisdom through the exercise and fulfillment of one's judgment. By supporting universal obligation to Heaven as mediated through a single, centralized system of political and legal authority, the early Mohists paved the way for critical developments in beliefs on individual authority and power in years to come.

A slew of other writings that date from the fourth century BCE joined early Mohist writings in placing humans under the authority of a single higher power that is expressed in systematic ways. It is perhaps not a mere coincidence that so many different texts from around this time assume a similar stance toward human relationship to the divine cosmos. Indeed, one might concur with Aihe Wang that the creation of new forms of cosmology was deeply intertwined with the project of empire formation.[3] In such a light, changes we see in fourth-century BCE intellectual orientations are perhaps instrumental in—as well as reflective of—the political changes occurring in states across the Central Plains at the time. We might thus view the unification of human relationship to a single, idealized source of authority as a harbinger of a new cosmological orientation. According to this orientation, all individuals alike are to participate more directly in a shared cosmic system. Such a belief no doubt served as a mirror for and a crucial element

Conclusion

in the formation of the highly systematic and centralized regimes that aimed to gain ever more direct power over the people.

Despite the proclaimed universality of cosmic authority at the time, some authors still found ways of limiting access to cosmic authority primarily to the ruling figure of a state. Certain authors of the fourth century BCE, including authors of *Laozi* and the "Heart Chapters" of the *Guanzi*, claimed that the sovereign, by means of the cultivation of his body, possessed the exclusive authority to harness and conform to cosmic power. Possessing a unique point of access to such power, the sovereign body served as the sole cosmic instrument, or conforming agent, that might tap into and help complete cosmic operations in the human world. Moreover, the self-attainment of the people, along with their ability to access the power of the cosmos, was contingent upon the bodily cultivation of the sovereign leader. So while the authors of such writings invoked the human body in general as the key medium for accessing cosmic power, they pointed singularly to the body of the sovereign as a superior and ultimate vehicle for transforming and controlling society through his cosmic conformism.

Writings on the conformism of the sovereign body are similar to writings of the early Mohists insofar as they both presuppose a necessary hierarchy of mediation for sovereign authority—whether such a hierarchy consists in a layered chain of command or in a more centralized structure in which the people are directly related to the sovereign head. Regardless of the different political structures implied, all such theories on human conformity appear to agree on the paramount importance of the throne in mediating the universal powers and authority of the cosmos. Though we now lack information on the specific contexts in which these texts were created and their ideas propagated in society, it seems fair to surmise that this discourse on sovereign power and universal human relationship to the cosmic authority of the head of state bore a close relationship to changes in state power structures at the time.

Certain political changes occurring during the fourth century BCE suggest a fundamental compatibility between transformations in cosmological theory and state centralization. Precisely around the mid-fourth century BCE, the state of Qin, according to the initiative of Shang Yang (the prime minister of Qin, d. 338 BCE), institutionalized a series of centralizing political reforms that substantially altered the face of its politics and helped contribute to its unification of China more than a century later. Although the exact extent to which these reforms were adopted by other states at the time is unknown, contemporaneous claims on sovereign conformism suggest something intriguing. They suggest that sometime during the fourth century, centralizing structures of sovereignty were being discussed, and might have even been in place, in regions as far as the states of Qi (where the *Guanzi* chapters allegedly arose) and Chu (where the Confucian texts and Laozian "short texts" from Guodian were found).[4] Moreover, the emphasis that the authors of these texts place on total and direct sovereign control over the people, as opposed to partial and indirect control as per the older, Zhou kinship system, is significant. Such an emphasis demonstrates how authors tried to appeal to the centralizing aspirations of sovereigns of the day—aspirations that would have been in line with the ideals of a strong central throne promulgated by Shang Yang in Qin.[5]

Not only do the many centralizing theories of the fourth century BCE attempt to increase a sovereign's power by giving him exclusive access to cosmic authority, they also appear to shape the nature of his authority as well. The authors discussed in chapter two address issues of sovereign authority by finding a way to qualify it. The claims for sovereign authority mediated through a hierarchy of conformist bureaucrats, as represented through early Mohist writings, or the claims for more direct, centralized sovereign control over the populace, as represented through the various writings of chapter two, all represent attempts to control the authority of the sovereign by placing absolute authority in an objective position beyond the individual—and thus beyond the sovereign himself. Because the authors of these writings constrain the sovereign by having his words, deeds, laws, and methods of governance agree with cosmic authority, they can afford to grant sovereigns direct, total control over the populace. After all, the ultimate authority derives not from the sovereign but from the cosmos. So while authors of such conformist texts made moves to broaden the scope of a sovereign's political efficacy, they at the same time tried to tame and restrain the nature of his authority according to religious beliefs in the cosmos.

Other writers of the fourth century BCE target a different audience for their writings, providing an alternative political and religious agenda to that of sovereign conformism. These writings give evidence of a belief in a distinctively individual claim to divine agency or control. Such a belief is similar in structure to a belief in bodily conformism of the sovereign head, but it is expanded to include all individuals as potential mediums of cosmic authority. In our discussion, we saw how the earliest writings from *Zhuangzi* carved out the idealized, cosmic power of the individual despite considerations of social position and rank. They rendered the relationship between individual and cosmos more direct, and, indeed, more immediate than in the sovereign-oriented texts on conformism.

Conclusion

Zhuangzi's writings reveal that individuals could exist for whom personal goals were considered more important than political or social efficacy in the world.[6] In all probability, the increase in an intellectual elite's competitive access to political power through social mobility, along with an increase in the power of the central throne, left intellectuals whose ideals did not support state centralization and strengthening without any reasonable hope of employment at court. This would have helped raise consciousness of the discrepancy between one's own lofty aims and the realities of sociopolitical power.

In terms of individualism, the authors of both the *Laozi* and *Zhuangzi* glorified a fundamental contradiction: the selfless self of the cosmic Dao. Insofar as the self was considered to be the locus or arena for efforts relating to idealized control and action in the world as well as the object that should be denied or negated in such a process, such a belief does not constitute "individualism" according to our definition. However, in many ways, the individual body was especially valued as the critical site of self-transformation and cultivation. Moreover, what emerged as an idealized "no-self" was not something that was identical with all other things of the universe; rather, it was powerful and valuable in its own special way. Above, I have suggested that this type of bodily conformism should be construed as a hidden form of individualism, which, because it did not give proper credit to or associate the powers of the self with the individual, cannot technically be labeled "individualistic" in the way later writings could be. Nonetheless, it is important that we recognize the strong individualistic tendencies in such ostensibly conformist writings and duly note how they perhaps served as key templates for more explicit forms of individualism that were being propounded around the same time or shortly thereafter.

Sometime during the fourth century BCE, authors began defining and elaborating on universal characteristics innate to humans in an effort to demonstrate the individual's direct access to the cosmos from within. They began to discuss *xing* as a universal power that bears a special relationship to cosmic power and authority. In their writings we see the development of a wide-ranging discourse on the universal efficacy of the body and the role it plays as a direct medium for the attainment and communication of idealized, and often spiritual, forms of authority and power. Such writings confirm the rise of an individualistic preoccupation with the powers of the self.

The rise of ideologies that recommended the cultivation of universal, innate human agencies marked an important—though closely linked—departure from conformist ideologies. It marked the beginning of more explicit forms of individualism in early China. Mencius' claims linking the sources of moral motivation to one's *xing*, discussed in chapter three, illustrate this shift in a particularly bold fashion. In a debate that dichotomized the issue of moral agency in terms of internal and external sources of moral motivation, Mencius formulated an ethics that accords aspects of human biology a relatively powerful moral agency. Mencius' attempt to naturalize moral motivation through the concept of *xing* speaks of universal access to moral cultivation irrespective of sociopolitical position and environment. By proposing that each individual focus on revitalizing his or her own innate agency for moral thought and conduct, Mencius was among the first in a wave of thinkers to locate the ideal agencies of the natural (and at once spiritual) cosmos in the self.

Individualism in the context of early China thus emerged as a spiritual orientation that posited universal access to divine or cosmic authority from within an individual's body. From the fourth century BCE on, many authors embraced such a notion completely, while others qualified it in a variety of ways. Of the authors who promoted a more extreme form of individualism, Yang Zhu was perhaps the most renowned. In my analysis of Yang Zhu's purported beliefs, I agreed with A. C. Graham that we should not take Mencius' critique of Yang Zhu as a fair reading of the latter's ideas. This means we should not view Yang Zhu as a promoter of unprincipled selfishness.[7] Instead, we might try to place Yang Zhu's emphasis on the self into the context of the contemporary debate over *xing* and the extent to which such an agency should determine or guide an individual's life. In such a light, we might view Yang Zhu's ideas not as a glorification of hedonism but as a religious orientation that considered the natural powers of human life and vitality to constitute the utmost good and ultimate spiritual goal.[8]

From the perspective on individualism as outlined in this book, Yang Zhu and Mencius might have actually agreed with each other in their hopes that individuals might rediscover from within their innate power of *xing*. Though each author allegedly attributed very different qualities to *xing* and understood the innate self to be capable of completely different goals, each of their emphases on individualized, natural sources of authority as determinants for behavior appears to be similar and significant.

Another radical individualist was the Primitivist, whose ideas can be found among many other types of writings in the *Zhuangzi* "Outer Chapters." The Primitivist viewpoint exhorted individuals to preserve one's *xing* and recover one's perfected nature as it originally existed at birth. Not unlike later, Neo-Confucian naturalists who averred that adult humans have sullied their natures so as not to recognize their original perfection, the Primitivist author advocated what Philip Ivanhoe calls a "recovery model"

Conclusion

of self-cultivation.[9] He thus shared an individualistic bent with Mencius and Yang Zhu by positing that one's self or individual body might serve as the idealized source of authority over one's actions, life, and process of development.

Third-century-BCE authors like Han Feizi and Xunzi, though they supported the use of institutional or external controls in society and were far from being individualistic thinkers in any sense of the term, were nonetheless deeply influenced by the rise of a discourse on innate human agencies. Such a discourse shaped the ways they argued their points against selfishness and the negative agencies of human beings. Whether Han Feizi and Xunzi discussed the nature of *xing* openly or not, they based their accounts of self-cultivation and/or social control on the assumption that innate human agencies are powerful determinants of behavior.

Textual evidence for a syncretic approach to self-cultivation and/or social order corresponds approximately to the early imperial period in China. In syncretic writings, we saw a new, eclectic approach to controlling the cosmos, society, and the human body. Authors acknowledged the importance of cultivating innate agencies while at the same time honoring and accounting for hierarchy, diversity, and particularity of power among humans. This type of approach, which defined social and institutional norms in tight relationship to cosmic wholes and universalized powers inherent in the individual, found a way of accommodating two different poles in a debate over the internal and external, or individualistic and institutional approaches to controlling self and society. It is one of many ways intellectuals accommodated the needs of newly developing centralized states, and indeed the empire, with the needs of the empowered individual.

Individualistic ways of thinking about the self during the Warring States and early imperial periods were not all meant to be egalitarian or universal in a truly universal sense. Indeed, it is likely that the widespread interest in delineating the powers of innate human nature stemmed not so much from concerns of sociopolitical equality as from what Aihe Wang refers to as concerns to tighten the relationships between natural human powers (of particular classes of individuals) and the idealized social order.[10] Such a concern to bring humans closer to cosmic authority and power would have allowed people of disenfranchised, but nonetheless elite, positions to claim moral or spiritual superiority over others in power who did not possess their expert knowledge of humans in relationship to the cosmos. Their moral or spiritual authority would have been considered a marketable commodity for which kings, princes, and ministers at various courts would have vied to procure.

Despite what may have been the underlying motivation for this discourse on universal individual agency, and despite the perhaps limited application of these ideals to the upper levels of court leadership and the educated elite, these ideological changes do hint at widened human access to self-cultivation and differentiated modes of power in comparison with earlier times. The textual evidence examined in this book suggests that an increased rise in human agency in the social sphere—one that began to spill beyond the elite *shi* stratum well into the merchant and perhaps even artisan classes—took place over the course of the fourth century BCE.[11] Since the realm of the mind is often both reflective and generative of social and political realities, the discussions we have encountered in these texts likely can be connected with an actual transformation in society in which individuals from an increasingly broad social spectrum were viewed as charged entities with which to be reckoned in political and social affairs.

Conformity and Individualism in Early China

I have outlined in this book not merely a variety of beliefs that support the power and agency of the individual in one way or another, but also a widespread belief in the importance of universal conformism to the greater cosmos, which appears to have been closely linked to the formation of an explicit form of individualism. Now it is fruitful to consider how conformism and individualism in early China differ conceptually from our own notions of the two. Conformist ideologies of the fourth century BCE emerged in relationship to the adoption and refinement of centralizing policies and state structures, as well as changing religious orientations. They advocated homogenous forms of social behaviors in agreement with universal laws or forces of the cosmos, and they thereby encouraged the effacement of dangerous individual or private ambitions and desires. In contrast to our own notion of conformity, which signifies the degradation of the self, conformist behaviors in early China dignified the self by helping preserve individual responsibility with respect to a universal goal and cosmic relationship. Notions of conformity encouraged all individuals to participate in the public good through a collective system of justice, ethics, or cosmic power. Through conformity, one could fulfill one's particular religious role and responsibility. Thus it served as a critical means for individuals to achieve spiritual attainment and contribute to social order.

In China of the fourth century BCE, conformity in no way connoted what it often connotes today: a lack of personal choice, uniqueness, distinction, creativity, and will. While characteristics such as uniqueness and

Conclusion

creativity were not a central concern for most early Chinese authors,[12] notions of personal choice, judgment, and the exertion of one's intellect, will, or moral agency were crucially associated with conformist ideologies. As seen in the writings of the early Mohists and certain chapters of the *Guanzi*, conforming individuals make decisions to carry out the dictates of their own rectified wills. While such decisions agree with a single higher power or authority, the decisions themselves are nonetheless made by individuals who must think and act on their own in order to ascertain and be sure that what they are doing complies with the higher authority. In effect, they must choose to cultivate personal responsibility vis-à-vis this higher authority, and this act of choosing entails a high degree of personal autonomy and achievement.

Similarly, the type of individualism that emerged during the Warring States period differs considerably from certain types of individualism that Europeans and Americans have inherited from the Enlightenment.[13] Individualism in the context of early China did not have so much to do with separation and individual achievement based on difference from others as it did with participation and individual achievement based on shared connectedness with others and the cosmos.[14] Of paramount importance is the fact that the individual was considered to be a unique and critical participant in a larger whole.[15] In this holistic vision of the individual, the central concern is the individual's fulfillment of universally shared qualities and participation in the becoming not just of him or herself but of all of society and the cosmos as well. Insofar as interdependence and not independence was the pursued goal, this form of individualism shared much in common with ideologies of conformism stemming from the same cultural and sociopolitical context. Both outlooks demonstrate how individual power or agency might be construed in terms of connection rather than isolation and atomistic spheres of authority.

Writings from early China clearly indicate that autonomous, individual agency and conforming agency both draw upon and take meaning from the larger whole. Individuals are not encouraged to detach themselves from the collective whole that is their environment, as such a whole helps define their persons and personal trajectories. Certainly, such individuals may assert their power, authority, and uniqueness from within such a whole, but they are not advised to separate themselves from it. The fundamentally integrated form of individualism that develops in early China is therefore not unrelated to ideals of conformism to a larger whole. The difference lies merely in distinguishing between internal and external sources of authority and power, and hence sources of control. From these writings, therefore, we gain sight of a holistic individual, whether conformist or relationally autonomous, and we gain the insight that conformism and individualism need not be radically different stances from each other.

In Donald Munro's edited volume on individualism in Confucian and Daoist traditions, many of the authors persuasively argue that holism, and not individualism, best characterizes certain Chinese orientations toward the self and individual. In an unrelated volume on the self in Chinese culture, Herbert Fingarette shows how Confucius shares in what he terms "the pan-Asian ideal of selflessness as crucial to salvation."[16] In this book I agree with most of these authors in stressing the emphasis in early Chinese thought on ideals that couch the self within a larger whole. Yet I do not agree with the basic assertion of most of these authors that "individualism" and "selfhood" are not key concepts in such a context. Therefore, I have gone a step further to claim that individualism need not be set apart from holism and that, indeed, "individuals" in the context of early Chinese thought are strengthened and made whole by attaining a seamless, harmonious relationship with their environment. Rather than view selflessness as crucial to salvation (whose salvation if not that of the self?), I differ with Fingarette by claiming that "selflessness" in the early Chinese context must be defined in terms of a new form of "selfhood." Such a selfhood is identified through the image of the holistic individual, who achieves salvation for himself or herself from within a much larger web of social and cosmic interconnectedness and agency.

By discussing early Chinese views on human agency and the self in terms of cosmic and holistic individualism, I hope readers will withdraw their commitment to a narrow, historically specific meaning of the term and embrace it as a theoretically powerful and useful tool in cross-cultural comparison. The concept of individualism as a hermeneutic device can probe any culture and historical context for beliefs relating to the self-determining powers and personal authorities of individuals. When applied to the context of early China, we see that there were many authors who supported a belief that the individual could and should rely on his or her own powers of self-determination and spiritual fulfillment in perceiving of and acting in the world. This strong conception of the power and authority of the individual resonates throughout Chinese and indeed East Asian history, accounting for a healthy conception of the self and its potentials and prerogatives from within a sometimes highly collectivistic and family-oriented framework.

Postscript

A Note on Chinese Individualism, Human Rights, and the Asian Values Debate

> Heaven's love for the people is very great. Would it then allow one man to preside over them in an arrogant and willful manner, indulging his excesses and casting aside *the nature Heaven and Earth allotted them?* Surely it would not! [italics mine]
> —Duke Xiang 14, *Zuo zhuan*[1]

> What is necessary is an impartial study of the different elements and values in the Chinese tradition and in Confucianism, including those that stand in a positive, neutral, or negative relationship to liberty, autonomy, equality, democracy, rights, etc. Only then will we be in a position to think about what form of LCD [liberal constitutional democracy] will be appropriate to China, what elements and values need to coexist with one another, and what kind of creative transformation is desirable for the Chinese tradition.
> —Albert Chen, "Is Confucianism Compatible with Liberal Constitutional Democracy?"[2]

Translating concepts from one cultural, historical context to the next is never an easy task. In using the term "individualism" in my analysis of intellectual developments related to the self, I show readers that certain early Chinese views can justifiably be compared with, or translated as, "individualism." By granting Chinese history its own idealistic notions of the self and analyzing such notions according to how they dignify and empower the individual, I refute the well-worn accusation that Chinese cultures lack a concept of individual prerogatives. In ancient China, indeed, an individualistic movement developed to promote the cultivation of an individual's own idealized powers and authorities. This form of individualism was ultimately grounded in a religious concept of the self as recipient of innate, divine powers, and it was also deeply intertwined with sociopolitical changes associated with the growth of powerful, centralized states.

Against the popular stereotype of Chinese culture as a culture that stresses not the individual but the effacement of the individual within the family, society, and cosmos, I argue that certain key aspects of Chinese culture are rooted in the power of the individual to cultivate himself or herself as a vital agent within a web of social and cosmic agents. The individual is not effaced; he or she is empowered and in control. To be sure, the individual stands at the heart of any transformation of the self and its surrounding environment.

Though the period I examined in this book certainly cannot and should not represent Chinese tradition as a whole, or even its contemporary forms, this so-called "classical period" plays a critical role in the development of a Chinese cultural identity that shaped history in critical ways. If one were to continue my analysis of the self throughout Chinese history and up until the modern day, one would no doubt witness not the destruction of individualism in favor of an exclusively social concept of the self but the construction and reconstruction of various forms of individualism in light of the family, society, and the larger cosmos. Individualism developed in China just as it took on other forms in other societies. It developed solidly there, and it never left.

The issue of individualism in China is a touchy subject that relates directly to a current, ongoing political debate between universal human rights advocates and Asian values supporters. The idea—albeit a false one—that traditional Asian values do not embrace individualism is constructed upon a particular reading of Chinese history that still exists today; namely, that there has never been an emphasis on individual prerogative and authority in the development of Chinese culture; that Chinese society has traditionally stressed one's social role and the subservience of individual concerns to those of the group, etc. Having refuted such claims in this book, I contend that individualism has been a powerful ideal throughout Chinese history, and thus should be regarded as a crucial element of Asian values.[3] While it is unclear that "rights"—in the sense of inalienable claims or moral entitlements to certain political and social goods—are endorsed in early Chinese texts, the very fact that individuals, their thoughts, judgments, potentials, wills, and cosmic powers do matter and were greatly valued should be reason enough to reconsider the human rights debate in such a light. Marina Svensson has recently claimed that "since China already has had a one-hundred-year-long history of human rights debates, one should think that the issue of whether human rights are compatible with the Chinese tradition could be laid to rest safely and finally."[4] No doubt, studies that contribute to a fuller history of the individual in Chinese history can give even more depth and understanding to such debates.

It is important that we remain open to the ways in which the idea of individualism takes on different forms from our own ideas of it in the current day. In addition, we must take note of the ways constructions of Asian identity are manipulated, either by oneself or the other, to assert power in any given relationship. Western imperialists are not the only ones to have denied China's claims on individualism; the Chinese have done it themselves in recent history, as Lydia Liu demonstrates in the quote cited at the beginning of the preface.[5] More recently, some Asian governments have tried to justify their claims to power and the creation of policy by reclaiming the uniqueness of Asian values. They deny the universal applicability of Western human rights discourse on the individual. While the notion of universal human rights is indeed fraught with problems regarding the truly universal nature and relevance of its ideals, the solution to such a problem cannot lie in a defensive posture that sinks into cultural relativism. Having argued against the denial of Chinese forms of individualism, I thus urge scholars and politicians alike to rethink the long history of Chinese and "Asian" conceptions of the self and come up with a more culturally and universally acceptable—not an autocratic and self-serving—version of "Asian values" and human rights.[6]

At the same time, I propose that we try to contextualize our own beliefs on human rights and individualism so that we might better understand the cultural and political implications of claims for universal human rights. Closely linked to our own notions of individualism, the concept of universal human rights is based on a culturally constructed belief in individuals as fully autonomous beings and/or sovereign subjects.[7] It represents a legal concept construed to ensure the allowance, entitlement, or claim of individuals on certain material and intellectual safeguards associated with being fully autonomous beings. Outside legal contexts, the concept of human rights serves as a rhetorical claim for social ideals that express themselves in terms of individual, atomistic properties and traits rather than sociopolitical goals and imperatives. Ethically, it is a historically constructed concept that has great potential for universal applicability, if it could be defined in terms that allow for cross-cultural forms of individualism and the recognition of human dignity. As an ethical movement that seeks to ensure the nobility and dignity of the individual, human rights discourse has the potential to encourage all governments and peoples to uphold individualistic values in keeping with their own traditions and histories. But in order to reconceive its relevance for Chinese concepts of the fully attained individual, it is important that one first clarify how Chinese traditions and histories differ from those that gave birth to the concept of universal human rights.

The observations of Stephen Angle on the recent history of human rights in China are worth considering in this light:

> For a range of reasons, as Chinese rights discourse develops in the twentieth century it will continue to posit a closer, more harmonious relationship between individual and collectivity than is found in at least some versions of Western rights theorizing. One strand of the nineteenth-century Chinese discourse, though, does highlight the *quan* [powers, rights] of individuals: These are the writings that place at their center the claim that "every person has the *quan* of self-mastery (*ren ren you zizhu zhi quan*)."[8]

Here is an analysis of individual rights in nineteenth- and twentieth-century China that appears to accord with some of the core themes of classical views on the individual. "Individualism" exists in China insofar as the individual is understood in terms of his or her relationship to a collectivity. Furthermore, one finds a strong and explicit acknowledgment of a particular power of individuals, stemming from the primary and enduring tradition of self-cultivation in Chinese thought. In Angle's sources, such an aspect is expressed as "self-mastery."[9]

In my analysis of ancient texts, this power of the individual is similarly associated with his or her achievements regarding self-cultivation, but not so much in terms of mastering the self as in fulfilling one's innate cosmic powers. Thus, if one were to artificially apply a language of claims, moral entitlements, or divinely given prerogatives to the type of early Chinese individualism highlighted in this book, one might say that some authors thought that individuals had the "right" to fulfill the moral or natural agencies and potentials endowed them by the cosmos at large. In a thoughtful piece on the role of Confucianism in challenging human rights discourses, Henry Rosemont frames his questions in terms of "rights-bearing individuals"—relevant to more Western traditions—and "role-bearing persons"—relevant to Confucian ideologies.[10] Perhaps we are now justified in adding another type to the mix of Chinese thought: that of "agency-fulfilling individuals."[11]

NOTES

Preface

1. Lydia H. Liu, "Translingual Practice: The Discourse of Individualism between China and the West," in Wimal Dissanayake, ed., *Narratives of Agency: Self-making in China, India, and Japan* (Minneapolis: University of Minnesota Press, 1996), pp. 27–28.

2. Ibid. John Greenwood questions the fundamental distinction between Western "individualism" and Eastern "collectivism" in his article "Individualism and Collectivism in Moral and Social Thought," in Kim-chong Chong, Sor-hoon Tan, and C. L. Ten, eds., *The Moral Circle and the Self: Chinese and Western Approaches* (La Salle, Ill.: Open Court, 2003), pp. 163–173.

3. See Randall Peerenboom, *China Modernizes: Threat to the West or Model for the Rest?* (Oxford: Oxford University Press, 2007); Ann Kent, *China, the United Nations, and Human Rights: The Limits of Compliance* (Philadelphia: University of Pennsylvania Press, 1999); Joanne R. Bauer and Daniel A. Bell, eds., *The East Asian Challenge for Human Rights* (Cambridge: Cambridge University Press, 1999); and Wm. Theodore de Bary and Tu Weiming, *Confucianism and Human Rights* (New York: Columbia University Press, 1998). See also Wm. Theodore de Bary, *Asian Values and Human Rights: A Confucian Communitarian Perspective* (Cambridge, Mass.: Harvard University Press, 1998), pp. 8–12, for a critique of the Asian values platform. For helpful accounts of the history of human rights in contemporary China, see Stephen Angle, *Human Rights in Chinese Thought: A Cross-Cultural Inquiry* (Cambridge: Cambridge University Press, 2002); and Marina Svensson, *Debating Human Rights in China: A Conceptual and Political History* (New York: Rowman & Littlefield, 2002). Svensson provides an interesting critique of an "Orientalist" view of human rights as foreign and inappropriate for Asia (pp. 51–64).

4. Indeed, Western-style human rights presents a case for the moral entitlement, claims, or prerogatives of every individual to such basic "goods" as freedom of speech, a voice in choosing one's political representatives, etc. If other cultural traditions also deem valuable certain basic "goods" of the individual, then it is important to find out what such goods are, whether there is any overlap or agreement with those values found in the West, and whether it makes sense to frame such goods in terms of each individual's moral entitlement to them.

5. Wm. Theodore de Bary has broached these issues in his discussions on the relationship between Confucian communitarianism and the individual. His work provides a careful critique of "spokesmen for authoritarian regimes" who, he claims, use the notion of "Asian values" conveniently to deflect international criticisms of their regimes' human rights record. De Bary, *Asian Values*, p. 8. De Bary goes so far as to speak of a strong tradition of "personalism," not "individualism," in East Asian Confucian cultures. I do not adopt the term "personalism" in this book because I wish to more directly compare early Chinese notions of individual power with our more broadly understood notion of "individualism." I also feel that the term "personalism" is more appropriate for the limited arena of Confucianism in Chinese history, while it is less fruitful with respect to notions of individual power outside such a tradition.

6. For a collection of the most important and thought-provoking essays concerning individualism in China to date, see Donald Munro, ed., *Individualism and Holism: Studies in Confucian and Taoist Values* (Ann Arbor: Center for Chinese Studies, University of Michigan, 1985). While the analyses in Munro's volume are for the most part insightful and engaging, most conclude that the term "individualism" as it is derived from Enlightenment Europe is not appropriate for the Chinese context. In this book, on the contrary, I define individualism not *against* holism but *in terms of* it.

7. An excellent source on the history of modern conceptions of the individual and/or self that help support this description is Charles Taylor's *Sources of the Self: The Making of the Modern Identity* (Cambridge, Mass.: Harvard University Press, 1989). See also Louis Dumont's *Essays on Individualism: Modern Ideology in Anthropological Perspective* (Chicago: University of Chicago Press, 1986). A recent text that discusses the compatibility of East Asian cultures with notions of a liberal democracy, and which provides provocative suggestions for the political systems in such areas, is Daniel A. Bell, *Beyond Liberal Democracy: Political Thinking for an East Asian Context* (Princeton, N.J.: Princeton University Press, 2006).

8. For discussions of this type, see Chad Hansen, "Individualism in Chinese Thought," in Munro, *Individualism and Holism*, pp. 35–56. Michael Nylan discusses the topic in relationship to intellectual currents at the end of the Han Dynasty and similarly concludes that the notion is not relevant to the period. See her "Confucian Piety and Individualism in Han China," *Journal of the American Oriental Society* 116.1 (1996): pp. 1–27.

9. Indeed, this latter emphasis on family values as opposed to individualism has become such a trope that some China scholars will introduce China and Chinese culture to the lay audience in such terms.

10. On this view, many scholars would claim that the term "individualism" simply is not relevant or appropriate to Chinese circles and that other terms should be created or invoked to describe the practices, beliefs, and traditions that might be compared to the "individualism" of the West. I do not see the need in developing neologisms when a term already exists to engage readers immediately in a cross-cultural comparison of conceptual relationships and disjunctions.

11. Joan Wallach Scott's *Only Paradoxes to Offer: French Feminists and the Rights of Man* (Cambridge, Mass.: Harvard University Press, 1996) provides a fascinating account of how gender fits into historical debates on citizenship and rights in eighteenth- and nineteenth-century France. Such a discussion directly engages competing forms of individualism from within the Western context itself.

12. I explain my reasons for using the term "individual" as a substitute for "self" in the introduction. Many scholars have addressed the relationship between human rights and China through a discussion of Confucian communitarianism and its emphasis on collective, social rites, rather than on individualism per se. For more on this manner of connecting China and human rights, see Roger Ames, "Continuing the Conversation on Chinese Human Rights," *Ethics and International Affairs* 11 (1997): pp. 177–205. See also the various essays in de Bary and Tu Weiming, *Confucianism and Human Rights;* and Roger Ames, "Rites as Rights: The Confucian Alternative," in Leroy S. Rouner, ed., *Human Rights and the World's Religions* (Notre Dame, Ind.: University of Notre Dame Press, 1988), pp. 199–216.

For scholarship exploring the relationship between Confucianism and liberal democracy, see Li Minghui 李明輝, *Ruxue yu xiandai yishi* 儒學與現代意識 (Taipei: Wenjin Chubanshe, 1991), pp. 1–18; Li Minghui, *Dangdai Ruxue zhi ziwo zhuanhua* 當代儒學之自我轉化 (Taipei: Academia Sinica, Wenzhesuo, 1994), pp. 1–21; and He Xinquan 何信全, *Ruxue yu xiandai minzhu* 儒學與現代民主 (Taipei: Academia Sinica, Wenzhesuo, 1996), pp. 1–11.

For scholarship concerning Chinese notions of the self—not necessarily "individual"—throughout various periods of history, see Kwong-loi Shun and David Wong, eds. *Confucian Ethics: A Comparative Study of Self, Autonomy, and Community* (Cambridge: Cambridge University Press, 2004); David Hall and Roger Ames, *Thinking from the Han: Self, Truth, and Transcendence in Chinese and Western Culture* (Albany: State University of New York Press, 1998); and Roger Ames, Wimal Dissanayake, and Thomas Kasulis, eds., *Self as Person in Asian Theory and Practice* (Albany: State University of New York Press, 1994).

13. C. B. Macpherson, *The Political Theory of Possessive Individualism* (Oxford: Clarendon Press, 1962), p. 3.

14. This type of individualism stems directly from Immanuel Kant's influential writings on the free and rational nature of individual moral authority. Immanuel Kant, *Foundations of the Metaphysics of Morals,* trans. Lewis White Beck (Indianapolis, Ind.: Bobbs-Merrill, 1969).

15. Henry Rosemont, Jr., "Whose Democracy? Which Rights? A Confucian Critique of Modern Western Liberalism," in Kwong-loi Shun and David Wong, eds. *Confucian Ethics: A Comparative Study of Self, Autonomy, and Community* (Cambridge: Cambridge University Press, 2004), pp. 49–71. Rosemont argues forcefully for a reconceptualization of the meaning of human rights in light of a community- and responsibility-driven sense of the individual. While I agree with much of his presentation of the Confucian individual, I disagree with statements that downplay Confucian concepts of individual autonomy in an effort to claim an exclusively

relational status for the individual. For scholarship on the importance of rituals and an ethics of responsibility, see the various essays in Mary Bockover, ed., *Rules, Rituals, and Responsibility: Essays Dedicated to Herbert Fingarette* (Chicago: Open Court, 1991).

16. The approach I have in mind would be based on an acknowledgment, acceptance, and reformulation of certain early Chinese contributions, as well as on a creative and appropriate assimilation of new inputs from other cultures.

Introduction

1. It is important to note that this type of religious or cosmic authority was not regarded as a god or anything similar to the Abrahamic or Greek notions of a transcendent authority, reality, or truth that exists outside the realm of human experience. Cosmic and religious authority in the Chinese tradition was always considered relevant to and immanent in human life, events, and natural processes. See David Hall and Roger Ames, *Thinking Through Confucius* (Albany: State University of New York Press, 1987), pp. 12–21.

2. Mark Csikszentmihalyi discusses the topic of embodied morality in *Material Virtue: Ethics and the Body in Early China* (Leiden: Brill, 2004).

3. The gaps in our knowledge about the dating, authorship, and place of origin of most texts from early China prevent us from making tight connections between ideas and specific people, policies, or agendas of the day. I thus often refer to a time-scale of centuries rather than years or decades, and to a geographic scope that includes the entire multistate sphere of political and intellectual interactions.

4. Two very interesting accounts on the issue of schools of thought in early China are Kidder Smith, "Sima Tan and the Invention of Daoism, 'Legalism,' et cetera," *Journal of Asiatic Studies* 63.1 (2003), and Mark Csikszentmihalyi and Michael Nylan, "Constructing Lineages and Inventing Traditions through Exemplary Figures in Early China," *T'oung Pao* 89:1–3 (2003): pp. 55–99.

5. In using such a methodology, I join a host of Warring States scholars who have shown that historical context and ideological meaning are mutually defining.

6. Though I mention the West here, I hope that readers will understand that it is very much a constructed concept. Some works that problematize the East-West distinction in scholarship and the popular imagination are Jerry Bentley, *Shapes of World History in Twentieth-Century Scholarship* (Washington, D.C.: American Historical Association, 1996); Richard Vinograd, *Boundaries of the Self: Chinese Portraits, 1600–1900* (Cambridge: Cambridge University Press, 1992); and Miranda Brown, "Neither 'Primitive' nor 'Others,' But Somehow Not Quite Like 'Us': The Fortunes of Psychic Unity and Essentialism in Chinese Studies," *Journal of the Economic and Social History of the Orient* 49.2 (2006): pp. 219–252.

7. Max Weber, *The Religion of China: Confucianism and Taoism*, trans. Hans Gerth (New York: The Free Press, 1951), p. 249.

8. Ibid., p. 248.

9. Ibid., p. 249.

10. Coined by Joseph Wu as "the fallacy of 'the misplaced hamburger,'" which draws an analogy with an American who would order a hamburger in a Chinese restaurant and then ask him or herself why Chinese restaurants do not serve hamburgers. See Paul Goldin, *After Confucius: Studies in Early Chinese Philosophy* (Honolulu: University of Hawai'i Press, 2005), p. 154 n. 8.

11. For example, Joseph Needham's entire *Science and Civilization* project on China, though undoubtedly a monumental achievement, approaches the issue of science in China by asking the fundamental question: "Why didn't China develop science?" Similarly, comparative philosophers to this day still discuss the relevance of the term "philosophy" to China. The very fact that Chinese philosophy is barely represented in departments of philosophy at American universities reflects the failure of the academy not just to incorporate difference but also its failure to understand Chinese philosophy in terms of its own unique attributes as philosophy, and not only in terms of rigid definitions of philosophy determined by the Greco-Roman and European traditions.

12. For the notion of "China-centered" histories, see Paul Cohen, *Discovering History in China: American Historical Writing on the Recent Chinese Past* (New York: Columbia University Press, 1984).

13. Roger Ames, "Reflections on the Confucian Self: A Response to Fingarette," in Mary Bockover, ed., *Rules, Rituals, and Responsibility: Essays Dedicated to Herbert Fingarette* (La Salle, Ill.: Open Court, 1991), p. 105. Other key works include de Bary, *Asian Values and Human Rights;* Henry Rosemont, "Two Loci of Authority: Autonomous Individuals and Related Persons," in Peter Hershock and Roger Ames, eds. *Confucian Cultures of Authority* (Albany: State University of New York Series in Asian Studies Development, 2006), pp. 1–20; and Henry Rosemont, "Rights-Bearing Individuals and Role-Bearing Persons," in Mary Bockover, ed., *Rules, Rituals, and Responsibility: Essays Dedicated to Herbert Fingarette* (Chicago: Open Court, 1991), pp. 71–101.

14. See the various essays in Ames, Dissanayake, and Kasulis, *Self as Person in Asian Theory and Practice*. Rosemont is particularly clear about this distinction between "person" and "individual" in relationship to Chinese thought. See Rosemont, "Rights-Bearing Individuals and Role-Bearing Persons," pp. 71–101.

15. See Hansen, "Individualism in Chinese Thought," pp. 35–55; and Rosemont, "Rights-Bearing Individuals and Role-Bearing Persons," pp. 71–101.

16. Hansen, "Individualism in Chinese Thought," p. 54.

17. Ibid.

18. Irene Bloom, "Confucian Perspectives on the Individual and the Collective," in Irene Bloom, J. Paul Martin, and Wayne L. Proudfoot, eds., *Religious Diversity and Human Rights* (New York: Columbia University Press, 1996), p. 117.

19. Yü Ying-shih 余英時, "Individualism and the Neo-Taoist Movement in Wei-Chin China," in Donald Munro, ed., *Individualism and Holism: Studies in Confucian and Taoist Values* (Ann Arbor: Center for Chinese Studies, University of Michigan, 1985), pp. 121–155.

20. More on this period and its individualistic movement can be found in Richard Mather, "The Controversy over Conformity and Naturalness during the Six Dynasties," *History of Religions* 9.2–3 (1967): pp. 160–180; and Richard Mather, "Individualist Expressions of the Outsiders during the Six Dynasties," in Donald Munro, ed., *Individualism and Holism: Studies in Confucian and Taoist Values* (Ann Arbor: Center for Chinese Studies, University of Michigan, 1985), pp. 199–214.

21. Nylan, "Confucian Piety and Individualism in Han China," p. 25.

22. Ibid.

23. Ibid.

24. Ames, "Reflections on the Confucian Self," p. 105.

25. Wm. Theodore de Bary uses this term in his work on Confucian traditions. See De Bary, *Asian Values and Human Rights,* pp. 146–147. See also preface, note 5.

26. For example, commonly held American assertions about individualism include the following: "I am an individual because I have the prerogative or power to do what I want as long as it does not adversely affect others," which satisfies the first criteria, while the statement "I am an individual because I decide what I wish to wear and how I wish to express myself" satisfies the second.

27. For example, the notion of creativity is often not primary in discussions of individual power and authority in early China. See Michael Puett, *The Ambivalence of Creation* (Stanford, Calif.: Stanford University Press, 2000).

28. For a helpful account of the *zong fa* ("lineage law") system of the Spring and Autumn, see Mark Lewis, *Sanctioned Violence in Early China* (Albany: State University of New York Press, 1990), pp. 8, 28–36.

29. Hsu Cho-yun discusses these changes at length in *Ancient China in Transition: An Analysis of Social Mobility, 722–222 B.C.* (Stanford, Calif.: Stanford University Press, 1968). See also Yuri Pines, *Foundations of Confucian Thought: Intellectual Life in the Chunqiu Period, 722–453 BCE* (Honolulu: University of Hawai'i Press, 2002). Pines gives a solid account of the rise and fall of ministerial power during the Spring and Autumn period and the effects such a development had on concepts of loyalty, the ruler-minister relationship, etc.

30. On the introduction of these administrative districts and their relationship to policies of universal military service, see Mark Lewis, "Warring States Political History," in Michael Loewe and Edward Shaughnessy, eds., *Cambridge History of Ancient China: From the Origins of Civilization to 221 B.C.* (Cambridge: Cambridge University Press, 1999), pp. 613–614. See also Zhu Fenghan 朱鳳瀚 and Xu Yong 徐勇, eds., *Xian Qin shi yanjiu gai yao* 先秦史研究概要 (Tianjin: Tianjin jiaoyu, 1996); and Zhu, Ruikai 祝瑞開, *Xian Qin shehui he zhuzi sixiang xin tan* 先秦社會與諸子思想新 (Fujian: Renmin, 1981).

31. The hereditary aristocracy did not lose its power in some states of the late Spring and Autumn and early Warring States periods. Examples of a thriving hereditary aristocracy and servile class in the state of Chu, for example, are reflected in legal documents from Baoshan tomb 2 (~322 BCE). See Susan Weld, "Chu Law

in Action: Legal Documents from Tomb 2 at Baoshan," in Constance Cook and John S. Major, eds., *Defining Chu: Image and Reality in Ancient China* (Honolulu: University of Hawai'i Press, 1999), pp. 77–97. See also Hsu Cho-yun, *Ancient China in Transition*, pp. 97–98; and Yü Ying-shih, *Shi yu zhongguo wenhua* 士與中國文化 (Shanghai: Shanghai renmin shuju, 1987).

32. See Yuri Pines, *Envisioning Empire: Chinese Political Thought of the Warring States Era* (Honolulu: University of Hawai'i Press, 2009), chapter 5. See also Hsu Cho-yun, *Ancient China in Transition*, 96.

33. Confucius, *Analects*, 9.13.

34. That is, especially among the lower-level, educated elite. Such a claim most likely does not apply as readily to commoners, although some merchants fared well in late Warring States China.

35. Yang Kuan 楊 寬, *Zhanguo shi* 戰 國 史 (Shanghai: Shanghai renmin chubanshe, 1980), pp. 176–185. Lewis, "Warring States Political History," p. 649.

36. See Zhu Fenghan 朱鳳瀚, *Shang Zhou jiazu xingtai yanjiu* 商周家族形態研究 (Tianjin: Guji chubanshe, 1990).

37. Lewis, *Sanctioned Violence in Early China*. For an in-depth look at the iron industry in ancient China, see Donald B. Wagner, *Iron and Steel in Ancient China* (Leiden: E. J. Brill, 1993).

38. Lewis, Sanctioned Violence, 54–67.

39. The most influential book to date on the social changes of this period is still Hsu Cho-yun's *Ancient China in Transition*. Hsu's claims concerning the rise in social mobility and fundamental growth of kingly power and the *shi* class have influenced greatly my thinking about discourses on human agency. To a large degree, my analysis of the intended social scope of such discourses signifies an attempt to use intellectual history, and not statistical data primarily from a single source, to help support Hsu's insightful but still debatable claims. Though the textual sources I use for my historical analysis are surely just as unrepresentative of whole societies as Hsu's, they can at least provide alternative textual corroboration of his finds.

40. Here I define one's ability to demonstrate agency in the world through a rise in social mobility. According to this definition, one's agency in the world can be expressed through one's heightened influence in the sociopolitical world. While the reasons for the alleged rise in social mobility are yet unclear, one may build a case for it by considering known historical changes of the period. Methods of centralization were designed so that state leaders could diminish the power of the local lords and aristocratic noblemen more easily than before. In addition to usurping the power of local lords over their small kingdoms, such rulers exterminated many rival aristocratic families. One likely result of this was the dispersal of the intellectual class (and hence their beginning as itinerant intellectuals, as well as their more marked independence from state service). This would likely have led to an increase in education among a greater variety of people, as well as a ruler's increasing promotion of individuals of nonaristocratic background into his service.

41. For an account of the growth of correlative cosmologies, a phenomenon related to universalistic ideologies, see John Henderson, *The Development and Decline of Chinese Cosmology* (New York: Columbia University Press, 1984); *Bulletin of the Museum of Far Eastern Antiquities (Special Issue: Reconsidering the Correlative Cosmology of Early China)* 72 (2000). See also Gu Jiegang, ed. *Wu de zhong shi shuo xia de zheng zhi he li shi* 五德終始說下的政治和歷史 (Hong Kong: Longmen Publishing, 1970); A. C. Graham, *Yin-Yang and the Nature of Correlative Thinking* (Singapore: The Institute of East Asian Philosophies, 1986); Aihe Wang, *Cosmology and Political Culture in Early China* (Cambridge: Cambridge University Press, 2000); and Michael Puett, *To Become a God: Cosmology, Sacrifice, and Self-Divinization in Early China* (Cambridge, Mass.: Harvard University Asia Center, 2002).

42. I use the term "debate" here to point to an intellectual involvement in a shared topic of concern, irrespective of the degree to which the actual players in a debate were consciously aware of their shared interest and the direction of their thoughts and responses.

43. *Webster's New Collegiate Dictionary* (Springfield, Mass.: G. & C. Merriam Company, 1979).

44. Henry Rosemont, "Who Chooses," in Henry Rosemont, Jr., ed. *Chinese Texts and Philosophical Contexts* (La Salle, Ill.: Open Court, 1991), pp. 227–263.

45. Ibid.

46. Copious scholarship has been written on this topic. For starters, a very good discussion of responsibility can be found in Bernard Williams, *Shame and Necessity* (Berkeley: University of California Press, 1993), pp. 50–74. See also the many essays in Mary Bockover, ed., *Rules, Rituals, and Responsibility: Essays Dedicated to Herbert Fingarette* (La Salle, Ill.: Open Court, 1991).

47. Gideon Yaffe discusses the origins of the notion of "free agency" in the thought of John Locke. Gideon Yaffe, *Liberty Worth the Name: Locke on Free Agency* (Princeton, N.J.: Princeton University Press, 2000).

48. Howard Harrod, *The Human Center: Moral Agency in the Social World* (Philadelphia: Fortress Press, 1981), p. 11.

49. In the language of contemporary action theory, the notions of agency and conformity are not juxtaposed or commonly considered to be a pair. See Jerome Segal, *Agency and Alienation: A Theory of Human Presence* (Savage, Md.: Rowman & Littlefield Publishers, Inc., 1991), pp. 3–4. See also Charles Taylor, *Human Agency and Language* (Cambridge: Cambridge University Press, 1985), for a discussion that views human agency as a product of notions of the self and personhood.

50. For contemporary debates and problems surrounding the issues of free will and control, see Daniel Dennett, *Elbow Room: The Varieties of Free Will Worth Wanting* (Cambridge, Mass.: MIT Press, 1997).

51. The distinction between active and passive agency I delineate here is related to a distinction commonly made in early modern philosophy between active and passive power.

52. In the context of early Chinese discourse, such sources of authority and power are never located outside of human experience, nor are they ever conceived of as radically disassociated or cut off from individuals and "human becoming" in the world. I have benefited from Roger Ames' ideas on "human becoming," in "What Ever Happened to 'Wisdom'? Confucian Philosophy of Process and 'Human Becomings,'" *Asia Major*, 3rd series 21.1 (2008): pp. 45–68.

53. Isaiah Berlin identifies two senses of autonomy that relate to "negative" and "positive" formulations of liberty. According to the former, "autonomy is the absence of constraints on individual action," while autonomy according to the positive conception is concerned with sources of control and the agency and desires individuals have to direct, master, and control their lives. In this book, I refer to this positive sense of "autonomy" in terms of "individual agency." See Kim-chong Chong, "Autonomy in the *Analects*," in Kim-chong Chong, Sor-hoon Tan, and C. L. Ten, eds., *The Moral Circle and the Self: Chinese and Western Approaches* (La Salle, Ill.: Open Court, 2003), pp. 277–278.

54. For a critique of "free will," see Dennett, *Elbow Room*.

55. For the European tradition, see Charles Taylor, *Sources of the Self: The Making of the Modern Identity* (Cambridge, Mass.: Harvard University Press, 1989), pp. 321–367. Roger Ames distinguishes between the "unique individual" and the "autonomous individual," claiming that the latter is irrelevant for Chinese traditions. Ames, "Reflections on the Confucian Self," pp. 108–110.

56. Charles Taylor is careful to point out that "modern moral culture," consists in multiple sources, or "fractured horizons." See his *Sources of the Self*, pp. 314–317.

57. Henry Rosemont has also contributed much to the idea of Chinese communitarianism and relationalism as a corrective to the emphasis on autonomy in some Western circles. I disagree with Rosemont on the usage of the term "autonomy" in early Chinese contexts. Whereas he sees such an idea as unfit—choosing instead the term "relational persons"—to describe early Chinese orientations, I contend that the early Chinese individual can be both "relational" and "autonomous" at the same time. See especially Henry Rosemont, "Whose Democracy? Which Rights? A Confucian Critique of Modern Western Liberalism," in Kwong-loi Shun and David Wong, eds. *Confucian Ethics: A Comparative Study of Self, Autonomy, and Community* (Cambridge: Cambridge University Press, 2004), pp. 49–71.

58. I borrow Roger Ames' vocabulary of the "authoritative individual." See Roger Ames' insights into "authoritativeness" as it relates to the Ruist notion of *ren* in *Focusing the Familiar: A Translation and Philosophical Interpretation of the Zhongyong* (Honolulu: University of Hawai'i Press, 2001), pp. 74–75.

59. Henry Rosemont can be credited, along with Ames and many others, as one who has done much to proffer an alternative vision to predominant Western conceptions of the individual. See Rosemont, "Whose Democracy? Which Rights?" pp. 49–71; and Rosemont, "Two Loci of Authority: Autonomous Individuals and Related Persons," pp. 1–20.

60. For works on the self in China, see Roger Ames, Wimal Dissanayake, and Thomas Kasulis, eds., *Self As Image in Asian Theory and Practice* (Albany: State University of New York Press, 1994); Shun and Wong, *Confucian Ethics: A Comparative Study of Self, Autonomy, and Community;* and Kim-chong Chong, Sor-hoon Tan, and C. L. Ten, eds. *The Moral Circle and the Self: Chinese and Western Approaches* (Peru, Ill.: Open Court Press, 2003).

61. For a brief consideration of these terms and others that involve the self, see Herbert Fingarette, "The Problem of the Self in the Analects," in Kim-chong Chong, Sor-hoon Tan, and C. L. Ten, eds., *The Moral Circle and the Self: Chinese and Western Approaches*, pp. 285–287. See also Ames, "Reflections on the Confucian Self," pp. 106–110.

62. Taylor, *Sources of the Self*, pp. 146–158. Indeed, Taylor describes this dualistic type of thinking in detail throughout the early portions of this book, and not merely in relationship to Descartes, but to other influential late Renaissance and Enlightenment philosophers as well.

63. Steven Pinker provides an overview and critique of this orientation in *The Blank Slate: The Modern Denial of Human Nature* (New York: Penguin, 2003).

64. A powerful critique of this disembodied approach can be found in Edward Slingerland, *What Science Offers the Humanities: Integrating Body and Culture* (Cambridge: Cambridge University Press, 2008), pp. 1–73.

65. See especially Antonio Damasio, *Descartes' Error: Emotion, Reason, and the Human Brain* (New York: Quill, 2000), pp. 14–17. Roger Ames and David Hall point to the multiplicity of approaches to the self in the Western tradition, including the "materialistic-mechanistic axis of interpretation" that rivaled dualistic thinking, in "The Problematic of Self in Western Thought," in David Hall and Roger Ames, eds., *Thinking from the Han: Self, Truth, and Transcendence in Chinese and Western Culture* (Albany: State University of New York Press, 1998), pp. 4–21.

66. In addition to Damasio and Slingerland, mentioned above, see Mark Johnson, *The Body in the Mind: The Bodily Basis of Meaning, Imagination, and Reason* (Chicago: University of Chicago Press, 1987); George Lakoff and Mark Johnson, *Philosophy in the Flesh: The Embodied Mind and Its Challenge to Western Thought* (New York: Basic Books, 1999).

67. As an atomistic subset of the human race, the term "individual" has no direct counterparts in early Chinese thought. Thinkers simply use the term *ren* 人 (human) to point to singular and/or plural human beings.

Chapter One: Individual Agency and Universal, Centralized Authority in Early Mohist Writings

1. For a good general account of the importance of moral autonomy in the *Analects*, see Benjamin Schwartz, *The World of Thought in Ancient China* (Cambridge, Mass.: Harvard University Press, 1985), pp. 113–114. Schwartz refutes Herbert Fingarette's provocative claim that Confucius' "individual" is one without

"genuine choices." See Fingarette's *Confucius—The Secular as Sacred* (New York: Harper & Row, 1972).

2. The writings of the early Mohists most likely date to some time after Confucius' death in 479 BCE and before ~350 BCE. Angus C. Graham outlines a general chapter schematic for dating the various chapters of the Mohist corpus. See A. C. Graham, *Divisions in Early Mohism Reflected in the Core Chapters of Mo-tzu* (Singapore: Institute of East Asian Philosophies, 1985). Throughout this chapter, I abide by Graham's outline and refer to the early Mohists as authors of the "core chapters" of the Mohist text.

3. Henri Maspero seems to have been one of the first scholars to refer to Mohist claims in terms of an individual's conformity to the will of Heaven. He states that Mozi's "religion was a completely personal religion that consisted first of all in conforming to the will of Heaven, and which by its individualism was opposed to the totally social religion of ancient China." Henri Maspero, *La Chine antique, Annales du Musée Guimet*, no. 71 (Paris: Presses Universitaires de France, 1965), p. 389, translated in Scott Lowe, *Mo Tzu's Religious Blueprint for a Chinese Utopia: The Will and the Way* (New York: The Edwin Mellen Press, 1992), p. 17. While I do not go so far as to speak of the Mohist claim as an individualistic one that is opposed to the totally social religion of China, I think that Maspero points to a subtle and often overlooked aspect of early Mohist thought in relationship to the individual and his or her agency.

4. Chapters 11, 12, and 13. In these chapters, the term *"tong"* is used in three basic ways: (1) as a gerund meaning "upward conforming (conformity) or agreement," or as a modified verb meaning "to conform upward" (上 / 尚同); (2) as a verb in conjunction with the word for "one" (yi 一 / 壹), meaning "to unify and make agree"; and (3) as an adjective meaning "same as" or "similar to."

5. By "authority," I refer to that which enables one to make claims concerning ethical or epistemological truth—or what is right in any given situation as well as how we know things exist as they do.

6. Zhou Changyao gives an account of the relationship between traditional religious beliefs and Mohist beliefs. See Zhou Changyao 周長耀, *Mozi sixiang zhi yanjiu* 墨子思想之研究" (Taipei: Zhonghua lunli kexue jiaoyu xiehui, 1974), pp. 24–29.

7. Many philosophers have debated the relationship among Heaven's will, what is right, and utilitarianism. The debate begins with Dennis Ahern, "Is Mo Tzu a Utilitarian?" *Journal of Chinese Philosophy* 3.2 (1976): pp. 185–193. See also Rodney Taylor, "Religion and Utilitarianism: Mo Tzu on Spirits and Funerals," *Philosophy East and West* 29.3 (1979): pp. 337–346; Dirck Vorenkamp, "Another Look at Utilitarianism in Mo-Tzu's Thought," *Journal of Chinese Philosophy* 19.4 (1992): pp. 423–443; David Soles, "Mo Tzu and the Foundations of Morality," *Journal of Chinese Philosophy* 26.1 (March 1999): pp. 37–48; and Kristopher Duda, "Reconsidering Mo Tzu on the Foundations of Morality," *Asian Philosophy* 11.1 (2001): pp. 23–31.

I tend to agree with David Soles' account that Mozi is a Divine Will theorist who relies on "utilitarian considerations to reveal" such a will (Soles, "Mo Tzu and the Foundations of Morality," p. 43), but I would disagree with Soles' claim that Mozi is not a utilitarian. One problem with this debate is that these philosophers consider utilitarianism to be incompatible by definition with divine command theory. This posits an artificial dichotomy that falsely suggests a contradiction in early Mohist thought. I contend that the Mohists are both utilitarian *and* believe that Heaven possesses ultimate control over what is right and wrong. This is because Heaven produces the standards for right and wrong—rendering them compatible with utilitarian values of benefit and harm—in the first place. Bryan Van Norden has provided a similar criticism, showing that the problem lies in an assumption of divine command theory that what is "right" is necessarily independent of God and limits his powers. See Van Norden, *Virtue Ethics and Consequentialism in Early Chinese Philosophy* (Cambridge: Cambridge University Press, 2007), p. 149.

8. Sun Yirang 孫詒讓, *Mozi jian gu* 墨子閒詁 (Taipei: Huaqu shuju, 1987) 26 ("Tian Zhi, A" 天志上), p. 176 (hereafter *Mozi*).

9. See their only remaining chapter on ghosts and spirits, *Mozi* 31 ("Ming Gui, Xia" 明鬼下), pp. 200–226. This claim agrees with the one made in Taylor, "Religion and Utilitarianism: Mo Tzu on Spirits and Funerals," pp. 337–346.

10. "Gui Shen" 鬼神之明 (The perspicuity of ghosts and spirits) appears to be a direct rejoinder to the early Mohist view on the efficacy of ghosts and spirits, perhaps by an outlier to the Mohist faith. See the recent analysis and text given by Ding Sixin 丁四新, "Shangbo Chu jian 'Gui Shen' pian zhu shi" 上博楚简《鬼神》篇注释, http://www.bsm.org.cn/show_article.php?id=337. This view contrasts with the view presented in the Shanghai volume itself, written by Cao Jinyan, which states that the text constitutes some lost writings of the Mohist school. "Gui Shen zhi ming" 鬼神之明, in Ma Chengyuan 馬承源, ed., *Shanghai Bowuguan cang Zhanguo Chu zhu shu* 上海博物館藏戰國楚竹書, vol. 5 (Shanghai: Shanghai guji chubanshe, 2005), pp. 307–320.

11. *Mozi* 11 ("Shang Tong, A" 上同上), p. 70. A very similar statement is made in Chapter 12, where the author includes even more disasters such as "irregularities in climate, unseasonable snow, frost, rain, and dew, situations in which the five grains do not ripen, and disastrous illnesses and epidemics," p. 74. The third chapter of "Upward Conformity" promotes conformity with Heaven but does not speak about Heaven's recourse to punishments when humans do not conform.

12. The fact that *ming* is connected to Heaven is not stated explicitly in the text. It is possible that the Mohists expressly did not wish to draw this connection because it would go against their "correct" understandings of how Heaven functions in the world. Moreover, given the presumed link between the "Heavenly Mandate" (*Tian Ming*) and *ming* during the Zhou Dynasty, it was probably unnecessary for the Mohists to elaborate on this concept when their main goal was to refute it in their own terms. See Lisa Raphals, "Languages of Fate: Semantic Fields in Chinese and Greek," in Christopher Lupke, ed., *The Magnitude of Ming: Command, Allotment, and Fate in Chinese Culture* (Honolulu: University of Hawai'i Press, 2005), pp. 70–106.

Notes to Pages 4–7

13. Though the Ru vision of Heaven in the *Analects* does indeed delegate much power to *ming*, it is not the case in that text that the Master and his disciples completely deny individuals the agency to change or affect what happens to themselves in life. It seems likely that the early Mohists are presenting an extreme interpretation of *ming*—one that was not necessarily espoused by Ru of the time—to advance their rhetorical claims.

14. *Mozi* 35 ("Fei Ming, A" 非命上), p. 242.

15. *Mozi* 33–35 ("Fei Ming A, B, and C" 非命上中下), pp. 239–259.

16. Indeed, "choice," like "agency," is not an explicit linguistic or conceptual construct in the early Mohist writings.

17. One might ask how a choice that is made from within a retributive system of punishment and reward might actually constitute a real choice. While not conforming to Heaven's will certainly brings about devastating results in one's life, as well as unsatisfactory conditions in society, the mere fact that such conditions often prevail in the world suggests that individuals can and do repeatedly choose to ignore Heaven's will. Moreover, since conformity to Heaven is neither physically nor mentally forced upon individuals—since it is not necessary from the standpoint of one's immediate survival or the range of actions one can take, individuals are truly free to choose the course of their actions. Not conforming to Heaven's will is therefore a clear option for individuals, though not a good or ideal one.

18. This view of individual accountability is carried over into legal formulations of roughly the same time period as the early Mohists. See Susan Weld, "The Covenant Texts from Houma and Wenxian," in Edward Shaughnessy, ed., *New Sources of Early Chinese History: An Introduction to the Reading of Inscriptions and Manuscripts* (Berkeley, Calif.: The Society for the Study of Early China and The Institute of East Asian Studies, 1997), pp. 125–160. According to Weld, covenant texts from the state of Jin (dating to the 420s) emphasize "individual, as opposed to the collective, liability of the separate covenantors and that breach by one covenantor did not affect the obligations of all the others." (Weld, "Covenant Texts," pp. 138, 148–149.) This suggests that laws of the age were sensitive to the notion of personal liability and obligation, and that they attempted to carve out a sphere that viewed individual actions as wholly determined by the self.

19. *Mozi* 11, 12, and 13 ("Shang Tong, A, B, C"), 67–68, 71–73, and 82–84.

20. For a discussion of whether or not the early Mohists advocated a divine command theory—or a theory that what makes something right (*Yi*) is that Heaven declared it right—see Van Norden, *Virtue Ethics and Consequentialism*, pp. 145–149.

21. This is attested by the very fact that in the "Upward Conformity" chapters the people of the world (*tian xia*) collectively decide that they need to abide by a single moral authority at the top. See *Mozi* 13 ("Shang Tong, C"), p. 83.

22. The question arises as to how certain individuals might transcend the average state of man to apprehend Heaven's true view of morality. Unfortunately, this is not a topic explained by the early Mohists. Rather, the authors simply presume

throughout their discussions of upward conformity that such individuals exist, that such individuals have uncovered a standardized method of arriving at the correct view, and that their method might be utilized effectively by all individuals to fulfill Heaven's *Yi*. Therefore, in order for the notion of upward conformity to have meaning, morally worthy individuals must exist so that they might lead others—misguided yet autonomous individuals—away from their own, wrong-headed *yi* toward the right path of Heaven's *Yi*. See *Mozi* 11, 12, and 13 ("Shang Tong, A, B, and C"), 67–68, 71–73, and 82–84.

23. Indeed, the fact of an individual's fallibility does not detract from his or her autonomy. Instead, it strengthens the early Mohist notion that individuals each possess control over their own destinies, insofar as they have the capacity to make wrong decisions on their own.

24. As I show below, such individuals are not completely morally subservient to external moral authorities; they possess the ability to recognize that a view is worthy of adoption after having been exposed to it. Even in the "Upward Conformity" chapters, the early Mohists imply that the people can collectively recognize the correct view when presented with it, insofar as they willingly accept the authority of the Son of Heaven and his associates over and above that of their own. Other statements in the text imply widespread recognition of worthy people irrespective of their social position. In "Upward Conformity, B," for example, the Son of Heaven calls upon all people to alert him of worthies and bad people from among their midst. See *Mozi* 12 ("Shang Tong, B"), p. 72. This suggests that the people do not simply conform to moral authority based on the authority alone; they do so because they also recognize such authority as morally correct.

25. For more on the issue of human motivations in early Chinese thought, including comments on Mozi's "voluntarism," see David Nivison, "Philosophical Voluntarism in Fourth-Century China," in Bryan Van Norden, ed., *Ways of Confucianism* (Chicago: Open Court, 1996), pp. 130–132.

26. Zhang Qianfang, "Human Dignity in Classical Chinese Philosophy: Reinterpreting Mohism," *Journal of Chinese Philosophy* 34.2 (June 2007): p. 249.

27. *Mozi* 26 ("Tian Zhi, A" 天志上), p. 175.

28. Ibid., p. 179.

29. Ibid., p. 177.

30. *Mozi* 27 ("Tian Zhi, B"), p. 180. Following Sun Yirang's commentary, I take *zheng* 政 to be *zheng* 正, and *shan* 善 to be a mistake for *yan* 言.

31. In "Against Heaven's Command, B" the word *fa* ("standards" or "laws"), rather than the term translated here as "criteria," *yi* 儀, actually appears in a similar argument made in the following chapter. Compare the phrase in *Mozi* 36 ("Fei Ming, B"), p. 247, with that in *Mozi* 35 ("Fei Ming, A"), p. 240.

32. *Mozi* 35 ("Fei Ming, A"), p. 240. Much has been written about the "Three Proofs" (sometimes translated as "Three Gnomens" or "Three Gauges or Standards") in early Mohist epistemology. For more on this topic, see Van Norden, *Virtue Ethics and Consequentialism*, pp. 151–161; Hu Shih, *The Development of the*

Logical Method in Ancient China (Shanghai: Oriental Book Company, 1922), pp. 72–82; Yi-pao Mei, *Motse, the Neglected Rival of Confucius* (London: Probsthain, 1934), pp. 61–84; and Chad Hansen, *A Daoist Theory of Chinese Thought* (New York: Oxford University Press, 1992), pp. 143–148.

33. By the same logic that there is no such thing as interpreting Heaven's will, it is more apt to adopt the language of the early Mohists themselves and refer to the act of deciphering Heaven as "obtaining" rather than "creating" *fa*. See the quote directly below. *Mozi* 26 ("Tian Zhi, A"), p. 179.

34. Ibid. Slightly amended translation from Burton Watson, trans., *Basic Writings of Mo Tzu, Hsün Tzu, and Han Fei Tzu* (New York: Columbia University Press, 1964), p. 83.

35. Ibid.

36. See *Mozi* 26 ("Tian Zhi, A"), p. 179, for an example of the early Mohist use of tool metaphors as a means of conveying the importance of setting and using standards to evaluate claims to truth.

37. We will discuss the effect of these laws and standardized methods on the individual agency of ordinary folk, unlike Mozi himself, below.

38. Nivison has argued that Mozi is "not concerned with the moral cultivation of individual people" and that a "'worthy' official is simply one who does his job well." David Nivison, "Motivation and Moral Action in Mencius," in Bryan Van Norden, ed., *The Ways of Confucianism: Investigations in Chinese Philosophy* (Chicago: Open Court, 1996), p. 93. Nivison goes too far, though. While the early Mohists indeed do not expound on the moral or psychological traits and attitudes of such a person, one cannot conclude that they are oblivious to the moral meanings of *xian* in their time.

39. *Mozi* 9 ("Shang Xian, B"), p. 45.

40. *Mozi* 27 ("Tian Zhi, B"), p. 180.

41. While we as contemporary readers readily see that some degree of subjective interpolation is implied in the process of deciphering Heaven's laws, the early Mohist would not. For him, the rhetoric of upward conformity dictates that humans cannot create Heavenly justice. And so history and the events of the world should be decoded as transcriptions of Heaven's will, not interpreted or created to the slightest degree. This does not mean, however, that there is no room for human misapprehension of Heaven's will. For the early Mohist, Heavenly morality is objective, but it can be misapprehended through use of incorrect tools of translation.

42. Zhang Qianfang refers to the equality of people under Heaven in terms of Heavenly love (expressed through the ideal of universal caring) and "equality based on merits." See Zhang Qianfang, "Human Dignity in Classical Chinese Philosophy," p. 245.

43. Although *neng*, "ability," is not explicitly defined in terms of morality, it is clear from the sections of the Mohist corpus under discussion that it is conceived along moral as well as cognitive lines. Also, as stated above, men who are "achieved" are characterized as wise and noble individuals. They are therefore not merely able in an intellectual sense, but morally fit as well.

44. *Mozi* 8 ("Shang Xian, A"), p. 41.

45. Not defined by context, ability appears to be the result of either individual effort or innate talent, although the text does not clarify this point for us.

46. *Mozi* 8 ("Shang Xian, A"), pp. 40–41.

47. Two aspects of these passages are worthy of note. The use of the verb "to compete," with reference to the peasants, multitudes, and princes, is revealing. It suggests that while all men might have the opportunity to strive to better themselves intellectually and morally, not all men can actually succeed at achieving the ability necessary for positions of leadership in the meritocratic hierarchy. Furthermore, the conditional phrase in the passage just quoted, "if he had ability," reveals that not all individual farmers or craftsmen have the ability necessary for promotion by the sages, regardless of their aspirations. This type of wording suggests that though the ideal was open to everyone, not everyone would become an achieved individual.

Unfortunately, early Mohists do not delve into the reasons why certain individuals might have the necessary ability for promotion while others would not. They appear simply to be interested in asserting the possibility that men of any background might achieve or possess the moral and intellectual worth necessary for sociopolitical advancement.

48. See Zhang Qianfang's analysis of equal opportunity and "equality based on merit" in "Human Dignity in Classical Chinese Philosophy," pp. 245–246.

49. For another discussion of the social structure as presented by the early Mohists, see Van Norden, *Virtue Ethics and Consequentialism*, pp. 166–170.

50. *Mozi* 12 ("Shang Tong, B"), p. 78.

51. *Mozi* 13 ("Shang Tong, C"), p. 83.

52. Early Mohist teachings are far from egalitarian in at least two senses of the term: they neither endorse a view of equal individual potential, nor do they support a vision of equal power relations among individuals in society. To expect an egalitarian view in these two senses would be to miss the internal consistency of their ideals for social advancement by confusing them with their claims for equality with respect to Heaven.

53. The Mohist author plays on the connotations and cognates of the word for rulership or government (*zheng* 政) to imply rectitude and control by the right means. For a discussion of various translations of this term and alternative interpretations stemming from them in this passage, see Van Norden, *Virtue Ethics and Consequentialism*, pp. 147–149.

54. Here I take the term "*ci*" 次 to refer to the cognate "*zi*," 資 "resources." According to this reading, one does not take oneself to be a resource for political action; hence, one does not rely on oneself.

55. *Mozi* 26 ("Tian Zhi, A"), pp. 176–177.

56. That the Mohists fully endorsed a highly structured, top-down system of authority is confirmed in their own social groups. Mohists were perhaps the only collectivity in the Warring States period to group themselves together according to what might be called "schools," or tight-knit paramilitary and study societies. All

Mohists within a given school were expected to defer to the absolute authority of the *Juzi* 巨子, or Mohist leader. As Van Norden shows, such a top-down system does not necessarily imply that it was utterly authoritarian in approach, as the early Mohist system allowed for mechanisms by which subordinates might remonstrate or address their grievances to superiors. Van Norden, *Virtue Ethics and Consequentialism*, pp. 168–169.

57. Without able and intelligent men like the Mohists in leadership positions, there would be no means of ensuring that orders from above are indeed worthy of being followed, and the world would be in a state of chaos, as it was before the existence of standards and government. *Mozi* 11 ("Shang Tong, A"), p. 67.

58. As we will see below, however, their notion of meritocracy does not seem to apply to the ruler at the top center.

59. *Mozi* 35 ("Fei Ming, A"), p. 242. Amended from Watson, *Basic Writings*, p. 119.

60. The idea of a meritocracy is linked to early Mohist religious beliefs in an important way: policies on political advancement, employed by the sage-kings, appear to derive from Heaven's system of justice. Thus, hierarchies of authority and power differentials are rooted in Heaven's will. *Mozi* 9 ("Shang Xian, B"), p. 45. Translated by Watson, *Basic Writings*, pp. 22–23.

61. Indeed, the position of the Son of Heaven does not appear to be open to meritocratic appointment from the top (from Heaven), although there is some evidence that the early Mohists thought his position should be in agreement with public opinion from below. See *Mozi* 11, "Upward Conformity, A," p. 68, and *Mozi* 12, "Upward Conformity B," p. 71.

62. *Mozi* 26 ("Tian Zhi, A"), pp. 176–177.

63. The legend of Emperor Yao yielding to Emperor Shun was becoming popular at least by the middle Warring States period. For a treatise that directly addresses and supports the issue of "yielding the throne," see *Tang Yu zhi Dao*," in *Jingmen shi bowuguan*, ed., *Guodian Chu Mu Chu Jian* (Beijing: Wen wu, 1998), p. 157. For scholarship on this issue, see Gu Jiegang, *Shan rang chuan shuo qi yu Mo jia kao* 禪讓傳說起于墨家考 (Beijing: National Beiping Research Institute, 1936); and Yuri Pines, "Disputers of Abdication: Zhanguo Egalitarianism and the Sovereign's Power," *T'oung Pao* 91.4–5 (2005): pp. 243–300.

64. *Mozi* 27 ("Tian Zhi, B"), p. 181. Translated by Watson, *Basic Writings*, p. 85.

65. *Mozi* 39 ("Fei Ru, C" 非儒下), p. 268. Amended from Watson, *Basic Writings*, p. 129. Bryan Van Norden also mentions the phenomenon of remonstrating with a superior. Van Norden, *Virtue Ethics and Consequentialism*, pp. 168–169.

66. By suggesting that rulers can be wrong without suggesting that they be replaced according to a meritocratic system based in Heavenly justice, the early Mohists demonstrate that they do not expect meritocracy to apply to the royal line of transmission itself.

67. *Mozi* 35 ("Fei Ming, A"), p. 244.

68. Why, after all, would they so deeply criticize the Ru for their beliefs in fate, and for their inability as ministers to speak up and criticize rulers who are wrong and misguided in their understanding of Heaven's will?

69. *Mozi* 13 ("Shang Tong, C"), p. 82.

70. Ibid., pp. 82–83.

71. Ibid.

72. Ibid., p. 83.

73. Ibid., p. 87.

74. *Mozi* 12 ("Shang Tong, B"), pp. 78–79.

75. *Mozi,* 13 ("Shang Tong, C"), p. 83.

76. Though we were not able to discuss this topic here, the famous early Mohist notion of "impartial caring" (*jian ai* 兼愛) is part and parcel of this objectification of values and norms for behavior. For more on this, see Van Norden, *Virtue Ethics and Consequentialism,* pp. 179–197.

77. Interestingly, mindful conformists are not the main concern of the early Mohists, who focus much of their attention on defining the necessary roles of the Son of Heaven and his advisors—the "achieved men"—in society.

Chapter Two: Centralizing Control

1. The *Shang jun shu,* which allegedly contains some of the writings of Shang Yang (d. 338 BCE), minister of the state of Qin, also dates to this period and advocates conformism to regulations and laws, not to psycho-physiological likeness. I do not use this text because I have already made my point about conformism by examining the early Mohists, and the *Shang jun shu* does not fit into the type of text outlined in this chapter.

2. Li Ling proposes that mantic practices of a variety of sorts—associated in the Han period with practitioners known as *fangshi* (方士)—stemmed from popular practices throughout Central States and coastal Shandong peninsula. See Li Ling 李零, *Zhongguo fang shu kao* 中国方术考 (Beijing: Dongfang, 2001), p. 19.

Two theories regarding the influx and influence of alien religious complexes on Central Plains civilizations are also worth considering. The first concerns the independent religious systems of the coastal regions of ancient China. The second theory, proposed by Victor Mair, speaks of the shaping of Laozian thought (and hence, early "Daoism") by yogic traditions of the thirteen *Upanishads,* attached to the *Vedas* of ancient India. For the first theory, see Chia-li Luo, "Coastal Culture and Religion in Early China: A Study through Comparison with the Central Plain Region" (PhD diss., Indiana University, 1999). For the second theory, see Victor Mair, trans., *Tao Te Ching: The Classic Book of Integrity and the Way* (New York: Bantam, 1990). Harold Roth writes at length about the early mystical traditions of "inward training," but not about possible origins for such a practice. See Harold Roth, *Original Tao, Inward Training (Nei-yeh) and the Foundations of Taoist Mysticism* (New York: Columbia University Press, 1999).

3. Puett, *To Become a God*. While Puett does not speak so much about the body as he does the "spirit"—which he carefully distinguishes from "form"—his notion that the sagely individual should in some fashion "embody" the larger divinity of the cosmos is a development in keeping with the claims presented in this chapter. Ibid., p. 221.

4. Csikszentmihalyi, *Material Virtue*.

5. Mark E. Lewis, *The Construction of Space in Early China* (Albany: State University of New York Press, 2006), pp. 13–76. Lewis' work serves as a critical backdrop to the claims I will make in this chapter concerning the sage-king's central and exclusive conformity to the cosmos.

6. Nathan Sivin, "State, Cosmos, and Body in the Last Three Centuries BC," *Harvard Journal of Asiatic Studies* 55.1 (1995): pp. 5–37.

7. For other important works on the body and cosmos, see Donald Harper, "Warring States Natural Philosophy and Occult Philosophy," in Edward Shaughnessy and Michael Loewe, eds., *The Cambridge History of Ancient China: From the Origins of Civilization to 221 BC* (Cambridge: Cambridge University Press, 1999), pp. 813–884. See also Roth, *Original Tao*.

8. Lewis, *The Construction of Space*, pp. 13–76.

9. One sees a faint hint of this in the *Analects* in the images of the wind bending the grass and the Pole Star ordering other astral entities. This represents the power exerted by a virtuous ruler over his subjects.

10. Michael Puett gives a convincing account of the development of notions of self-divinization during this period in *To Become a God*, pp. 109–144.

11. The problems attendant upon trying to date the text of the received version of *Laozi* have been multiplied by the discovery of the Guodian bamboo slips. For more on this, see Edward Shaughnessy, "The Guodian Manuscripts and Their Place in Twentieth-Century Historiography on the *Laozi*," *Harvard Journal of Asiatic Studies* 65.2 (December 2005), which discusses the views of textual scholars like Harold Roth, Wang Bo, Li Xueqin, etc. Most of these scholars agree that the Guodian find demonstrates that the ideas of the *Laozi* can be traced back at least to the late fourth century BCE.

For an excellent review of the debates surrounding the texts and dating of the *Laozi*, see Shaughnessy, "The Guodian Manuscripts," pp. 417–458; Roth, *Original Tao*, pp. 173–190; and William Baxter, "Situating the Language of the *Lao Tzu*: The Probable Date of the *Tao Te Ching*," in Michael LaFargue and Livia Kohn, eds., *Lao-Tzu and the Tao-Te-Ching* (Albany: State University of New York Press, 1994), pp. 231–253. For a recent translation that takes into account the newly published strips from Guodian and Mawangdui, see Roger Ames and David Hall, *Dao De Jing: A Philosophical Translation* (New York: Ballantine Books, 2003); and Robert Henricks, *Lao-tzu: Te-tao ching. A New Translation Based on the Recently Discovered Ma-wang-tui Texts* (New York: Ballantine, 1989).

12. *Laozi: jia, yi bing*. In *Jingmen shi bowuguan* 荊門市博物館, ed., *Guodian Chu mu zhu jian* 郭店楚墓竹簡 (Beijing: Wen wu Publishing Company, 1998), p. 62.

In both Mawangdui versions of the text, the character for "storehouse" (*ao* 奧) is *zhu* (注 "tendency," or the "way things flow"). *Mawangdui Han mu bo shu zheng li xiao zu* 馬王堆漢墓帛書整理小组, ed., *Laozi: Mawangdui Han mu bo shu* 老子: 馬王堆漢墓帛書 (Beijing: Wen Wu Publishing, 1976). See also Henricks, *Lao-tzu: Te-tao ching*, pp. 146–147.

13. For more on the equality of humans in both early Daoism and Confucianism, see Donald Munro, *The Concept of Man in Early China* (Ann Arbor: Center for Chinese Studies, University of Michigan, 2001), p. 1–22.

14. The dating of the *Guanzi* is extremely complicated and problematic and must be considered on a chapter-by-chapter basis. Allyn Rickett gives a good account of scholarly opinions on the dating of each individual chapter of the text. He generally dates the "Techniques of the Heart-mind" chapters to the early Han period, while attributing a much earlier date to the "Nei Ye." Notably, Rickett, following other scholars' leads, takes "Techniques of the Heart-mind, Lower" to be more related to the "Nei Ye" than to the other "Techniques of the Heart-mind" chapters. See W. Allyn Rickett, trans., *Guanzi: Political, Economic, and Philosophical Essays from Early China*, vol. 2 (Princeton, N.J.: Princeton University Press, 1998), pp. 15–97; Allyn Rickett, "Guanzi," in Michael Loewe, ed., *Early Chinese Texts: A Bibliographic Guide* (Berkeley: The Society for the Study of Early China, 1993); see also Roth, *Original Tao,* along with Roth's discussion of these texts in "Psychology and Self-Cultivation in Early Daoistic Thought," *Harvard Journal of Asiatic Studies* 51.2 (1991): pp. 599–650, in particular, pp. 608–611.

I follow Rickett and A. C. Graham's lead in dating chapter 49 of "Nei Ye" to the fourth century BCE. See A. C. Graham, *Disputers of the Tao: Philosophical Argument in Ancient China* (La Salle, Ill.: Open Court, 1989), p. 100. As for the "Techniques of the Heart-mind" chapters (Upper and Lower), I would argue that they could date from as early as the third century BCE. (This earlier dating does not include the commentarial portion of "Techniques of the Heart-mind, Upper," which occur in the latter two-thirds of that chapter and more clearly date to the Han Dynasty.) So even though the "Techniques of the Heart" chapters do not belong to the fourth century BCE, I include these chapters here because their central ideals show close affinity with traditions associated with the "Nei Ye" of the fourth century BCE. Notably, I do not include in my discussion other, more ostensibly Han texts and traditions that might be associated with the "Huang lao" 黃老 imperial cult.

15. Li Xiangfeng 黎翔鳳, *Guanzi jiaozhu* 管子校注 (Beijing: Zhonghua shuju, 2004), 36 (*Xin Shu, Shang* 心術上; "Techniques of the Heart-mind, Upper"), p. 767 (hereafter *Guanzi*).

16. Such would be consistent with texts such as the *Analects,* which focus on such transmitters of moral culture and authority. For more on the special relationship that develops between the sage and *tian* (Heaven) in Ru texts like the *Five Phases* and *Mencius,* see Csikszentmihalyi, *Material Virtue,* pp. 59–200.

17. Mark Csikszentmihalyi aptly describes certain authors' emphasis on the connection between the sage and the spiritual cosmos by speaking of "the sage's transcendent body." Mark Csikszentmihalyi, *Material Virtue*, pp. 161–200.

18. *Guanzi*, 49 (*Nei Ye* 內業; "Inward Training"), p. 937.

19. The arrangement of the text titled *Cheng Zhi Wen Zhi* as published in 1998 has since been subjected to much criticism. Some scholars argue for a complete rearrangement of the strips. In my translations and use of the title of this text, I will refer to Zhou Fengwu's rearrangement and title. See Zhou Fengwu 周鳳五, "Du Guodian Chu jian 'Cheng Zhi Wen Zhi' zha ji 讀郭店竹簡成之聞之札記," *Gu wen zi yu wen xian shi kan hao* 古文字與古文獻試刊號 (October 1999), pp. 42–54. See also Guo Yi 郭溢, "Guodian Chu jian 'Cheng Zhi Wen Zhi' pian shu zheng 郭店楚簡成之聞之篇疏証," in *Guodian Chu jian yanjiu* 郭店楚簡研究 [*Zhongguo zhexue* 中國哲學, vol. 20], ed. Jiang Guanghui 姜廣輝 (Shenyang: Liaoning jiao yu chu ban she, 1999), pp. 277–291.

20. "Cheng Zhi Wen Zhi" 成之聞之 ("Tian Jiang Da Chang" 天降大常). In *Guodian Chu mu zhu jian* 郭店楚墓竹簡, ed. *Jingmen shi bowuguan* 荊門市博物館 (Jingmen: Wen wu, 1998), p. 168.

21. Yang Bojun 楊伯峻, *Lunyu yi zhu* 論語譯注 (Hong Kong: Zhonghua shu ju, 1989), 3.14, p. 28 (hereafter *Analects*).

22. The most thorough account in English of the dating and philosophy of the *Wu Xing* can be found in Csikszentmihalyi, *Material Virtue*, pp. 62–100.

23. *Wu Xing* 五行, in *Jingmen shi bowuguan* 荊門市博物館, ed., *Guodian Chu mu zhu jian* 郭店楚墓竹簡 (Beijing: Wen Wu Publishing Company, 1998), p. 149.

24. The term *De* can also be associated with the influential, moral power of an individual. *De* certainly connotes that type of power here, and so it seems fitting that intellectuals would begin to associate it with the way of Heaven. For a much more detailed study of the role of Heaven in the *Wu Xing* text, see Csikszentmihalyi, *Material Virtue*, especially pp. 161–200.

25. For more on these concepts, see Mizoguchi Yuzo 溝口雄三, *Chugoku no kō to shi* 中国の公と私 (Tokyo: Kembusha, 1995), pp. 3–13, 42–56; Paul Goldin, "Han Fei's Doctrine of Self-Interest," in *After Confucius: Studies in Early Chinese Philosophy* (Honolulu: University of Hawai'i Press, 2005), pp. 58–65; and Nylan, "Confucian Piety and Individualism in Han China," p. 7.

26. For more on *wu-wei* as a governmental ideal in Warring States thought, see Roger Ames, *The Art of Rulership: A Study of Ancient Chinese Political Thought* (Albany: State University of New York Press, 1994), pp. 28–64. For the concept as a religious ideal, see Edward Slingerland, *Effortless Action: Wu-wei as Conceptual Metaphor and Spiritual Ideal in Early China* (Oxford: Oxford University Press, 2003).

27. This famous line does not appear in the corresponding Mawangdui chapter, although it might have existed in Mawangdui 48 at the point of the lacuna in both versions A and B. See Henricks, *Lao-tzu*, pp. 260–261.

28. Chen Guying 陳鼓應, *Laozi zhuyi ji pingjie* 老子注譯及評介 (Beijing: Zhonghua shuju, 2001), ch. 37, p. 209 (hereafter *Laozi*). It is worth noting that the Mawangdui version of this chapter deviates slightly from the received version translated here. Instead of having leaders rid the people of their desires (*yu* 欲), the text speaks of not disgracing (*ru* 辱) the people. See Henricks, *Lao-tzu*, pp. 260–261.

29. This basic critique of action motivated for the benefit of the self can be seen throughout the *Laozi* in a variety of forms. For example, a critique of *yu-wei* 有為, the opposite of *wu-wei*, is placed in a context in which the sovereign is seen to exact too much from his populace for the purpose of his own selfish needs and desires (*Laozi*, ch. 75, p. 339.). Here, *yu-wei* involves intentional action carried out to gratify the ruler's person. The text goes on to state, "Because the ruler at the top seeks out the luxuries of life, the people below do not treasure life (and attempt to overthrow him). It is only he who does not act in the interests of life (*wu yi sheng wei zhe* 無以生為者) who is truly good at valuing life" (*Laozi*, ch. 75, p. 339.). The individual terms "*wu*" and "*wei*" in this context are separated by an objective: "in the interests of life."

I would like to suggest that this particular linguistic usage of *wu-wei* is an instance of the manner in which the term, taken together as *wu-wei*, is understood throughout the text. In other words, there is an implied generalized object that acts as the direct object of the transitive verb "*wei*." The correct understanding of the term according to this type of translation, then, always involves the notion of having an objective or purpose for one's action and should be rendered "not acting with the purpose [in the interest] of X (*wu yi* 'X' *wei zhe* 無以 'X' 為者)."

30. Critical differences still remain. In the *Laozi*, the notion of *wu-wei* functions not within a hierarchy of top-down authority, but within a more centralized schema in which a single central figure possesses direct authority over everyone else. All others must rely on this central figure in their own engagements with the Dao. In effect, the central agent initiates all other activity, serving as a catalyst for universal conformity to the Dao.

Also, one will recall that in early Mohist thought, while decision making is rhetorically limited to Heaven, individual humans are fundamentally responsible for choosing and deciding their fates. In texts like the *Laozi*, to the contrary, authors more directly advocate the abdication of all agencies associated with the self.

31. "Cheng Zhi Wen Zhi" 成之聞之 ("Tian Jiang Da Chang" 天降大常), p. 168.

32. *Laozi*, ch. 37, p. 209 speaks famously of the non-agency (*wu-wei*) of the Dao. Lords and kings are asked to "preserve" this very attribute, so that the myriad things can transform of themselves.

33. Since this text exclusively highlights the relationship between the sovereign and his people and thereby promotes the self-cultivation of the ruler, it is fair to assume that this author's references to the sage and gentleman are directed toward the ruler.

34. One must then ask what the author means by Heaven in the text. Here it appears to be a source of universal moral patterns external to the human realm. Because of the emphasis in this text on Heaven's normative patterns (including normative decrees, *ming* 命), and not its non-normative aspects (also associated with *ming*), one suspects that this Heaven might be conceptualized in more systematic terms than the one described in, for example, the *Analects*. For a lengthy discussion of Heaven in *Ru* religious thought, see Robert Eno, *The Confucian Creation of Heaven: Philosophy and the Defense of Ritual Mastery* (Albany: State University of New York Press, 1990).

35. *Laozi*, ch. 55, p. 276. Indeed, my use of the term "conformism" here in relationship to what many would call "mysticism" is unconventional. By using "conformism," I hope merely to highlight the dynamic of external vs. internal sources of authority that I believe is vital to an understanding of how individualism develops in early China.

36. Mark Lewis describes this phenomenon not so much as a normative ideal for the body as a reality concerning the identical energies of the composite body with those of the cosmos. See Lewis, *The Construction of Space*, pp. 36–61.

37. In my translation, I follow Yu Yue's 俞樾 comment that the word *mu* 慕 is an error for the word *zuan* 纂, "to edit, arrange, place in order." *Guanzi jiaozhu*, p. 781.

38. *Guanzi*, 37 ("*Xin Shu, Xia*" 心術下; Techniques of the Heart-mind, Lower), p. 780.

39. Ibid.

40. Ibid. Translation adapted from Rickett, "Guanzi," vol. 2, p. 61.

41. In this last statement, I am following the Mawangdui B and Guodian A versions that uses the term *shi* 始 "to begin," instead of *ci* 辭. *Laozi*, ch. 2, p. 64. See *Laozi: Mawangdui Han mu bo shu* 老子:馬王堆漢墓帛書, ed., *Mawangdui Han mu bo shu zheng li xiao zu* 馬王堆漢墓帛書整理小组 (Beijing: Wen Wu Publishing, 1976); and *Laozi jia* (A), *Laozi: jia, yi, bing*, in *Guodian Chu mu zhu jian*, p. 112. For an excellent discussion of the notion of *zuo*, see Puett, *Ambivalence of Creation*, pp. 22–91.

42. Indeed, the phrase *ke tuo Tian Xia* 可拖天下 implies that such a person could be entrusted as the agent of the world. This phrase is reminiscent of the philosophy of self-preservation that is attributed to Yang Zhu, who is famous for claiming that he would not pull a hair from his head to benefit the world. Cf. Yang Bojun 楊伯峻. *Mengzi yi zhu* 孟子譯注, 7A26, p. 313 (hereafter *Mencius*). See chapter three for more on Yang Zhu.

43. *Laozi*, ch. 13, p. 109. I follow the Mawangdui versions in my translation. Certainly, if one were to follow the received version, one would arrive at a very different interpretation—one that focuses more explicitly on self-abnegation of the body.

44. So pronounced is the *Laozi*'s emphasis on the body that scholars associate some passages (like ch. 10, p. 96) with traditions of meditative and breathing

practices found in other texts. See Roth, *Original Tao,* pp. 144–153. Edward Slingerland notes that the emphasis on the body in such passages represents "an entirely new level of sophistication concerning the psycho-physiological makeup of the self." *Effortless Action,* p. 116.

45. For a comprehensive evaluation of the scholarly literature on this issue, see Slingerland, *Effortless Action,* pp. 107–117. See especially his discussion of the fundamental paradox of *wu-wei* in the *Laozi;* namely, trying not to try. For a critique of Slingerland's description of *wu-wei* as a characteristic of persons and not a manner of acting, see P. J. Ivanhoe, "The Paradox of Wuwei?" *Journal of Chinese Philosophy* 34.2 (June 2007): pp. 277–287.

46. *Laozi,* ch. 55, p. 276. There are not many variations of this passage in the different versions of the text.

47. I assume here that both these forces exist throughout the cosmos, as is implied in many supposedly early texts. The "Nei Ye" provides us with an explicit statement about the pervasive presence of *jing* in the cosmos and, interestingly, in human beings as living creatures of the cosmos. See *Guanzi,* 49 ("Nei Ye"), p. 931.

48. I depart from standard translations of this sentence here, which usually take *shen* to refer to the concerns or needs of a person. My interpretation takes *shen* more literally as a body, understanding the externalization of one's body to be a process of mentally externalizing one's sense of person.

49. *Laozi,* ch. 7, p. 87.

50. Such a duality can be found in mystical traditions throughout the world. Compare especially with Martin Buber's *I and Thou* (New York: Charles Scribner's Sons, 1958).

51. Michael Puett discusses the phenomenon of becoming like a spirit through physiological techniques in the "Nei Ye." See Puett, *To Become a God,* pp. 109–117.

52. Robin Yates discusses the phenomenon of man mirroring Heaven in "Body, Space, Time and Bureaucracy: Boundary Creation and Control Mechanisms in Early China," in John Hay, ed. *Boundaries in China* (London: Reaktion, 1995), pp. 69–73.

53. *Laozi,* ch. 30, p. 188. Translation adapted from Henricks, *Lao-Tzu,* pp. 246–247.

54. See *Laozi* chapters 4, 6, 25, 32, 34, among many other passages that describe the traits of the Dao.

55. *Laozi jia* (A), *Guodian Chu mu zhu jian,* p. 111. Interestingly, the corresponding sections of this text in the received and Mawangdui versions pointedly criticize Ru virtues altogether different from the apparently Mohist ones listed here.

56. The received version of the *Laozi* also voices a strong critique of knowledge and knowing. See *Laozi,* chapters 3, 10, 18, 19, 57, 65, and 81.

57. As religious specialists, it is likely that such men would have been in a position to judge the ruler's bodily practices as correctly in accord with the Dao or not, thereby controlling the decision-making process to a large extent.

58. Unfortunately, we do not have any evidence about the actual lives of the authors or proponents of these texts that would support or deny this hypothesis.

59. There are many scholars who do not read the *Laozi* as a political text. For readings of the text that are more philosophical, religious, or poetic in interpretation, see Ames and Hall, *Dao De Jing;* and Michael LaFargue, "Recovering the *Tao-te-ching's* Original Meaning: Some Remarks on Historical Hermeneutics," in Livia Kohn and Michael LaFargue, eds., *Lao-Tzu and the Tao-Te-Ching,* pp. 231–253 (Albany: State University of New York Press, 1994), pp. 231–253.

60. Again, I group the "Techniques of the Heart-mind" chapters from the *Guanzi* into this account primarily because the "Nei Ye" likely dates to around that time, and the other three chapters—while clearly later in date—take the focus of the "Nei Ye" as their basis.

61. See Mark Lewis' discussion of Shang Yang's reforms in "Warring States Political History," pp. 611–616.

62. While the *Laozi,* Ru texts found at Guodian, and *Guanzi* were clearly connected to the states of Chu and Qi, there is no reason to believe that these texts did not have a relationship to the state of Qin.

63. See above, where I mention that the real, non-rhetorical power may have been reserved for the intellectuals and priests themselves.

64. The Guodian "Zi Yi" is differently arranged but virtually identical with the "Zi Yi" chapter in the present recension of the *Li Ji, Book of Rites.* In addition, this passage must be compared with the recent bamboo slips of the Shanghai Museum, which also feature this text. See Ma Chengyuan 馬承源, ed., *Shanghai Bowuguan cang Zhanguo Chu zhu shu,* vol. 1 ("*Shangbo*") 上海博物館藏戰国楚竹書（一）(Shanghai: Shanghai guji, 2001), pp. 171–213. The subject of the text is the transformation of the people through the good model of the sage ruler. The "Zi Yi" attempts to outline which qualities are fundamental for a ruler in order to make his subjects morally behaved as part of a well-ordered country. In this respect, it is very much a political treatise designed for the ruler as audience. Because it closely follows the moral foundations laid out by Confucius, replete with quotations from the "Master," many of which are still locatable in the *Analects,* it undoubtedly can be linked with Ru traditions.

65. I follow Qiu Xigui's suggestion and take "*fa*" 法 as "*fei*" 廢, "to abandon." *Guodian Chu mu zhu jian,* p. 132.

66. For a theory relating why different terms are used in the Shangbo, Guodian, and the received versions of this passage, see Feng Shengjun 馮勝君, "*Du Shangbo jian 'Zi Yi' Li Ji yi ze*" 讀上博簡《緇衣》札記一則, (http://www.jianbo.org/Wssf/2002/fengshengjun02.htm). *Zi Yi* 緇衣, in *Jingmen shi bowuguan* 荊門市博物館, ed., *Guodian Chu mu zhu jian* 郭店楚墓竹簡 (Beijing: Wen Wu Publishing Company, 1998), p. 129.

67. Admittedly, the text also includes recommendations for not only *junzi* as rulers and leaders of the people, but for "great ministers" 大臣 and "great men" 大人 as well. In almost all of its discussions, such lofty people are compared to the

people below, as though the author assumes they will be in positions of leadership and governance over them. The two-part hierarchy between leaders and people is therefore prevalent throughout the text.

68. *Analects* 2.1, p. 11.

69. *Guanzi,* 49 ("Nei Ye"), pp. 935–937.

70. *Guanzi,* 37 ("Techniques of the Heart, Lower"), pp. 781–782.

71. I follow the received version here, as such a passage parallels two passages in the Guodian *Laozi* (versions A and C) that speak of the myriad things following along with "that which is so" (*zi ran* 自然) and also "not daring to act" (*fu gan wei* 弗敢為) or "not being able to act" (*fu neng wei* 弗能為). See *Laozi, Guodian Chu mu zhu jian,* pp. 112 and 121, strips 12 and 13 (version *jia*, A), and strip 14 (version *bing*, C).

72. *Laozi,* ch. 3, p. 71.

73. Many scholars have written about the potentially devious power of the ruler in the *Laozi,* especially as it relates to the statement in chapter 65, which recommends making the people ignorant. See Slingerland, *Effortless Action,* pp. 110–113.

74. The reader should note that just because the *Laozi* is framed in terms of a certain political philosophy on kingship, this does not mean that the religious universalism inherent in the concept of *ziran* ("so of itself") does not "leak out at the edges," thereby creating a problem with such a framework. I highlight here a narrow, political reading of the text so as to hint at how the text might have been used as a religious text from within a highly politicized context in the fourth century BCE. I am not interested in describing how the text can be applied to everyone, even today, because such a reading can be found in virtually every analysis or translation of the text. For a sharp critique of contemporary translations of the *Laozi,* see Paul Goldin, "Those Who Don't Know Speak: Translations of *Laozi* by People Who Do Not Know Chinese," in Paul Goldin, *After Confucius* (Honolulu: University of Hawai'i Press, 2005), pp. 119–133.

75. *Wu-shi* 無事 oftentimes appears to be a more specific application of *wu-wei* in that it only concerns the sage's non-involvement in statewide policy. However, this is not the case in the following passage, which features *wu-shi* as a generalized behavioral stance toward political rule: "Put a state in order by means of correctness (*zheng* 政; probity, straightforwardness), utilize the military by means of *qi* and take hold of the world by means of *wu-shi*." *Laozi,* ch. 57, p. 284. Here, *wu-shi,* like *wu-wei,* concerns the issue of a sovereign's power of authority over an entire state. The authors of *Laozi* do not use the two terms consistently and frequently interchange the two, so that it is difficult to discern a difference between them.

76. *Laozi,* ch. 57, p. 284. The Mawangdui versions are identical with the received version here. This passage does not occur in the versions of the Guodian *Laozi* according to such a sequence.

77. I agree with P. J. Ivanhoe that, though the text does not speak of human nature, it presupposes a certain "benign" concept of the natures or "so of themselves"

of human beings. Unlike Ivanhoe, however, I would not go so far as to claim that the *Laozi* and early chapters of *Zhuangzi* offer an explicit notion of an original human nature. See P. J. Ivanhoe, "Zhuangzi on Skepticism, Skill, and the Ineffable Dao," *Journal of the American Academy of Religion* 61 (1993): pp. 639–654.

78. See *Laozi*, ch. 37, p. 209.

79. Also apparent in the quote: "The people, without having to be commanded [verbally, or in any tangible way], reach an equilibrium of their own accord." *Laozi*, ch. 32, p. 194.

80. *Laozi*, ch. 29, p. 183, describes the immanent yet normative nature of the diverse Dao in the world, a non-random diversity aptly characterized through the notion of "individualized conformity" (*zi* 自): "As for he who wishes to take control of the world, I can see that he has no way to succeed. For the world is a spiritual vessel, and you cannot control or direct it." The irony of this passage lies in the fact that such an inherently spiritual world can only be fully realized by humans as such through *wu-wei* techniques pursued by the head of state, not by people "of themselves."

81. As mentioned above, this reading prioritizes the fundamentally political aspects of the text. Those who wish to ignore such aspects might easily gravitate to passages that do not make such political stipulations, which are indeed present throughout the text. By focusing on the implications of the text's political statements, I hope to highlight how the text was put together for primarily political purposes, even though it was likely compiled from religious ideas that addressed the more universal powers of every individual, and not just the sovereign. Thus it seems likely that this text manifests a political usage of a religious orientation, much more universal in its scope.

82. *Zi Yi*, in *Guodian Chu mu zhu jian*, p. 129.

83. For example, the ruler's humanity is correlated with humanity in the people. His desires are correlated with the people's desires. Correspondence and identical conformity are stressed, as opposed to a more abstract notion of modeling oneself after something. See Csikszentmihalyi, *Material Virtue*, pp. 59–100.

84. *Zi Yi*, in *Guodian Chu mu zhu jian*, p. 129.

85. I am following Qiu Xigui's interpretation of the graphs "*lei*" (類 category) and "*deng*" (等 order) for the two graphs in question. Ibid., p. 132.

86. Ibid., p. 129.

87. The Ru creation of such virtues as trust, "*xin*" 信, and loyalty, "*zhong*," 忠 are important overall outcomes of the power of moral influence. Such virtues reinforce concepts of conformity that permeate relationships of power in the text, stressing the goal of predictability in a subordinate's actions that the author highlights for his sovereign audience. They are discussed in the "Zi Yi" text toward the beginning of *Zi Yi*, in *Guodian Chu mu zhu jian*, p. 130.

88. Rather than speak of the people's own self-cultivation, it makes more sense in the Ru context to speak of their education, or "educational transformation" (*jiao*

hua 教化), as some modern Chinese say even today. This type of education differs from self-cultivation insofar as it is not sought out by the self but obtained passively.

89. Though discussion of the so-called "Huang-Lao" texts that date to the early Han also address these very issues of a sovereign's bodily authority, I do not discuss them here because of their late date. However, I include the "Techniques of the Heart-mind" chapters (dating most likely also to the early Han) only because they comment directly on the view outlined in a fourth-century BCE text, the "Nei Ye."

90. Wang, *Cosmology and Political Culture*, p. 80.

91. Although Aihe Wang contends that the king's monopoly on divine authority existed during the Shang, she implies that such a monopoly was still somewhat intact by the Warring States period when social and political forces arrived to dismantle it (Wang, *Cosmology and Political Culture*, pp. 75–80). This of course leads one to ask what was occurring in relationship to power during the early Zhou and Spring and Autumn periods.

Chapter Three: Decentralizing Control and Naturalizing Cosmic Agency

1. The absence of the term *xing* in writings that have been traditionally dated to a period earlier than ~320 BCE is astonishing when compared with writings dating to the turn of the fourth through the third centuries BCE. For example, while Zhuangzi's "Inner Chapters" do not mention the term even once, *xing* appears prominently in the "Later Chapters" of the book, starting with chapter 8. Similarly, in the Mohist corpus, chapters that have traditionally been attributed to the early Mohists do not present the term *xing* as a topic of debate. *Xing* as a term of art is neither featured in the *Laozi* nor in the "Nei Ye" chapter of the *Guanzi*, but it appears frequently in third-century BCE writings ostensibly influenced by the *Laozi*. Of course, generalized ideas or understandings of human nature can be found in any of these texts. And it is always possible that earlier authors might have been using the term for "life," *sheng* 生, in reference to "human nature," *xing*, since the two were interchangeable from an early date. I point here merely to the beginnings of an explicit philosophical discussion about the term and its meanings.

Recently discovered texts from Guodian and the Shanghai Museum strips (roughly dating to the same period, ~300 BCE) support the notion that *xing* emerges as an explicit topic of concern sometime toward the end of the fourth century BCE. The term *xing* makes a few appearances in the newly excavated texts, especially in the *Xing Zi Ming Chu* and *Xing Qing Lun*, which appear to be two versions of the same text. The author of this text does not go so far as to associate *xing* with special cosmic powers of the individual, as individualistic programs would do. However, he does posit a natural link between *xing* and the cosmic endowment of *ming* (Heaven's Command) in humans. For more on *xing* in this text, see Erica Brindley, "Music and Cosmos in the Development of 'Psychology' in Early China," *T'oung Pao* 92.1–3 (2006): pp. 1–49.

2. While some readers may wish to view Zhuangzi as a proponent of this type of individualism, I do not include him here because of a technicality. *Zhuangzi* expressly advocates moving beyond one's mundane "self" to embrace the powers of the Dao. For this reason, his thought does not fit the definition of individualism that I propound here, which links cosmic agency intrinsically to the self. Nonetheless, one cannot dispute the fact that Zhuangzi's philosophy generally resembles the type of orientation we describe; it thereby attests to a close affinity between the conformist and individualistic writings discussed in this book.

3. A. C. Graham was probably one of the first recent scholars to suggest this development in his *Disputers of the Tao*. Though he does not develop his thesis on individualism, he refers to certain movements in the fourth century BCE in terms of "egoism," "the discovery of subjectivity," "selfishness," and "the retreat to private life." See Graham, *Disputers of the Tao*, pp. 53–63, 95–105; and A. C. Graham, "Background of the Mencian Theory of Human Nature," in Xiusheng Liu and Philip Ivanhoe, eds., *Essays on the Moral Philosophy of Mengzi* (Indianapolis, Ind.: Hackett Publishing, 2002), pp. 6–7, 11. Mark Lewis also speaks of the discovery of the individual in *The Construction of Space in Early China*, p. 16. While many scholars loosely use the term "individualism" to refer to a specific type of philosophy (that associated with Yang Zhu) in the period, I am not aware of any scholar who defines individualism as broadly as I do here, or who identifies the phenomenon to be discussed in terms of a widely shared orientation on human agency.

4. Certainly, as with most of the other conformist texts analyzed in this book, such conformism is considered to be something positive: the highest spiritual ideal, rather than a negative way of being. While most scholars would probably not find the English term "conformism" to be quite fitting for Zhuangzi's thought, preferring instead the term "mysticism," I use conformism here to highlight the structural similarities between certain modes of religious thinking and more individualistic modes that develop around Zhuangzi's time. Furthermore, I use this term in a technical sense, more literally referring to the notion of "agreeing in form," and do not associate the current negative connotations of the term with it (as such connotations arise from a culturally specific sense of what it means to be an idealized individual or self).

5. Chris Jochim explains this emphasis on one's person and self by rejecting contemporary analyses of Zhuangzi's "no-self," insisting instead that Zhuangzi advocates the creation of an idealized "self." My claim differs slightly from this insofar as I underscore the power attributed to the locus of the individual and his or her surroundings in the text. My argument for "transcendent individualism" in Zhuangzi thus builds on Roger Ames' claim for the centrality of place and changing situation in Zhuangzian philosophy. See Chris Jochim, "Just Say No to 'No Self' in *Zhuangzi*," in Roger Ames, ed., *Wandering at Ease in the Zhuangzi* (Albany: State University of New York Press, 1998), pp. 35–74; and Roger Ames, "Knowing in the *Zhuangzi*: 'From Here, on the Bridge, over the River Hao,'" in Roger Ames, ed., *Wandering at Ease in the Zhuangzi* (Albany: State University of New York Press, 1998), pp. 219–230.

6. I believe that in this passage Zhuangzi hints at a larger meaning for the term *shi* (使). In a simple sense, the nominal usage of *shi* refers to an "assignment," "instruction," or "command," or to the "agent" who receives an assignment from his superiors (though it is unlikely that Zhuangzi refers in this passage to an actual person, not least because he does not use the term *zhe* (者) after *shi*). In the context, then, Yan Hui might be referring to the Master's assignment for him to fast his heart-mind. At the same time, the usage of the term *shi* seems unconventional, like many other terms in the text. One might plausibly interpret *shi* as an indirect reference to the command or agency of the Dao, as well as a direct reference to the assignment or guidance of the Master.

7. Wang Xiaoyu 王孝魚, *Zhuangzi jishi* 莊子集釋, vols. 1 and 2 (Taipei: Sanming, 1993), 4 ("*Ren jian shi*" 人間世), pp. 147–148 (hereafter *Zhuangzi*).

8. It is interesting to note, however, that Hui retrospectively finds it possible to describe the state of no-self as having been "his own" experience, implying a transient state of Dao embodiment in one's life.

9. Lee Yearley has also noted how Zhuangzi's attained persons "cease to be normal agents" with "either dispositional or reflective drives." Rather, they embrace what Yearley refers to as "transcendent drives." See "Zhuangzi's Understanding of Skillfulness and the Ultimate Spiritual State," in Paul Kjellberg and Philip J. Ivanhoe, eds. *Essays on Skepticism, Relativism, and Ethics in the Zhuangzi* (Albany: State University of New York Press, 1996), pp. 154, 176.

10. Notably, and in keeping with the texts on conformism outlined above, Zhuangzi overlooks one vital mechanism of human control in this equation: each person's choice to "lose oneself" with the Dao.

11. Slingerland, *Effortless Action*, 184.

12. Of course, this interpretation assumes that the *qi* (material-force) serves as the operational force of the heart-mind over and above the body.

13. "Attained Person" 至人, "Spiritual Person" 神人, and "Sage" 聖人 are among some of the common phrases Zhuangzi bandies about in his text. For more on these idealized types, see Shuen-fu Lin, "*Yi wu yi fei zhe: 'Zhuangzi Neipian' dui yu zui gao lixiang renwu de miaoshu* 以無翼飛者莊子內篇對於最高理想人物的描述, *Bulletin of the Institute of Chinese Literature and Philosophy, Academia Sinica* 26 (March 2005): pp. 1–36.

14. Michael Puett claims that Zhuangzi is not a relativist but "a cosmologist with a strong commitment to a certain view of the proper place of humanity in the universe." Puett, *To Become a God*, p. 133. While I agree with Puett that Zhuangzi might well understand how humans share certain traits with each other, as opposed to with storks, I believe he tries to push us to transcend all such categories as "humans" and "storks"—indeed, even "selves"—so that we become truly individual in relationship to the Dao. In other words, in my reading there is no such thing as a normative vision or role for individuals as "humans," but as individual manifestations of an ever-changing Dao. It is important to be able to transcend—at least in spirit—one's sense of humanity, just as it is important to transcend one's

sense of self, even though one's actions might still be constrained by the human form and its functions.

15. *Zhuangzi,* 1 ("*Xiao yao you*" 逍遙遊), p. 17.

16. Note that the key to understanding this interpretation lies in the fact that the Dao is not a "self"-propelling agent but an agent that takes over from where the self leaves off. For a wealth of literature on the concept of freedom in the *Zhuangzi,* see the many articles in Roger Ames, ed. *Wandering at Ease in the Zhuangzi* (Albany: State University of New York Press, 1998); and Scott Cook, "Harmony and Cacophony in the Panpipes of Heaven," in Scott Cook, ed., *Hiding the World in the World: Uneven Discourses on the Zhuangzi* (Albany: State University of New York Press, 2003), pp. 69–71. In Cook's volume, Alan Fox speaks of *wu-wei* in terms of "frictionless activity," which promotes a certain form of freedom. "Reflex and Reflectivity: *Wuwei* in the *Zhuangzi,*" p. 214.

17. Zhuangzi defines this as the reality or "correctness" of Heaven and Earth, the transformations of the Six *Qi,* and infinity itself. *Zhuangzi,* 1 ("*Xiao yao you*"), p. 17. (The Six *Qi* are glossed in the *Zuo Zhuan* as *yin, yang,* wind and rain, dark and light. Lewis, *The Construction of Space,* pp. 30–32).

18. *Zhuangzi,* 1 ("*Xiao yao you*"), pp. 1–11.

19. Lee Yearley, "Chuang Tzu's Cosmic Identification," in *Taoist Spirituality,* vol. 10 of Tu Wei-ming, ed., *World Spirituality: An Encyclopedic History of the Religious Quest* (New York: Crossroads, forthcoming).

20. It is important to understand that being in accordance with the Dao does not result in one's total loss of a sense for distinctions. The perspective of the Dao allows for the making of distinctions, but it does not allow for a human agent to attribute value to them based on terms of the self and objectives for the self. For this reason, there is no room for the existence of human designs and personal motivations.

21. Since, according to this vision, the state of not perceiving the boundaries of the self does not necessarily imply a lack of ability to function in the world and transform with the myriad things, these two perspectives on idealized attainment are not necessarily contradictory to each other. Rather, I see them as contrasting descriptions of the same phenomenon of selfless conformism.

22. While the term *zi ran* 自然 does not occur in the *Zhuangzi* but only in the *Laozi,* the basic idea that things transform of themselves still exists. Other turns of phrase are used instead, sometimes referring to one's nature and destiny (*xing ming* 性命), but these occur only in the "Outer Chapters."

23. Although chapter titles were most likely a later addition by compilers of the text during the Han Dynasty or even Guo Xiang 郭象 (d. 312), who edited the text, they are clearly intended to identify some key aspect of the text itself. For more information on the compilation of the *Zhuangzi,* see Harold Roth, "Who Compiled the *Chuang tzu?*" in Henry Rosemont, Jr., ed., *Chinese Texts and Philosophical Contexts* (La Salle, Ill.: Open Court Press, 1991), pp. 79–128.

24. For more comprehensive discussions of the theme of uselessness in the *Zhuangzi*, see Judith Berling, "Self and Whole in Chuang Tzu," in Munro, ed., *Individualism and Holism;* and John Major, "The Efficacy of Uselessness: A Chuang-tzu Motif," *Philosophy East and West* 25.3 (1975): pp. 265–279.

25. *Zhuangzi,* 4 ("*Ren jian shi*"), p. 174.

26. Ibid.

27. William Callahan has discussed the importance of non-human worlds in "Cook Ding's Life on the Whetstone: Contingency, Action, and Inertia in the *Zhuangzi,*" in Ames, ed. *Wandering at Ease in the Zhuangzi,* p. 180.

28. Ibid., p. 186.

29. *Zhuangzi,* 3 ("*Yang sheng zhu*" 養生主), p. 119.

30. Paul Kjellberg, "Sextus Empiricus, Zhuangzi, and Xunzi on 'Why Be Skeptical?'" In Kjellberg and Ivanhoe, *Essays on Skepticism,* pp. 1–25.

31. Paul Kjellberg, "Dao and Skepticism," *Dao* 6 (2007): p. 297.

32. The word *jie* (介) is glossed by commentators as *wu* (兀), "having the legs cut off."

33. *Zhuangzi,* 3 ("*Yang sheng zhu*"), p. 124.

34. Under this logic, one would assume that the ideal was open to other types of animals as well. For an in-depth account of early Chinese attitudes toward animals, see Roel Sterckx, *The Animal and the Daemon in Early China* (Albany: State University of New York Press, 2002).

35. As in the cases of Butcher Ding and Liezi. *Zhuangzi,* 3 ("*Yang sheng zhu*"), p. 119, and 7 ("*Ying di wang*" 應帝王), p. 306.

36. There are several examples from the "Inner Chapters" in which rulers and *shi*-elite men such as the sage Emperor Shun or Confucius are depicted as attained individuals. See *Zhuangzi,* 2 ("*Qi wu lun*" 齊物論), p. 89, and *Zhuangzi,* 4 ("*Ren jian shi*"), pp. 131–159.

37. One should keep in mind that at the time Zhuangzi was writing, the boundaries between the lower echelons of the *shi* and the commoners, or *shu* 庶, were already blurred, so it is not so surprising that he gives little credence to such social boundaries.

38. One might object that the terms "*wu-wei*" and "*wu-shi*" make their appearances in later chapters of the *Zhuangzi,* implying that they are important terms in his philosophical system. However, the appearance of these terms in the later *Zhuangzi* corpus in fact highlights their absence in the "Inner Chapters," suggesting later influence by Laozian-style thought.

39. That Zhuangzi does not mention the term *wu-wei* could be intentional, representing an effort to extend the process of self-cultivation to more people and varied audiences. Or it could be that Zhuangzi was drawing from a similar cultural tradition as the *Laozi* without having been aware of the particular vocabulary and writings of the latter. That the two texts shared a basic vision for the normative agency of humankind was not lost on later contributors to the *Zhuangzi* compilation, though, and it is probably because of this similarity in belief that later thinkers

associated the two and assumed the same strict intellectual lineage through the label "Daoist." While the relationship between the texts is far from clear, our analysis reveals a shared concern in both texts for the issue of human conformism to an impersonal Dao. Moreover, it demonstrates an agreement in the belief that an individual's personal embodiment of the Dao is the viable means to personal and social transformation of a positive sort.

40. See Yuri Pines, *Envisioning Eternal Empire: Chinese Political Thought of the Warring States Era* (Honolulu: University of Hawai'i Press, 2009).

41. For a study of the changing relationship of *shi* to the state during this period, which likely affected the stance we see in writings such as the *Zhuangzi*, see Pines, *Envisioning Eternal Empire*.

42. For an account of the process of self-divinization during this period, see Puett, *To Become a God*. Mark Lewis also thoroughly addresses this phenomenon in *The Construction of Space*, pp. 13–76, while Masayuki Sato mentions what he refers to as an analogical association among the human body, society, and the natural world in the third century BCE text of the *Xunzi*. See Masayuki Sato, *The Confucian Quest for Order: The Origin and Formation of the Political Thought of Xunzi* (Leiden: Brill, 2003), pp. 146–161.

43. John Locke, *An Essay Concerning Human Understanding*, book I, ch. 3, sect. 13 (Oxford: Clarendon Press, 1967), pp. 31–32.

44. The link between Mencius' concept of human nature and the divine cosmos—as Heaven—is strongly suggested in the text. See *Mencius* 7A1. For a more thorough account of Heaven in both the *Analects* and *Mencius*, see P. J. Ivanhoe, "Heaven as a Source for Ethical Warrant in Early Confucianism," *Dao* 6.3 (2007): pp. 211–220.

45. With the discovery of ancient Chu bamboo strips from Guodian and the Shanghai Museum, we can learn more about how the process of naturalizing morality develops in early China. See Csikszentmihalyi's *Material Virtue*, for an in-depth account of how authors begin to speak of a material component to virtue.

46. From the *Mencius* one senses that Gaozi was an important intellectual whose ideas posed a particular threat or challenge to Mencius. At the same time, Gaozi's ideas represent a neat ideological foil through which Mencius may convincingly showcase his own superior, and seemingly new, views on *xing*. Unfortunately, there are no extant writings that can definitively be attributed to Gaozi. Information regarding Gaozi's life, contemporary influence, and thinking is only to be found in the *Mencius*, which hardly represents a reliable or unbiased version of Gaozi's views.

The recent discovery of the Guodian corpus of texts has sparked a debate about the possibility that Gaozi or Zi Si was an author of one or several of them. For an evaluation of Gaozi as a possible author of these texts, see Pang Pu 龐樸, "Kong-Meng zhi jian: Guodian Chujian zhong de Rujia xinxing shuo 孔孟之間郭店楚簡中的儒家心性說," *Zhongguo zhexue* 20 (1999): p. 32; Paul Goldin, "Xunzi in the Light of the Guodian Manuscripts," *Early China* 25 (2000): pp. 113–146; and

Edward Slingerland, "The Problem of Moral Spontaneity in the Guodian Corpus," *Dao: A Journal of Comparative Philosophy* 7.3 (Fall 2008): pp. 237–256.

47. I use the notion of "moral motivation" in the *Mencius* to refer to a kind of moral agency, explained in this section in greater depth. For an important recent debate on Mencius' theory of human nature, see Roger Ames, "The Mencian Concept of *Ren xing*, Does It Mean 'Human Nature'?" in Henry Rosemont, ed., *Chinese Texts and Philosophical Contexts* (La Salle, Ill.: Open Court, 1991); and Irene Bloom, "Mengzian Arguments on Human Nature (Ren Xing)," in Xiusheng Liu and Philip J. Ivanhoe, eds., *Essays on the Moral Philosophy of Mengzi* (Indianapolis, Ind.: Hackett Publishing Co., Inc., 2002), pp. 64–100.

48. For an excellent discussion of some interpretations of Mencius' "internalist" views, see Kwong-loi Shun, *Mencius and Early Chinese Thought* (Stanford, Calif.: Stanford University Press, 1997). See also Xiusheng Liu's comments in "Mengzian Internalism," in Xiusheng Liu and Philip Ivanhoe, eds., *Essays on the Moral Philosophy of Mengzi* (Indianapolis, Ind.: Hackett Publishing Co., Inc., 2002), pp. 101–131.

49. *Mencius* 6A1. Yang Bojun, ed., *Mengzi yi zhu*, 6A1 (Hong Kong: Zhonghua shu ju, 1998), p. 253 (hereafter *Mencius*). I often consult translations by D. C. Lau, trans., *Mencius* (New York: Penguin, 1970).

50. *Mencius* 2A2, pp. 61–62.

51. In chapter two, I have translated *yi* as "justice" in the context of early Mohist writings and thought. With respect to the *Mencius*, however, I translate it as "rightness" to highlight its connotations of public morality in the text.

52. Two relevant studies on the thorny issue of "nimbus-like *qi*" are Xinyan Jiang's "Mengzi on Human Nature and Courage," and A. C. Graham, "The Background of the Mencian Theory of Human Nature," both in Xiusheng Liu and Philip J. Ivanhoe, eds., *Essays on the Moral Philosophy of Mengzi* (Indianapolis, Ind.: Hackett Publishing, 2002), pp. 143–162 and 1–63, respectively.

53. *Mencius* 2A2, p. 62.

54. For a more thorough account of the developing concept of material virtue and the *Mencius*, see Csikszentmihalyi, *Material Virtue*, pp. 101–160.

55. *Mencius* 6A2, p. 254.

56. literally, "going beyond one's forehead"

57. That is, humans are susceptible to being caused to go against or mask the functionality of their own *xing*. *Mencius* 6A2, p. 254.

58. Ibid. The use of this concept seems to have emerged during this period as part of the larger cultural debate on human agency that I outline here. In *Mencius* 2A1, an interesting quote, attributed to the people of the state of Qi, juxtaposes external force (*shi* 勢) with timing (*shi* 時), referring to forces outside an individual's control. *Mencius* 2A1, p. 57. On the concept of *shi* in the *Han Feizi*, see chapter four. See also Roger Ames' interpretations of *shi* in the *Huainanzi* in *The Art of Rulership*, pp. 65–107.

59. *Mencius* 6A2, p. 254.

60. A good example of the use of *xing* for *sheng* occurs in *Mozi*, chapter 3: "Acting according to pattern arises (*xing*) from being 'dyed' by what is proper." Sun Yirang, *Mozi jian gu* 3 ("Suo Ran" 所染), p. 16. According to Graham, Fu Sinian chooses not to distinguish *xing* from *sheng* at all for writings earlier than the Han. Graham decisively shows that Fu Sinian was misguided in this. See Graham, "The Background of the Mencian Theory of Human Nature," pp. 3–6. Also worthy of note is that the term *xing* in the recently published Guodian and Shanghai Museum texts is not written as *sheng*.

61. Bryan Van Norden also stresses the moral and cultural aspects of Mencius' views on human agency in "Mengzi and Xunzi: Two Views of Human Agency," in T. C. Kline III and P. J. Ivanhoe, eds., *Virtue, Nature, and Moral Agency in the Xunzi* (Indianapolis, Ind.: Hackett Publishing Company, Inc., 2000), pp. 103–134.

62. *Mencius* 6A3, pp. 254–255. This translation is a bit unorthodox insofar as it refuses to limit the semantic range of *sheng* in this sentence to "birth" or "what we have from birth." Instead, I attempt to retain the aspect of life in the present as well as at the moment of birth, concurring with A. C. Graham that *xing* in early China was deeply associated with the course of one's life and not merely a fixed essence, or nature, in the Platonic sense. A. C. Graham, "The Background of the Mencian Theory of Human Nature," in Xiusheng Liu and Philip Ivanhoe, eds., *Essays on the Moral Philosophy of Mengzi* (Indianapolis, Ind.: Hackett Publishing, 2002), pp. 1–4. See also Roger Ames, "The Mencian Concept of *Ren xing*, Does It Mean 'Human Nature'?" in Henry Rosemont, ed., *Chinese Texts and Philosophical Contexts* (La Salle, Ill.: Open Court, 1991), pp. 143–175.

63. Ibid.

64. *Mencius*, 6A2, p. 254.

65. Here I agree with Irene Bloom's thesis that Mencius wishes to transcend Gaozi's "narrowly biological conception" of human nature. See Bloom, "Mengzian Arguments on Human Nature," p. 93.

66. My analysis here is somewhat related to Kwong-loi Shun's discussion of the meaning and scope of the term ren-human in early texts of the Warring States period. See Kwong-loi Shun, *Mencius and Early Chinese Thought*, pp. 190–191. Also, my claim that Mencius seeks to identify what is universal to all humans corresponds to that of Bloom, "Mengzian Arguments on Human Nature," pp. 64–93.

67. *Mencius* 6A6, pp. 258–259.

68. *Mencius* 6A8, p. 263.

69. Ibid.

70. *Mencius* 2A2, pp. 61–62.

71. In section 2A2 Mencius prefaces his story about the man from Song with a section that has likely been miscopied or damaged, reading according to my interpretation as follows: "[In achieving morality through one's nimbus-like *qi*,] one must tend to the affair without neglecting it or 'aiding in its development.'" In this translation, I am taking *zheng xin* (正心) to have represented an alternate graph for *wang* (忘), which is thought to have been mistakenly transcribed at some point

in the copying of this text into the two vertically presented characters of *zheng xin* (and then repeated in the passage immediately afterwards in its correct form as *wang*).

72. In the sense of having a single target or aim.
73. *Mencius* 2A2, pp. 61–62.
74. Given Gaozi's vision of *xing*, it makes sense that Gaozi should account for morality in the human sphere by emphasizing a person's acquisition of it through a process of moral internalization.
75. Mencius intriguingly never explains how circumstances can obstruct one from developing morally while not actually affecting one's health and vitality.
76. P. J. Ivanhoe refers to Mencius' model of moral self-cultivation as a "developmental model" as opposed to the "acquisition model" of Confucius and the "reformation," "transformation," or even "transmutation" models of Xunzi. P. J. Ivanhoe, *Confucian Moral Self Cultivation* (New York: Peter Lang, 1993), pp. 20, 35, 45–46. Ivanhoe's various models of self-cultivation agree with my thesis concerning the internalization of human agencies in the fourth century BCE.
77. See Edward Slingerland's discussion of metaphor theory in relationship to early Chinese philosophical texts. Slingerland, *Effortless Action,* pp. 35–36.
78. As Graham notes, evidence for Yang Zhu's rough dates consists in a known audience with King Hui of Liang (369–319 BC). Graham, *Disputers of the Tao,* p. 54. See Edward Shaughnessy for reasons behind correcting, and thereby extending, the reign dates for King Hui of Liang to 319 BCE, "Calendar and Chronology," in Michael Loewe and Edward Shaughnessy, eds. *The Cambridge History of Ancient China: From the Origins of Civilization to 221 B.C.* (Cambridge: Cambridge University Press, 1999), p. 21.
79. Fung Yu-lan, *A History of Chinese Philosophy,* vol. 1, trans. Derk Bodde (Princeton, N.J.: Princeton University Press, 1967), pp. 137–141. A. C. Graham, influenced by Fung and Kuan Feng [*Zhuangzi zhexue taolun ju* (Beijing: Zhonghua shu ju, 1962)], argues strongly for the existence of Yangist teachings in what he labels the "Nurture of Life" chapters of the *Lüshi chunqiu* (chapters 1.2, 1.3, 2.2, 2.3, and 21.4) and the "Yangist" chapters of *Zhuangzi* (chapters 28–31). See Graham, *Disputers of the Tao,* p. 55.
80. Fung, *A History of Chinese Philosophy,* p. 137.
81. For a critical evaluation of A. C. Graham's accounts of Yangism, see Paul Goldin, "Review," *Early China* 28 (2003): pp. 204–211. Goldin reveals the unsystematic nature of the chapters in the *Zhuangzi* that Graham labels "Yangist" and problematizes Graham's tendency to group thinkers into schools of thought according to chapters in various composite texts.
82. Qian Mu 錢穆, *Xian qin zhu zi xi nian* 先秦諸子繫年 (Shijiazhuang: Hebei jiaoyu, 2000), pp. 278–282.
83. See, for example, Qian's claim that Yang Zhu's work does not appear in Han Dynasty lists of texts (the "Yi Wen Zhi" 藝文志 of the *Han Shu*). Ibid., p. 279.

84. To be precise, it is possible that Yang Zhu's writings have been transmitted to us in fragmentary form through various extant sources such as the *Zhuangzi*, *Lüshi chunqiu*, and (more unlikely) *Liezi*, but since Yang Zhu's name is not associated or only dubiously linked with any of these writings, we cannot prove that they belong to him or his followers. Chapters in *Zhuangzi* and *Lüshi chunqiu* that appear to adopt the terminology and general egoistic attitude attributed to Yang Zhu might actually represent another strand of thought that existed during the Warring States period but was separate from that of Yang Zhu. As for the "Yangist" chapter of the *Liezi*, it is highly unlikely to represent original material from the Warring States period and is perhaps only a later fantasy of what Yang Zhu symbolized. The dating of the *Liezi* is late (most likely of the late third to early fourth centuries CE), and most of it is probably a forgery by an ancestor of Zhang Zhan 張湛 (late fourth century), who wrote the first preface and commentary to the received work. See A. C. Graham, "The Date and Composition of *Liehtzyy*," *Asia Major* 8.2 (1961): pp. 140, 198.

85. *Mencius* 7B26, p. 335.

86. *Mencius* 3B9, p. 155. Because Mencius presents the concept of egoism alongside the confirmed tenet of the Mohist school, universal caring (*jian ai* 兼愛), it is possible that the term for egoism, *wei wo*, constitutes the very formulation of the concept propounded by Yang Zhu and his followers.

87. For an interesting thesis that Yang Zhu's emphasis on the human body was in fact part of a larger philosophy that rejected traditional and public authorities in favor of private, familial ones, see John Emerson, "Yang Chu's Discovery of the Body," *Philosophy East and West* 46.4 (October 1996): pp. 533–566. Because I disagree fundamentally with Emerson's depiction of traditional Chinese notions of an "empty" or "weak" self, I also tend to think of Yang Zhu's contributions not in terms of an emphasis on familial bodies but on individual bodies that likely bear connection—but not identity—with one's family and ancestral clan. Also, while Emerson's claim that Yang Zhu idealized "private" over "public" values is interesting and possibly true, there is—to my knowledge—virtually no linguistic or conceptual evidence to prove that Yang Zhu was concerned with such a debate.

88. Interpretations of the phrase describing Mozi's eagerness to help the world are but educated guesses. Yang Bojun suspects the phrase to have been an idiomatic expression, the meaning of which is now lost. Yang Bojun, *Mengzi yi zhu*, p. 313.

89. *Mencius* 7A26, p. 313.

90. Chen Qiyou 陳奇猷, *Lüshi chunqiu jiao shi* 呂氏春秋校釋. Vols. 1 and 2. (Shanghai: Xinhua shudian, 1995), 17.7 ("Bu Er" 不二), p. 1123 (hereafter *Lüshi chunqiu*). Translation adapted slightly from, John Knoblock and Jeffrey Riegel, *The Annals of Lü Buwei (Lüshi chun qiu): A Complete Translation and Study* (Stanford, Calif.: Stanford University Press, 2000), p. 433.

91. Liu Wendian 劉文典, *Huainan honglie jijie* 淮南鴻烈集解 (Beijing: Zhonghua shuju, 1997), 13 ("Fan Lun Xun" 氾論訓), p. 436 (hereafter *Huainanzi*). Translation adapted slightly from A. C. Graham, *Disputers of the Tao*, p. 54.

92. According to Graham's translations of what he believes to be the Yangist remnants in *Zhuangzi*, such "genuineness" refers to spontaneous human responses that accord with Heaven and not with common custom. Certainly, such a Zhuangzian reading of the term is conjectural, and we cannot know what Yang Zhu meant by "genuineness" without direct knowledge of and access to his writings.

93. See Emerson, "Yang Chu's Discovery of the Body," pp. 533–566.

94. For all we know, Yang Zhu might have possessed a mystical belief that every individual's pursuit of his or her own salvation might ultimately help bring about some kind of social order and contribute to the greater social good.

95. A. C. Graham supports this claim in his translation of certain passages in the *Zhuangzi* and *Lüshi chunqiu*, which he deems to be Yangist in orientation. Graham refers to Yang Zhu's advocates as individualists rather than egoists who might have valued selfishness. See Graham, *Disputers of the Tao*, 59–64. However, if the terminology Yang Zhu employed really did include "*wei wo*" ("for the self"), as Mencius indicates, the term "egoist," minus the connotation of someone who is selfish, might also be an appropriate description.

96. As observed so far, texts like the *Laozi* and the "Inner Chapters" of the *Zhuangzi*, which are earlier or roughly contemporaneous with the *Mencius*, do indeed associate cosmic power with the individual human body. However, they make a special point to claim that such power is not innate or intrinsic to it.

97. See especially A. C. Graham, who writes about the idea of individualism with reference only to Yang Zhu's philosophy and its legacy in other Warring States texts. See Graham, *Disputers of the Tao*, pp. 53–63; and "The Background of the Mencian Theory," pp. 6–7, 11.

Chapter Four: Two Prongs of the Debate

1. For an interesting account of the "Discovery of the Body" in Warring States and early imperial China, see Lewis, *The Construction of Space*, pp. 14–76.

2. The scope of my analysis of Primitivist discourse includes most of what is present in chapters 8–11 and 29 of the *Zhuangzi*. For an in-depth description of how Graham presents the Primitivist viewpoint, see Graham's translation of the *Zhuangzi*, especially "Part Four: The essays of the Primitivist and episodes related to them," in A. C. Graham, trans., *Chuang-tzu: The Inner Chapters: A Classic of Dao* (London: Mandala, 1981), pp. 195–217. See also Liu Xiaogan, "The Evolution of Three Schools of Latter-Day Zhuang Zi Philosophy (I)," trans. Ai Ping, *Chinese Studies in Philosophy* 23.2 (Winter 1991–1992): pp. 3–88.

3. One could also translate Liu's label as the "Anarchist School." Liu's and Graham's categories do not refer to the same set of writings. My own use of the label "Primitivist" refers to Graham's construction. It generally refers to a group of writings found in chapters 8–10 and in the introductory section of chapter 11 of the *Zhuangzi*. See Graham, *Chuang-tzu*, p. viii; and Liu, "Evolution of Three Schools," p. 49.

4. The so-called "later chapters" of the *Zhuangzi* reflect a wide array of viewpoints most likely stemming from different contexts and possibly even different

traditions. I adopt Graham's use of the word "Primitivist" here to point to a distinctive intellectual orientation that stands out from the rest. My own experience with the *Zhuangzi* as an eclectic document persuades me that it was likely compiled after the Warring States period and in a haphazard way.

5. Unlike Graham, I think it is possible that there are at least two authors who represent a Primitivistic perspective in these chapters. I also do not endorse the view that this perspective, or any other in the text, marks itself off according to neat breaks in chapters. As Goldin shows ("Review," p. 207), each chapter of the *Zhuangzi* "Outer Chapters" contains many eclectic parts and perspectives, and it makes little sense to mark off whole chapters in such a way.

6. The social criticism of the Primitivist appears to be strongly influenced by the *Laozi*. Yet, unlike *Laozi*, the Primitivist author makes explicit claims concerning *xing* and an individual's ideal relationship toward that nature.

7. For an interesting account of Warring States debates about the creation of culture, see Puett, *The Ambivalence of Creation*, pp. 1–140.

8. In this way, the Primitivist is even more radical than the authors of *Laozi*, who, in the end, still see a need for social organization, as well as the possession of basic weapons and technology. See *Laozi*, ch. 80.

9. *Mencius* 6A1, p. 253.

10. Graham, *Chuang-tzu*, p. 201. The Primitivist is not always consistent on this point and sometimes relegates moral and aesthetic culture to a distant second place.

11. Liu, "Evolution of Three Schools," pp. 57–63. In light of the Primitivist's criticism of Yangist orientations, however, it seems odd that Liu should include in his categorizations for the "Wu Jun school" the chapters of the *Zhuangzi* most famously known for their allegedly Yangist claims (chapters 28, 29, and 31; Graham includes these chapters, plus "Shuo Jian" chapter 30, labeled "Yangist miscellany." Graham, *Zhuangzi*, p. 224). The mixture of what seem to be at least two competing viewpoints in these later chapters, the Yangist and the Primitivist, serves to warn scholars of the dangers of thinking about the *Zhuangzi* in terms of whole chapters that belong together, without paying heed to thematic difference and conspicuously different claims and assumptions revealed within each chapter.

For example, while some stories in *Zhuangzi* chapters 28–31 noticeably do not pay attention to *xing*, focusing instead almost completely on preserving the physical body, there are other passages that strongly repeat Primitivist concerns for preserving a "natural" or "true" state of human conditions, especially in chapter 29, "Robber Zhi." Precisely because of the sharp criticism of Yang Zhu voiced in chapters 8–11 and absent from chapters 28, 29, and 31, there is perhaps good reason to believe that certain stories of Liu's "Wu Jun" chapters are not exclusively "Wu Jun," but a mixture of both Primitivist and Yangist viewpoints.

12. Wang Xiaoyu 王孝魚, *Zhuangzi ji shi* 莊子集釋 (Taipei: Wan juan lou, 1993), 10 ("Qu Qie" 胠篋), p. 353 (hereafter *Zhuangzi*).

13. Ibid. Li Zhu was purportedly a man of Huang Di's time with excellent eyesight. See Cheng Xuanyin's commentary at the beginning of *Zhuangzi*, 8 ("Pian Mu" 駢拇), p. 314.

14. *Zhuangzi*, 8 ("Pian Mu" 駢拇), p. 317.

15. Ibid., p. 321.

16. "Trying not to try" is what Edward Slingerland calls the "paradox of wu-wei." See Slingerland, *Effortless Action*, pp. 107–117, 210–215.

17. *Zhuangzi*, 8 ("Pian Mu" 駢拇), p. 323. The passive vocabulary that the Primitivist invokes appears to derive largely from the vocabulary of *wu-wei* utilized in the *Laozi*.

18. The Primitivist is careful to use language on *xing* that argues for the primacy of origins over constructed moral precepts, for his vision is not an ethical one. The "right" that appears in the text refers to something that is correct in the sense that it is "on the mark" or "as it is supposed to be." This distinction is especially significant in light of the author's attempts to propose the ideal alternative to the traditional ethical values of "*ren* and *yi*" 仁義. *Zhuangzi*, 8 ("Pian Mu" 駢拇), p. 327.

19. Ibid. The power of "destiny" (*ming* 命) also plays a crucial role in Primitivist thought. Unfortunately, the author is vague about what he perceives the relationship between *ming* and *xing* to be. In congruence with *xing*, *ming* seems to share the sense of an allotment that is originally so without the addition of cultural interference. Given the already long history of the term *Tian Ming* (天命 "Mandate of Heaven"), one might distinguish it from *xing* by its unembodied sense, in that it is not located intrinsically within any phenomenal object, but instead derives its authority directly from Heaven above. Furthermore, while *xing* appears to be the headquarters in each individual object and being that causes internal things to happen of themselves, *ming* appears to be the external headquarters responsible for occurrences outside a given thing.

20. It is possible to read *xing* here as a reference to *sheng* 生, "life," as the two graphs were sometimes interchangeable.

21. I have slightly altered Graham's translation here. Graham, *Chuang-Tzu*, p. 209–210. *Zhuangzi*, 10 ("Qu Qie" 胠篋), pp. 359–360.

22. The mentioning of *wu-wei* in this context, as a general attitude in accordance with one's *xing*, demonstrates an evolution of the term to fit contexts representing any person's accordance with Dao, not just that of the sage-king. This shows that the term comes to represent cultivation of the Dao beyond the specific political context in which the term seems to have developed in the *Laozi*.

23. Two examples occur at the beginning of *Zhuangzi*, 11 ("Zai You" 在宥), pp. 365–366, 369. See also p. 317. For some related scholarship on the role of *ming* in early Chinese thought, see Christopher Lupke, ed., *The Magnitude of Ming: Command, Allotment, and Fate in Chinese Culture* (Honolulu: University of Hawai'i Press, 2005).

24. The phrase used here is picked up from *Laozi*, ch. 13, a disputed section of the text. *Zhuangzi*, 11 ("Zai You" 在宥), p. 369.

25. In contrast to the *Laozi*, the Primitivist adopts a depoliticized view of government. Indeed, the Primitivist recommends focusing on the body to the exclusion of politics, stating, "How am I to have spare time for governing the world!" *Zhuangzi*, 11 ("Zai You" 在宥), p. 369. In this sense, the notion of *wu-wei* has evolved from a specifically political concept of body to a notion associated more generally with bodily states of being and spiritual cultivation that can be utilized to undermine politics itself.

26. *Zhuangzi*, 9 ("Ma Ti" 馬蹄), p. 334.

27. Ibid., p. 336.

28. It appears as though these passages were written by different authors with slightly different agendas and points of view.

29. For a compelling discussion of debates over artifice and nature that addresses these distinctions, see Puett, *The Ambivalence of Creation*.

30. *Zhuangzi*, 8 ("Pian Mu" 駢拇), p. 327.

31. Ibid.

32. Ibid.

33. Ibid.

34. Ibid.

35. Ibid., p. 317.

36. One is reminded of Mencius' metaphor of violating a willow tree to make cups and saucers, see *Mencius* 6A1.

37. *Zhuangzi*, 8 ("Pian Mu" 駢拇), p. 323.

38. The *Lüshi chunqiu*, produced as a whole text circa 239 under the sponsorship of the wealthy and powerful prime minister of Qin, Lü Buwei, is a compendium of varied writings that provide the Son of Heaven with coherent guidance in ruling according to the relevant powers of the cosmos. See James Sellmann, *Timing and Rulership in Master Lü's Spring and Autumn Annals (Lü shi chun qiu)* (Albany: State University of New York Press, 2002), pp. 1–5. The very structure and content of the *Lüshi chunqiu* suggests a goal of control, unity, and inclusion of society and the cosmos. It is no small detail, then, that the chapters relating to man's power through vitality and health should be situated near the beginning of the text—associated with categories of "spring" and the budding of life and vital powers in the cosmos. Chen Qiyou 陳奇猷, *Lüshi chunqiu jiao shi* 呂氏春秋校釋, vols. 1 and 2 (Shanghai: Xinhua shudian, 1995), 1.2 ("Ben Sheng" 本生), p. 21 (hereafter *Lüshi chunqiu*).

39. Notably, these writings address the "*Tianzi*," or "Son of Heaven," implying a more far-reaching area of control than the term for sovereign, "*junzi*."

40. For more on early imperial theocracies, see Puett, *To Become a God*, pp. 225–258.

41. These chapters are chapter 1.2, "Taking Life as One's Basis," 1.3, "Giving Weight to Self," 2.2, "Valuing Life," 2.3, "The Essential Desires," and 2.4, "Be Aware of What It Is For." Graham, "The Background of the Mencian Theory of Human Nature," pp. 6–7. See also the complete translation of this text by John Knoblock and Jeffrey Riegel, *The Annals of Lü Buwei*.

42. Graham, "The Background of the Mencian Theory of Human Nature," p. 3.
43. Ibid.
44. *Lüshi chunqiu,* 1.2 ("Ben Sheng" 本生), p. 21.
45. Ibid., pp. 20–21. By materialistic, I refer to such concepts as *qi* and essences (*jing*). These two concepts are found frequently in the *Lüshi chunqiu.* Although the connection between *xing* and essences is not made explicit, the fact that these essences are responsible for the Son of Heaven's political legitimacy suggests that they are a function of his *xing.* Ibid., p. 21.
46. Ibid., p. 20.
47. Ibid., p. 21.
48. For insights into an early Chinese epistemology of the senses, see Jane Geaney, *On the Epistemology of the Senses in Early Chinese Thought* (Honolulu: University of Hawai'i Press, 2002).
49. *Lüshi chunqiu,* pp. 20–21.
50. In the writings of the early Mohists, there is no sense that a powerful determining force exists within any individual, and humans were thought to be easily able to conform to external circumstances and the environment. Bryan Van Norden briefly discusses the malleability of humans in early Mohist writings in *Virtue Ethics and Consequentialism,* pp. 163, 167, and 195. See also David Nivison, "Weakness of Will in Ancient Chinese Philosophy," in Bryan Van Norden, ed., *The Ways of Confucianism: Investigations in Chinese Philosophy* (Chicago: Open Court, 1996), p. 83.
51. Liu Zehua provides some excellent textual passages that document this interest in institutional methods of control as a means of denigrating *si* (private) values. Liu Zehua 劉澤華, "Chunqiu Zhanguo de 'li gong mie si' guannian yu shehui de zhenghez" 春秋戰國的立公滅私觀念與社會的整合, in *Xierzhai wen gao* 洗耳齋文稿 (Beijing: Zhonghua shuju, 2003), pp. 337–373.
52. Xiong Gongzhe 熊公哲, *Xunzi jin zhu jin yi* 荀子今註今譯 (Taipei: Shang Wu, 1990), 6 ("Fei Shi Er Zi" 非十二子), p. 89 (hereafter *Xunzi*). On the relationship between "Five Phases" and "Five Virtues," see Gu Jiegang's *Wu de zhong shi shuo xia.* See also Pang Pu 龐樸, "Mawangdui boshu jiekai le Si-Meng wuxing shuo gu mi 堆帛書解開了思孟五行說古謎," in *Zhubo* Wuxing *pian jiaozhu ji yanjiu* 竹帛《五行》篇校注及研究 (Taipei: Wan juan lou, 2000).
53. *Xunzi,* 6 ("Fei Shi Er Zi" 非十二子), p. 91.
54. In other words, that human states of mind are inherently malleable. *Xunzi,* 4 ("Rong Ru" 榮辱), p. 58.
55. *Xunzi,* 4 ("Rong Ru"), p. 57.
56. For a recent account of Xunzi's theory of *xing,* see Dan Robins, "The Development of Xunzi's Theory of *xing,* Reconstructed on the Basis of a Textual Analysis of *Xunzi,* 23, '*Xing e*' (*Xing* is Bad)," *Early China* 26–27 (2001–2002): pp. 99–158. See the claim that Xunzi's theory on nature rests upon theories of psychology and virtue in Eric Hutton, "Does Xunzi Have a Consistent Theory of Human Nature?" in T. C. Kline III and P. J. Ivanhoe, eds., *Virtue, Nature, and Moral Agency in the Xunzi* (Indianapolis, Ind.: Hackett Publishing Company, Inc., 2000), pp. 220–236.

57. This kind of view is unique to Xunzi. The Guodian and Shanghai Museum text, *Xing Zi Ming Chu* (alternatively called *Xing Qing Lun* in the Shanghai manuscript publication), gives us additional insight into a perspective on *xing* and *qing* that differs in interesting ways from both Mencius and Xunzi. See Brindley, "Music and Cosmos in the Development of 'Psychology' in Early China," pp. 1–49.

58. Much work has been done on the topic of human agency and moral motivation in the *Xunzi* by Eric Hutton, P. J. Ivanhoe, T. C. Kline III, Bryan Van Norden, and David Wong. See their articles in T. C. Kline III and Philip J. Ivanhoe, eds., *Virtue, Nature, and Moral Agency in the Xunzi* (Indianapolis, Ind.: Hackett Publishing Company, 2000).

59. *Xunzi*, 4 ("Rong Ru"), p. 57.

60. Ibid.

61. For an account of the moral agency and charisma of the sages, see T. C. Kline III, "Moral Agency and Motivation in the *Xunzi*," in T. C. Kline III and P. J. Ivanhoe, eds., *Virtue, Nature, and Moral Agency in the Xunzi* (Indianapolis, Ind.: Hackett Publishing Company, Inc., 2000), pp. 155–175.

62. *Analects*, 17.2.

63. *Xunzi*, 4 ("Rong Ru"), p. 57.

64. Paul Goldin describes Xunzi's view of the person as "ultimately a union of xing and artifice" 偽 (*wei*). Paul Goldin, *Rituals of the Way: The Philosophy of Xunzi* (Chicago: Open Court, 1999), p. 75.

65. *Xunzi*, 23 ("Xing E" 性惡), p. 486.

66. Michael Puett has discussed this topic at length. See *The Ambivalence of Creation*. My interpretation also falls in line with that of David Wong. See his "Xunzi on Moral Motivation," in P. J. Ivanhoe, ed., *Chinese Language, Thought, and Culture: Nivison and His Critics* (Chicago: Open Court, 1996), pp. 202–223, in which Wong details how Xunzi accounts for "the path to moral transformation," p. 219.

67. *Xunzi*, 22 ("Zheng Ming" 正名), p. 454.

68. This of course is not to say that Xunzi expects all humans to fulfill such a potential. It is likely that he only conceives of *junzi* and sages as possessing the will, moral education, and personal wherewithal to put enough human effort to the task of moral cultivation.

69. *Xunzi*, 22 ("Zheng Ming"), p. 454.

70. Unfortunately, Xunzi does not mention how the ancient sages acquired their abilities to utilize their agencies in the proper fashion. One can speculate that they gained such abilities through the unique circumstances of their personal experiences and education—with or without a teacher and proper rites for guidance.

71. *Xunzi*, 23 ("Xing E"), p. 486.

72. One will recall from chapter three that Mencius conflates idealized human agency with morality in many ways. Such instances of not distinguishing between moral impulses and one's general agencies of thought perhaps serve as examples of what Xunzi criticizes as "utter abominations that do not adhere to correct standards of categorization." *Xunzi*, 6 ("Fei Shi Er Zi"), p. 89.

73. The nature of authorship in a text like the *Han Feizi* is still largely unknown. Since this text contains much material written in different styles and sometimes contains references to the same term or concept that betray very different understandings (which, in my opinion, cannot simply be attributed to different times in a single author's life), I believe that many authors contributed to the composition of this text. It is impossible to determine which sections belong to the historical figure of Han Feizi. For a contrary opinion, see Jean Levi's brief account of the date of compilation and authenticity in Michael Loewe, ed., *Early Chinese Texts: A Bibliographic Guide* (Berkeley: University of California Press, 1993), pp. 116–117.

I still refer to these authors by the name "Han Feizi" to underscore that these authors were all probably associated with a similar line of teachings as well as a master who influenced and encouraged their writings. For Han Fei's political philosophy, see Jiang Zhongyao 蔣重躍, *Han Feizi de zhengzhi sixiang* 韓非子的政治思想 (Beijing: Shifan daxue, 2000).

74. This statement should come as no surprise, especially in light of the fact that Xunzi—a foremost theoretician on human nature—was his erstwhile teacher.

75. Wang Xianshen 王先慎, ed., *Han Feizi ji jie* 韓非子集解 (Beijing: Zhonghua shuju, 1998), 50 ("Xian Xue" 顯學), p. 462 (hereafter *Han Feizi*). Adapted from Burton Watson's translation, *Han Fei Tzu: Basic Writings* (New York: Columbia University Press, 1964), pp. 126–127.

76. *Han Feizi*, 40 ("Nan Shi" 難勢), p. 389.

77. Qing Dynasty commentator Wang Xianshen argues that the words should have been attributed to Zi Xi for this passage to make sense. See *Han Feizi*, p. 191.

78. *Han Feizi*, 23 ("Shuo Lin, B" 說林下), p. 191. The speaker is allegedly Confucius. This statement, which forcefully proclaims the deterministic powers of *xing* over people, seems highly unlikely to have derived from Confucius' or even his disciples' mouths.

79. See Fung Yu-lan, *A History of Chinese Philosophy*, especially pp. 96–103.

80. While these chapters are generally not considered to be part of the earliest Mohist writings, the visions of person and power that they present correspond to their overarching philosophy. For more on their dating, see Wu Yujiang 吳毓江, "*Mozi* gepian zhenwei kao" 墨子各篇真偽考, in Wu Yujiang, *Mozi jiaozhu* 墨子校注 (Beijing: Zhonghua shuju, 1994), pp. 1025–1055.

81. *Mozi*, 3 ("Suo Ran" 所染), p. 11.

82. See *Mozi*, 3 ("Suo Ran"), p. 16.

83. *Han Feizi*, 50 ("Xian Xue" 顯學), p. 462. Adapted from Burton Watson's translation, 127.

84. To be sure, the importance of choosing the right environment is not new to Han Feizi. "Cosmetics" as a metaphor can even be found in the *Analects;* the early Mohists stressed the importance of "dyeing"; and Xunzi emphasized the importance of choosing a good environment.

85. *Han Feizi*, 19 ("Shi Xie" 飾邪), p. 123.

86. For more on this topic, see Goldin, "Han Fei's Doctrine," pp. 58–59.

87. *Han Feizi,* 19 ("Shi Xie"), p. 123. This is the claim in the following quote: "Now, it is the people's nature to detest labor and find pleasure in idleness. Idleness brings sloth, sloth brings intractability, and intractability brings disorder." *Han Feizi,* 54 ("Xin Du" 心度), p. 474. Also, see the quote in the previous note.

88. For the Ru, it was especially important to love and care for one's parents (*Analects,* 17.21), just as it was important for a ruler to love and care for his people (*Analects,* 1.5).

89. Here, Han Feizi clearly used the term *xing* to designate not human nature as it relates to individuals but a characteristic that develops as a matter of course in human relationships. *Han Feizi,* 47 ("Ba Shuo" 八說), p. 428.

90. Ibid.

91. Han Feizi makes the same point in *Han Feizi,* 49 ("Wu Du" 五蠹), p. 446. Interestingly, he refers to the natural conditions of the parent-child relationship through the term *xing* as in the example above.

92. *Han Feizi,* 54 ("Xin Du"), p. 474.

93. Ibid.

94. *Han Feizi,* 49 ("Wu Du"), p. 447.

95. There are many interesting discussions in the available literature on *shi*-authority. I find Roger Ames' translation of *shi* as "political purchase" to be most helpful. See also his account of the history of such a term in military, "legalistic," and other miscellaneous treatises, in Ames, *The Art of Rulership,* pp. 65–107. In general here, it is used to refer both to political power obtained through sociopolitical status and to environmental conditions/forces that determine the outcome of events.

96. Literally, "that by which they rode"

97. *Han Feizi,* 40 ("Nan Shi"), p. 388. It is helpful to consider the quote from *Zhuangzi,* described in chapter three, on Liezi riding the wind. *Zhuangzi,* 1 ("Xiao Yao You"), p. 17. Whereas for Shenzi, riding on the wind—analogous to possessing the authority of one's position—is desirable, Zhuangzi wishes to do away with all such external instruments of control.

98. *Han Feizi,* 40 ("Nan Shi"), pp. 389–390.

99. Ibid., p. 392.

100. Ibid., pp. 392–393. There is, he claims, "one case of social order for every thousand cases of disorder."

101. Ibid.

102. Ibid.

103. Note that Han Feizi acknowledges the potentially bad situation of having *shi* fall into the hands of evil rulers, but he considers this an inevitable price to pay for a system that functions most of the time.

104. Especially consider the ideologies of Mencius, the Primitivist, and those of the *Lüshi chunqiu,* which claim that an individual's perfection or the key to it is inborn. In these ideologies, as in the passage here, one either embellishes oneself or makes oneself whole—never fundamentally changing what a person has from the beginning.

105. It is also not present in what are considered to be the earlier chapters of the *Analects* of Confucius, which are approximately contemporary with the writings of the early Mohists.

106. This is clearly the case in the *Analects* and the *Mozi*. For comments on the *Analects*, see Benjamin Schwartz, *The World of Thought in Ancient China* (Cambridge, Mass.: Harvard University Press, 1985), pp. 118–120. We have already discussed the fact that the Mohists considered humans to be extremely malleable creatures.

Chapter Five: Servants of the Self and Empire

1. The two texts examined in this chapter, the *Zhong yong* and the Syncretist writings from the *Zhuangzi*, do not have precise datings. In my discussion of these texts, I highlight thematic aspects that seem to suggest a third-century BCE dating, but one can never be sure. Parts of the Syncretist writing analyzed at the end of this chapter utilize the term "imperial king," suggesting a Qin or even Han Dynasty dating.

2. For two very different translations of this text, see Roger Ames and David Hall, *Focusing the Familiar: A Translation and Philosophical Interpretation of the Zhongyong* (Honolulu: University of Hawai'i Press, 2001); and Andrew Plaks, trans., *Ta Hsüeh and Chung Yung (The Highest Order of Cultivation and On the Practice of the Mean)* (New York: Penguin Putnam, 2004).

3. Admittedly, one must qualify such a statement with respect to the *Mencius*. Certain passages in that text suggest the need for external inputs in order for one's innate moral agency to be properly fulfilled. Recall *Mencius* 1A7, which calls for careful attention to education and the basic needs of the people. Or 6A15, where "petty men" fail—out of a lack of concentration (*si* 思)—to follow their noble parts. Such passages do indeed suggest that positive interventions from the outside are necessary to ensure one's proper fulfillment of *xing*. I would interpret all these examples, however, as instances that demonstrate what constitutes a healthy environment for the positive and natural growth of *xing*. By asserting that positive environments do matter, Mencius does not diminish his claim about the powerful nature of *xing*, but qualifies it as not something entirely self-evident, self-driven, and likely to succeed regardless of circumstance.

4. See especially the Ru texts from Guodian for more examples of this.

5. *Zhong yong*, in Xie Yongying 謝冰瑩 et al., eds., *Si Shu Du Ben* 四書讀本 (Taipei: San min, 1991), chapter 20, p. 43 (hereafter *Zhong yong*).

6. The term *cheng* is one of the most fundamental concepts discussed in this text. In the passages that refer to *cheng*, some of which will be analyzed below, I believe it stands for a process of properly fulfilling life that is at once moral and immanent in the natural world. A fitting translation would be to "fulfill life properly," with "properly" being used in both senses of what is morally and naturally appropriate. Because such a translation is a bit unwieldy, I will usually refer to the term as "to fulfill," so as to imply both the constant state of transformation in life

as well as one's dynamic movement toward an ultimate embodiment of the moral sage. In its adjectival form, I use the word "fulfilled." For a thorough explanation of *cheng* as "creativity" in this text, see Roger Ames and David Hall, *Focusing the Familiar,* pp. 31–38.

7. *Zhong yong,* chapter 1, p. 22.

8. This claim can be found in the *Xing zi ming chu* text from Guodian. While this text also explicitly incorporates both internal human agencies and external sources of authority in its Dao, I do not include it in this discussion for an important reason. The discussion of *xing* in *Xing zi ming chu* is not at all concerned with defending or refuting a claim for innate moral potentials. Rather, it is concerned with introducing the notion that the moral Dao is somehow linked to innate human agencies. While the author of *Xing zi ming chu* thus fits into the larger discourse on innate human agencies dating from the fourth century BCE, he appears to represent an earlier period of the debate when individualistic claims like that of Mencius had still not been made.

9. *Zhong yong,* chapter 21, p. 47

10. *Zhong yong,* chapter 25, p. 50.

11. *Zhong yong,* chapter 22, p. 48.

12. In such a way, the *Zhong yong* is more like Mencius than the writings discovered at Guodian. For an account of formulations on *xing* and its relationship to music in the "Xing Zi Ming Chu," see Brindley, "Music and Cosmos." See also Goldin, "Xunzi in the Light of the Guodian Manuscripts," pp. 117–120.

13. One may argue that Xunzi also believed that external inputs should serve to bring out potentials associated with the self. However, such potentials lay not in the realm of *xing* or any "ready-made," divine-given power or potential for morality. Rather, for Xunzi, such potentials lay in the human capability to expend effort, work hard, and accumulate knowledge to forge or create a moral sense where there was originally none.

14. The "Heaven Chapters" (chapters 12–14) refers to a set of three chapters in the *Zhuangzi* which most scholars agree are among the latest writings in the compilation. Many scholars also believe these chapters to have been written by the author of the renowned chapter, "Tian Xia," chapter 33. A. C. Graham goes on to include chapter 15, "Finicky Notions," as belonging to what he categorizes as "Syncretist" writings, covering the bulk of chapters 12–15 and 33. In the present analysis, I join Graham and take a majority of the stories located in chapters 12–14, all of 15, and all of 33 to have been authored by people who assumed a "Syncretist" perspective.

Mixed in with the Syncretist writings are quite a few Primitivist excerpts and stories, some more obviously Primitivist than others. But among the writings that I would label Syncretist, there seems to be one author who might also have written the entire chapter 33, and who viewed himself as distinct from both Zhuangzian and Laozian thought. For the Syncretist's judgments of Zhuangzi, Laozi, and others, see Zhuangzi, annot. Wang Xiaoyu 王孝魚, *Zhuangzi ji shi* 莊子集釋 (Taipei: Wan juan lou, 1993), 33 ("Tian Xia" 天下), pp. 1095–1099 (hereafter *Zhuangzi*).

15. Graham, *Chuang-Tzu, The Inner Chapters: A Classic of Dao* (London: Mandala, 1991), pp. 255–285. In these pages, Graham gives a general description of what distinguishes this line of thought from other parts of the *Zhuangzi*. Although I often refer to the term "Syncretist" in the singular form, this does not preclude the possibility that these writings might have been penned by multiple authors who shared similar perspectives.

16. While Graham dates this writing to the interval between the fall of Qin and the support of Ru forms of study by Emperor Wu of the Han, there is no evidence to suggest it could not have been written anytime during the Qin or Han periods, when the term "Di" (august thearch) came into usage to denote the emperor. Graham arrives at his dating through a process of elimination: There was no other likely time, he claims, given that the Qin court favored legalism and important factions in the early Han court embraced the ideas of "Huang and Lao." I contend that just because a particular strain of thinking dominated at court does not mean that other ideologies and perspectives were not simultaneously created to have been presented to the throne, whether such perspectives were ultimately successful or not.

17. *Zhuangzi*, 13 ("Tian Dao" 天道), p. 457.

18. Ibid.

19. Ibid.

20. Ibid.

21. Ibid.

22. Taking *gui*, "ghost," to be a scribal error for *po* 魄, "corporeal numen," the counterpart of *hun* 魂, "ethereal numen," usually juxtaposed in southern religious traditions.

23. *Zhuangzi*, 13 ("Tian Dao"), pp. 462–463.

24. I translate *wu-wei* differently here from my translation of the term in *Laozi* as "non-purposive action." This is because the term now has a counterpart to specify activity and action.

25. *Zhuangzi*, 13 ("Tian Dao"), pp. 457–458.

26. One might account for this difference by assuming two different authors and occasions for the writing of these passages. However, I present an explanation for the discrepancies based on an assumption that the claims made in each can be viewed as consistent with a single perspective.

One can also point to the fact that the previous passages refer to the role of the sage and sometimes the "Son of Heaven," rather than the imperial king and his ministers, to argue for different occasions in the writing of these passages. Such a discrepancy in the subject, and the presumed audience of the writing, suggests that the passages could have been written on different occasions.

27. *Zhuangzi*, 13 ("Tian Dao"), p. 465.

28. Ibid.

29. Ibid.

30. Ibid., p. 467.

31. Ibid., p. 469.

32. Such rhetoric reflects the "internal-external" discourse on control that concerns so many other authors of the late Warring States period. The "root" applies to fundamental agencies cultivated within the human body that guide and provide the primary impetus for activities in the "extremities"—or those institutional controls not essentially associated with the cosmic human body.

33. *Zhuangzi,* 13 ("Tian Dao"), pp. 465–468.

34. By the third century BCE, the phrase "techniques of the heart-mind" had become a common reference to heart-mind cultivation used by various intellectuals to serve different goals. The earliest reference to the phrase appears in the *Xing zi ming chu* (dating to the fourth century BCE) text of the Guodian finds. The "Techniques of the Heart-mind" chapters of the *Guanzi* also mention the phrase, but this occurs in a commentarial section to "Techniques of the Heart-mind, Lower," and not in the original text of the chapter. The titles of the chapters "Techniques of the Heart-mind, Lower and Upper" were most likely given by the author of the commentarial section, or thereafter—in any case, probably not at least until the third century BCE.

35. *Zhuangzi,* 13 ("Tian Dao"), p. 468.

36. Almost the exact judgment appears in the "Tian Xia" chapter of the *Zhuangzi,* in reference to the intellectuals the Syncretist systematically describes and critiques. In that context the phrase runs, "They are *shi* of one frame of reference," *Zhuangzi,* 33 ("Tian Xia" 天下), p. 1069, and is meant to be applied to the thinkers of the "100-schools," not dialecticians.

37. *Zhuangzi,* 13 ("Tian Dao"), p. 473.

38. Unfortunately, given only the vague mention in the *Shi ji* of Huang-Lao thought that prevailed at the Han court before Emperor Wu, I see no way of demonstrating that this portion of the *Zhuangzi* might have constituted part of such a political philosophy.

39. The lack of social mobility implied in the Syncretist writings suggests an attempt to control and regulate one's access to authority and expression of individual powers. This would especially be the case if these writings date to the Qin or early Han empires. Imperial rulers of this period were notably more suspicious of individuals not related by blood or lifetime service to the throne. Their appointments to high government positions were largely based on private connections rather than ideals of meritocracy, which would have allowed a broader array of individuals to compete for appointment based on the fulfillment of their potentials.

Chapter Six: Conclusion

1. Karyn Lai. "Understanding Change: The Interdependent Self in Its Environment," in Karyn Lai, ed., *New Interdisciplinary Perspectives in Chinese Philosophy. Journal of Chinese Philosophy* (December 2007) p. 94.

2. One can readily apprehend the breadth of its influence on other, later spiritual traditions, such as Buddhism, which in China and other parts of East Asia adopts a special emphasis on the Buddha nature of every individual.

Scholars of Buddhism generally do not contest the claim that this emphasis on Buddha nature is uniquely East Asian. For a good study of the textual origins of the concept, see Sallie B. King, *Buddha Nature* (Albany: State University of New York Press, 1991). For more on the distinctively Chinese origins of this concept, see Peter Hershock, *Chan Buddhism* (Honolulu: University of Hawai'i Press, 2004), pp. 49–53, 129–130.

3. Wang, *Cosmology and Political Culture in Early China*, pp. 206–216.

4. Of course, just because a text is found somewhere does not mean that its values were being applied to the government in that location. Nonetheless, it does suggest that intellectuals in these places were aware of the existence of such political modes of thought.

Some of the most important first measures toward state centralization actually occurred in Chu, which instituted the *jun-xian* administrative system even before the Qin. See Yang Fanzhong 楊范中 and Zhu Maxin 祝馬鑫, "Chunqiu shiqi Chuguo jiquan zhengzhi chutan 春秋時期楚國集權政治初探," *Jianghan luntan* 江漢論壇 4 (1981): pp. 104–108.

5. Judging from what we know of the textual histories of these texts, none of these texts is suspected to have had any particular historical relationship to the Qin state outside of the fact they might have been circulating there as in other states of the late Zhou politico-economic sphere.

6. It is interesting to note that although Confucius can be seen as one of the first thinkers to proclaim the primacy of personal moral cultivation over political success, his views as presented in the *Analects* for the most part still support a type of self-cultivation that is inherently socially and politically effective in its own right. See *Analects*, 2.21.

7. See Graham, *Disputers of the Tao*, pp. 54–59.

8. Ibid., p. 53. Philip Ivanhoe argues convincingly against viewing Yang Zhu as a hedonist. See Ivanhoe, *Confucian Moral Self Cultivation*, p. 24 n. 9.

9. Ivanhoe, *Confucian Moral Self Cultivation*, p. 46.

10. Wang, *Cosmology and Political Culture*, pp. 80–81.

11. This is congruent with Hsu Cho-yun's claims concerning the increase in social mobility during the Warring States period. See *Ancient China in Transition*.

12. An exception being Zhuangzi, who emphasized both the creative powers of the Dao and the unique qualities it endows upon all things.

13. Certainly, my case for such a contrast is weakened when comparing early Chinese thought with many premodern or even minority strands of thought in the West. It is not my purpose here to discuss the presence of holistic and interdependent notions of the individual in the West, but to highlight the dominant view that has shaped our current constructions of individualism.

14. Note David Hall's and Roger Ames' important insight into this distinction: "The distinction between Western forms of individualism and the Confucian concept of the person lies in the fact that difference is prized in Western societies as a mark of creativity and originality, while in China the goal of personality

development involves the achievement of interdependence through the actualization of integrative emotions held in common among individuals. Such an ethos is based upon a rejection of those idiosyncratic emotions and actions that are not expressible through immanent norms of custom and tradition. The actions of individuals who dare to stand away from and challenge tradition and the visions of the past are interpretable by the Confucian as consequences of self-serving effrontery in the face of the legitimate continuities of a received tradition." In Hall and Ames, *Thinking through Confucius*, p. 23.

15. For more on this type of holism, see Munro, ed., *Individualism and Holism*.

16. Herbert Fingarette, "The Problem of the Self in the *Analects*," in Kim-chong Chong, Sor-hoon Tan, and C. L. Ten, eds., *The Moral Circle and the Self: Chinese and Western Approaches* (La Salle, Ill.: Open Court, 2003), p. 291.

Postscript

1. Duke Xiang 14, *Zuo Zhuan*, a sixth- through fourth-century BCE Chinese text. *The Tso Chuan: Selections from China's Oldest Narrative History*, trans. Burton Watson (New York: Columbia University Press, 1989), p. 16.

2. Albert Chen, "Is Confucianism Compatible with Liberal Constitutional Democracy?" *Journal of Chinese Philosophy* 34.2 (June 2007): pp. 209–210. A skeptical position on the desirability of trying to draw "equivalences or congenial values to human rights in Confucianism" (p. 9) can be found in Svensson, *Debating Human Rights in China,* pp. 55–58.

3. As mentioned in the preface, scholars have for years been re-evaluating China's "classical" tradition in light of the concept of human rights. See Jung H. Lee, "Preserving One's Nature: Primitivist Daoism and Human Rights," *Journal of Chinese Philosophy* 34.4 (December 2007): pp. 597–612. A plethora of literature now discusses the relationship between democracy and Chinese culture, often drawing upon classical texts and thinkers. For a good overview that also provides provocative suggestions for China's current political system, see Bell, *Beyond Liberal Democracy*.

4. Svensson, *Debating Human Rights in China*, p. 8.

5. Liu, "Translingual Practice," pp. 27–28.

6. Much work is currently being done on topics such as the self in Asian society and human rights in Asia. But there could be an even greater dialog that attempts to connect the two spheres. For a powerful reconsideration of human rights as they potentially relate to the Chinese tradition as a whole, including a careful consideration of the goals of harmony vs. unity, see Xia Yong's 夏勇 works: *Renquan gainian qiyuan* 人權概念起源 (Beijing: Zhengfa University Press, 1992); and "Renquan yu Zhongguo chuantong" 人權與中國傳統, in Liu Nanlai et al., eds., *Renquan de pubianxing he teshuxing* 人權的普遍性和特殊性 (Beijing: Social Sciences Documents Press, 1996.) For a consideration of Xia's 1996 article, see Angle, *Human Rights in Chinese Thought*, pp. 231–233.

7. These are the specific definitions of "individualism" that Simone de Beauvoir advocates in her book *The Second Sex*. See also Rosemont, "Two Loci of Authority," pp. 1–20.

8. Angle, *Human Rights in Chinese Thought*, 130.

9. As Angle shows, the language of "self-mastery" was especially endorsed by public intellectuals such as Kang Youwei (1858–1927), who argued that individuals do not "in fact have free will, since God made us that way," but that "since we are all equal, we ought to be masters of ourselves." See ibid., 132–133.

10. See Rosemont, "Rights-Bearing Individuals and Role-Bearing Persons," pp. 71–101.

11. Thus, according to the language of human rights, such individuals would be entitled to the fulfillment of themselves as integral members of a complicated web of traditional authorities (state, culture, society, family), cosmic powers (natural transformations of the Dao), and responsibilities (filial piety, loyalty incumbent in one's position, trustworthiness toward friends, etc.). One might imagine, for example, a type of human rights in China that is based on a concept of the moral imperative of the individual to seek spiritual cultivation qua harmony with and participation in one's larger community and natural environment. In such a scenario, the emphasis would not be on an individual's claims to something like "free speech" (in terms of the freedom to say anything you wish regardless of the response it might garner), but to "free judgment," "free thought," "free will," and even "free speech" in terms of a constant interaction between individual inputs and pre-existing moral and spiritual teachings and guidelines.

Works Cited

Ahern, Dennis. "Is Mo Tzu a Utilitarian?" *Journal of Chinese Philosophy* 3.2 (1976): pp. 185–193.

Ames, Roger. *The Art of Rulership: A Study of Ancient Chinese Political Thought.* Albany: State University of New York Press, 1994.

———. "Continuing the Conversation on Chinese Human Rights." *Ethics and International Affairs* 11 (1997): pp. 177–205.

———. "Knowing in the *Zhuangzi*: 'From Here, on the Bridge, over the River Hao.'" In *Wandering at Ease in the Zhuangzi*, ed. Roger Ames, pp. 219–230. Albany: State University of New York Press, 1998.

———. "The Mencian Concept of *Ren xing*, Does It Mean 'Human Nature'?" In *Chinese Texts and Philosophical Contexts*, ed. Henry Rosemont, pp. 143–175. La Salle, Ill.: Open Court, 1991.

———. "The Problematic of Self in Western Thought." In David Hall and Roger Ames, *Thinking from the Han: Self, Truth, and Transcendence in Chinese and Western Culture.* Albany: State University of New York Press, 1998.

———. "Reflections on the Confucian Self: A Response to Fingarette." In *Rules, Rituals, and Responsibility: Essays Dedicated to Herbert Fingarette*, ed. Mary Bockover, pp. 103–114. La Salle, Ill.: Open Court, 1991.

———. "Rites as Rights: The Confucian Alternative." In *Human Rights and the World's Religions*, ed. Leroy S. Rouner, pp. 199–216. Notre Dame, Ind.: University of Notre Dame Press, 1988.

———, ed. *Wandering at Ease in the Zhuangzi.* Albany: State University of New York Press, 1998.

———. "What Ever Happened to 'Wisdom'? Confucian Philosophy of Process and 'Human Becomings.'" *Asia Major,* 3rd series 21.1 (2008): pp. 45–68.

Ames, Roger, and David Hall, trans. *Dao De Jing: A Philosophical Translation.* New York: Ballantine Books, 2003.

———, trans. *Focusing the Familiar: A Translation and Philosophical Interpretation of the Zhongyong.* Honolulu: University of Hawai'i Press, 2001.

Ames, Roger, Wimal Dissanayake, and Thomas Kasulis, eds. *Self as Person in Asian Theory and Practice.* Albany: State University of New York Press, 1994.

———, eds. *Self As Image in Asian Theory and Practice.* Albany: State University of New York Press, 1998.

Angle, Stephen. *Human Rights in Chinese Thought: A Cross-Cultural Inquiry.* Cambridge: Cambridge University Press, 2002.

Bauer, Joanne, and Daniel Bell, eds. *The East Asian Challenge for Human Rights.* Cambridge: Cambridge University Press, 1999.

Baxter, William. "Situating the Language of the *Lao Tzu:* The Probable Date of the *Tao Te Ching.*" In *Lao-Tzu and the Tao-Te-Ching,* ed. Michael LaFargue and Livia Kohn, pp. 231–253. Albany: State University of New York Press, 1994.

Bell, Daniel A., *Beyond Liberal Democracy: Political Thinking for an East Asian Context.* Princeton, N.J.: Princeton University Press, 2006.

Bentley, Jerry. *Shapes of World History in Twentieth-Century Scholarship.* Washington, D.C.: American Historical Association, 1996.

Bloom, Irene. "Confucian Perspectives on the Individual and the Collective." In *Religious Diversity and Human Rights,* ed. Irene Bloom, J. Paul Martin, and Wayne L. Proudfoot, pp. 114–151. New York: Columbia University Press, 1996.

———. "Mengzian Arguments on Human Nature (Ren Xing)." In *Essays on the Moral Philosophy of Mengzi,* ed. Xiusheng Liu and Philip J. Ivanhoe, pp. 64–100. Indianapolis, Ind.: Hackett Publishing Co., Inc., 2002.

Bockover, Mary, ed. *Rules, Rituals, and Responsibility: Essays Dedicated to Herbert Fingarette.* La Salle, Ill.: Open Court, 1991.

Brindley, Erica. "Music and Cosmos in the Development of 'Psychology' in Early China." *T'oung Pao* 92.1–3 (2006): pp. 1–49.

Brown, Miranda. "Neither 'Primitive' nor 'Others,' But Somehow Not Quite Like 'Us': The Fortunes of Psychic Unity and Essentialism in Chinese Studies," *Journal of the Economic and Social History of the Orient* 49.2 (2006): pp. 219–252.

Buber, Martin. *I and Thou.* New York: Charles Scribner's Sons, 1958.

Bulletin of the Museum of Far Eastern Antiquities (Special Issue: Reconsidering the Correlative Cosmology of Early China) 72 (2000).

Callahan, William. "Cook Ding's Life on the Whetstone: Contingency, Action, and Inertia in the *Zhuangzi.*" In *Wandering at Ease in the Zhuangzi,* ed. Roger Ames, pp. 175–195. Albany: State University of New York Press, 1998.

Chen, Albert H. Y. "Is Confucianism Compatible with Liberal Constitutional Democracy?" *Journal of Chinese Philosophy* 34.2 (June 2007): pp. 195–216.

Chen Guying 陳鼓應. *Laozi zhuyi ji pingjie* 老子注譯及評介. Beijing: Zhonghua shuju, 2001. Cited as *Laozi* in the notes.

Chen Qiyou 陳奇猷. *Lüshi chunqiu jiao shi* 呂氏春秋校釋, vols. 1 and 2. Shanghai: Xinhua shudian, 1995. Cited as *Lüshi chunqiu* in the notes.

"Cheng Zhi Wen Zhi" 成之聞之 ("Tian Jiang Da Chang" 天降大常). In *Guodian Chu mu zhu jian* 郭店楚墓竹簡, ed. *Jingmen shi bowuguan* 荊門市博物館. Jingmen: Wen wu, 1998.

Chong, Kim-chong, Sor-hoon Tan, and C. L. Ten, eds. *The Moral Circle and the Self: Chinese and Western Approaches.* La Salle, Ill.: Open Court, 2003.

Works Cited

Chunqiu Zuo zhuan. See Yang Bojun 楊伯峻. *Chunqiu Zuo zhuan zhu* 春秋左傳注, vols. 1–4.

Cohen, Paul. *Discovering History in China: American Historical Writing on the Recent Chinese Past.* New York: Columbia University Press, 1984.

Cook, Constance, and John S. Major, eds. *Defining Chu: Image and Reality in Ancient China.* Honolulu: University of Hawai'i Press, 1999.

Cook, Scott, ed. *Hiding the World in the World: Uneven Discourses on the Zhuangzi.* Albany: State University of New York Press, 2003.

Csikszentmihalyi, Mark. *Material Virtue: Ethics and the Body in Early China.* Leiden: Brill, 2004.

Csikszentmihalyi, Mark, and Michael Nylan. "Constructing Lineages and Inventing Traditions through Exemplary Figures in Early China." *T'oung Pao* 89 (2003).

Damasio, Antonio. *Descartes' Error: Emotion, Reason, and the Human Brain.* New York: Quill, 2000.

de Bary, William Theodore. *Asian Values and Human Rights: A Confucian Communitarian Perspective.* Cambridge, Mass.: Harvard University Press, 1998.

de Bary, W. T., and Weiming Tu. *Confucianism and Human Rights.* New York: Columbia University Press, 1998.

Dennett, Daniel. *Elbow Room: The Varieties of Free Will Worth Wanting.* Cambridge, Mass.: MIT Press, 1997.

Ding Sixin 丁四新. "Shangbo Chu jian 'Gui Shen' pian zhu shi" 上博楚简《鬼神》篇注释. http://www.bsm.org.cn/show_article.php?id=337.

Dissanayake, Wimal, ed. *Narratives of Agency: Self-making in China, India, and Japan.* Minneapolis: University of Minnesota Press, 1996.

Duda, Kristopher. "Reconsidering Mo Tzu on the Foundations of Morality." *Asian Philosophy* 11.1 (2001): pp. 23–31.

Dumont, Louis. *Essays on Individualism: Modern Ideology in Anthropological Perspective.* Chicago: University of Chicago Press, 1986.

Emerson, John. "Yang Chu's Discovery of the Body." *Philosophy East and West* 46.4 (October 1996): pp. 533–566.

Eno, Robert. *The Confucian Creation of Heaven: Philosophy and the Defense of Ritual Mastery.* Albany: State University of New York Press, 1990.

Feng Shengjun 馮勝君. "*Du Shangbo jian 'Zi Yi' Li Ji yi ze*" 讀上博簡《緇衣》札記一則. http://www.jianbo.org/Wssf/2002/fengshengjun02.htm.

Fingarette, Herbert. *Confucius: The Secular as Sacred.* New York: Harper and Row, 1972.

———. "The Problem of the Self in the *Analects*." In *The Moral Circle and the Self: Chinese and Western Approaches,* ed. Kim-chong Chong, Sor-hoon Tan, and C. L. Ten, pp. 283–294. La Salle, Ill.: Open Court, 2003.

Fung Yu-lan. *A History of Chinese Philosophy,* vols. 1 and 2. Translated by Derk Bodde. Princeton, N.J.: Princeton University Press, 1967.

Geaney, Jane. *On the Epistemology of the Senses in Early Chinese Thought.* Honolulu: University of Hawai'i Press, 2002.

Goldin, Paul. *After Confucius: Studies in Early Chinese Philosophy*. Honolulu: University of Hawai'i Press, 2005.

———. "Han Fei's Doctrine of Self-Interest." In *After Confucius: Studies in Early Chinese Philosophy*, pp. 58–65. Honolulu: University of Hawai'i Press, 2005.

———. "Review." *Early China* 28 (2003): pp. 204–211.

———. *Rituals of the Way: The Philosophy of Xunzi*. Chicago: Open Court, 1999.

———. "Those Who Don't Know Speak: Translations of *Laozi* by People Who Do Not Know Chinese." In *After Confucius: Studies in Early Chinese Philosophy*, pp. 119–133. Honolulu: University of Hawai'i Press, 2005.

———. "Xunzi in the Light of the Guodian Manuscripts." *Early China* 25 (2000): pp. 113–146.

Graham, A. C. "The Background of the Mencian Theory of Human Nature." In *Essays on the Moral Philosophy of Mengzi*, ed. Xiusheng Liu and Philip Ivanhoe, pp. 1–63. Indianapolis, Ind.: Hackett Publishing, 2002.

———, trans. *Chuang-tzu: The Inner Chapters: A Classic of Dao*. London: Mandala, 1991.

———. "The Date and Composition of *Liehtzyy*." *Asia Major* 8.2 (1961): pp. 139–198.

———. *Disputers of the Tao: Philosophical Argument in Ancient China*. La Salle, Ill.: Open Court, 1989.

———. *Divisions in Early Mohism Reflected in the Core Chapters of Mo-tzu*. Singapore: Institute of East Asian Philosophies, 1985.

———. *Yin-Yang and the Nature of Correlative Thinking*. Singapore: The Institute of East Asian Philosophies, 1986.

Greenwood, John. "Individualism and Collectivism in Moral and Social Thought." In *The Moral Circle and the Self: Chinese and Western Approaches*, ed. Kim-chong Chong, Sor-hoon Tan, and C. L. Ten, pp. 163–173. La Salle, Ill: Open Court, 2003.

Gu Jiegang 顧頡剛. *Shan rang chuan shuo qi yu Mo jia kao* 禪讓傳說起于墨家考. Beijing: National Beiping Research Institute, 1936.

———. *Wu de zhong shi shuo xia de zheng zhi he li shi* 五德終始說下的政治和歷史. Hong Kong: Longmen Publishing, 1970.

Guanzi. See Li Xiangfeng 黎翔鳳. *Guanzi jiaozhu* 管子校注.

"Gui Shen zhi ming" 鬼神之明. In *Shanghai Bowuguan cang Zhanguo Chu zhu shu* 上海博物館藏戰國楚竹書. Vol. 5, ed. Ma Chengyuan 馬承源, pp. 307–320. Shanghai: Shanghai guji chubanshe, 2005.

Guo Qingfan 郭慶藩, *Zhuangzi jishi* 莊子集釋, vols. 1 and 2. Taipei: Sanming, 1993.

Guo Yi 郭溢. "Guodian Chu jian 'Cheng Zhi Wen Zhi' pian shu zheng" 郭店楚簡成之聞之篇疏証. In *Guodian Chu jian yanjiu* 郭店楚簡研究 [*Zhongguo zhexue*中國哲學 vol. 20], ed. Jiang Guanghui 姜廣輝, pp. 277–291. Shenyang: Liaoning jiao yu chu ban she, 1999.

Guodian Chu mu zhu jian 郭店楚墓竹簡. See *Jingmen shi bowuguan* 荊門市博物館. Jingmen: Wen wu, 1998.

Works Cited

Hall, David, and Roger Ames. *Thinking Through Confucius.* Albany: State University of New York Press, 1987.

———. *Thinking from the Han: Self, Truth, and Transcendence in Chinese and Western Culture.* Albany: State University of New York Press, 1998.

Han Feizi. See Wang Xianshen 王先慎. *Han Feizi ji jie* 韓非子集解.

Hansen, Chad. *A Daoist Theory of Chinese Thought.* New York: Oxford University Press, 1992.

———. "Individualism in Chinese Thought." In *Individualism and Holism: Studies in Confucian and Taoist Values,* ed. Donald Munro, pp. 35–55. Ann Arbor: Center for Chinese Studies, University of Michigan, 1985.

Harper, Donald. "Warring States Natural Philosophy and Occult Philosophy." In *The Cambridge History of Ancient China: From the Origins of Civilization to 221 BC,* ed. Edward Shaughnessy and Michael Loewe, pp. 813–884. Cambridge: Cambridge University Press, 1999.

Harrod, Howard. *The Human Center: Moral Agency in the Social World.* Philadelphia: Fortress Press, 1981.

He Xinquan 何信全. *Ruxue yu xiandai minzhu* 儒學與現代民主. Taipei: Academia Sinica, Wenzhesuo, 1996.

Henderson, John B. *The Development and Decline of Chinese Cosmology.* New York: Columbia University Press, 1984.

Henricks, Robert G., trans. *Lao-tzu, Te-Tao Ching: A New Translation Based on the Recently Discovered Ma-wang-tui Texts.* New York: Ballantine, 1989.

Hershock, Peter. *Chan Buddhism.* Honolulu: University of Hawai'i Press, 2004.

Hsu, Cho-yun. *Ancient China in Transition: An Analysis of Social Mobility, 722–222 B.C.* Stanford, Calif.: Stanford University Press, 1968.

Hu Shih. *The Development of the Logical Method in Ancient China.* Shanghai: Oriental Book Company, 1922.

Huainanzi. See Liu Wendian 劉文典, *Huainan honglie jijie* 淮南鴻烈集解.

Hutton, Eric. "Does Xunzi Have a Consistent Theory of Human Nature?" In *Virtue, Nature, and Moral Agency in the Xunzi,* ed. T. C. Kline III and P. J. Ivanhoe, pp. 220–236. Indianapolis, Ind.: Hackett Publishing Company, Inc., 2000.

Ivanhoe, P. J. *Confucian Moral Self Cultivation.* New York: Peter Lang, 1993.

———. "Heaven as a Source for Ethical Warrant in Early Confucianism." *Dao* 6.3 (2007): pp. 211–220.

———. "The Paradox of Wuwei?" *Journal of Chinese Philosophy* 34.2 (June 2007): pp. 277–287.

———. "Zhuangzi on Skepticism, Skill, and the Ineffable Dao," *Journal of the American Academy of Religion* 61 (1993): pp. 639–654.

Jiang, Xinyan. "Mengzi on Human Nature and Courage." In *Essays on the Moral Philosophy of Mengzi,* ed. Xiusheng Liu and Philip J. Ivanhoe, pp. 143–162. Indianapolis, Ind.: Hackett Publishing, 2002.

Jiang Zhongyao 蔣重躍. *Han Feizi de zhengzhi sixiang* 韓非子的政治思想. Beijing: Shifan daxue, 2000.

Jingmen shi bowuguan 荊門市博物館. *Guodian Chu mu zhu jian* 郭店楚墓竹簡. Beijing: Wen Wu Publishing Company, 1998.

Jochim, Chris. "Just Say No to 'No Self' in *Zhuangzi*." In *Wandering at Ease in the Zhuangzi*, ed. Roger Ames, pp. 35–74. Albany: State University of New York Press, 1998.

Johnson, Mark. *The Body in the Mind: The Bodily Basis of Meaning, Imagination, and Reason*. Chicago: University of Chicago Press, 1987.

Kant, Immanuel. *Foundations of the Metaphysics of Morals*. Translated by Lewis White Beck. Indianapolis, Ind.: Bobbs-Merrill, 1969.

Kent, Ann. *China, the United Nations, and Human Rights: The Limits of Compliance*. Philadelphia: University of Pennsylvania Press, 1999.

King, Sallie B. *Buddha Nature*. Albany: State University of New York Press, 1991.

Kjellberg, Paul. "Dao and Skepticism." *Dao* 6 (2007): pp. 281–299.

Kjellberg, Paul, and Philip J. Ivanhoe, eds. *Essays on Skepticism, Relativism, and Ethics in the Zhuangzi*. Albany: State University of New York Press, 1996.

Kline, T. C., III. "Moral Agency and Motivation in the *Xunzi*." In *Virtue, Nature, and Moral Agency in the Xunzi*, ed. T. C. Kline III and P. J. Ivanhoe, pp. 155–175. Indianapolis, Ind.: Hackett Publishing Company, Inc., 2000.

Kline, T. C., III, and P. J. Ivanhoe, eds. *Virtue, Nature, and Moral Agency in the Xunzi*. Indianapolis, Ind.: Hackett Publishing Company, Inc., 2000.

Knoblock, John, and Jeffrey Riegel. *The Annals of Lü Buwei (Lüshi chun qiu): A Complete Translation and Study*. Stanford, Calif.: Stanford University Press, 2000.

Kohn, Livia, and Michael LaFargue, eds., *Lao-Tzu and the Tao-Te-Ching*. Albany: State University of New York Press, 1994.

Lai, Karyn. "Understanding Change: The Interdependent Self in Its Environment." In *New Interdisciplinary Perspectives in Chinese Philosophy*, ed. Karyn Lai. Journal Supplement Series to the *Journal of Chinese Philosophy* (2007): pp. 81–99.

Lakoff, George, and Mark Johnson, *Philosophy in the Flesh: The Embodied Mind and Its Challenge to Western Thought*. New York: Basic Books, 1999.

Laozi. See Chen Guying 陳鼓應, *Laozi zhuyi ji pingjie* 老子注譯及評介.

Laozi: jia, yi bing (A, B, and C). In *Guodian Chu mu zhu jian* 郭店楚墓竹簡, ed. *Jingmen shi bowuguan* 荊門市博物館, pp. 111–122. Beijing: Wen wu Publishing Company, 1998.

Lau, D. C., trans. *Mencius*. New York: Penguin, 1970.

Lee, Jung H. "Preserving One's Nature: Primitivist Daoism and Human Rights." *Journal of Chinese Philosophy* 34.4 (December 2007): pp. 597–612.

Lewis, Mark. *The Construction of Space in Early China*. Albany: State University of New York Press, 2006.

———. *Sanctioned Violence in Early China*. Albany: State University of New York Press, 1990.

———. "Warring States Political History." In *The Cambridge History of Ancient China: From the Origins of Civilization to 221 B.C.*, ed. Michael Loewe and Edward Shaughnessy, pp. 587–650. Cambridge: Cambridge University Press, 1999.

Li Ling 李零. *Zhongguo fang shu kao* 中国方术考. Beijing: Dongfang, 2001.

Li, Minghui 李明輝. *Dangdai Ruxue zhi Ziwo Zhuanhua* 當代儒學之自我轉化. Taipei: Academia Sinica, Wenzhesuo, 1994.

———. *Ruxue yu Xiandai Yishi* 儒學與現代意識. Taipei: Wenjin chubanshe, 1991.

Li Xiangfeng 黎翔鳳. *Guanzi jiaozhu* 管子校注. Beijing: Zhonghua shuju, 2004.

Lin Shuen-fu. "*Yi wu yi fei zhe: 'Zhuangzi Neipian' dui yu zui gao lixiang renwu de miaoshu*" 以無翼飛者莊子內篇對於最高理想人物的描述. *Bulletin of the Institute of Chinese Literature and Philosophy, Academia Sinica* 26 (March 2005): pp. 1–36.

Liu, Lydia H. "Translingual Practice: The Discourse of Individualism between China and the West." In *Narratives of Agency: Self-making in China, India, and Japan*, ed. Wimal Dissanayake. Minneapolis: University of Minnesota Press, 1996.

Liu Wendian 劉文典, *Huainan honglie jijie* 淮南鴻烈集解. Beijing: Zhonghua shuju, 1997.

Liu Xiaogan 劉笑敢. "The Evolution of Three Schools of Latter-Day Zhuang Zi Philosophy (I)." Translated by Ai Ping. *Chinese Studies in Philosophy* 23.2 (Winter 1991–1992): pp. 3–88.

Liu, Xiusheng. "Mengzian Internalism." In *Essays on the Moral Philosophy of Mengzi*, ed. Xiusheng Liu and Philip Ivanhoe, pp. 101–131. Indianapolis, Ind.: Hackett Publishing Co., Inc., 2002.

Liu Zehua 劉澤華. "Chunqiu Zhanguo de 'li gong mie si' guannian yu shehui de zhenghe" 春秋戰國的立公滅私觀念與社會的整合. In *Xierzhai wen gao* 洗耳齋文稿, pp. 337–373. Beijing: Zhonghua shuju, 2003.

Locke, John. *An Essay Concerning Human Understanding*. Oxford: Clarendon Press, 1967.

Loewe, Michael, ed. *Early Chinese Texts: A Bibliographical Guide*. Berkeley: The Society for the Study of Early China, 1993.

Loewe, Michael, and Edward Shaughnessy, eds. *The Cambridge History of Ancient China: From the Origins of Civilization to 221 B.C.* Cambridge: Cambridge University Press, 1999.

Lowe, Scott. *Mo Tzu's Religious Blueprint for a Chinese Utopia: The Will and the Way*. Lewiston, N.Y.: The Edwin Mellen Press, 1992.

Lüshi chunqiu. See Chen Qiyou 陳奇猷. *Lüshi chunqiu jiao shi* 呂氏春秋校釋, vols. 1 and 2.

Luo, Chia-li. "Coastal Culture and Religion in Early China: A Study through Comparison with the Central Plain Region," Ph.D. dissertation, Indiana University, 1999.

Lupke, Christopher, ed. *The Magnitude of Ming: Command, Allotment, and Fate in Chinese Culture*. Honolulu: University of Hawai'i Press, 2005.

Ma Chengyuan 馬承源, ed. *Shanghai Bowuguan cang Zhanguo Chu zhu shu* 上海博物館藏戰國楚竹書. Shanghai: Shanghai guji chubanshe, 2005.

Macpherson, C. B. *The Political Theory of Possessive Individualism: Hobbes to Locke*. Oxford: Clarendon Press, 1962.

Mair, Victor, trans. *Tao Te Ching: The Classic Book of Integrity and the Way*. New York: Bantam, 1990.

Major, John S. "The Efficacy of Uselessness: A Chuang-tzu Motif." *Philosophy East and West* 25.3 (1975): pp. 265–279.

Mather, Richard. "The Controversy over Conformity and Naturalness during the Six Dynasties." *History of Religions* 9.2–3 (1967): pp. 160–180.

———. "Individualist Expressions of the Outsiders during the Six Dynasties." In *Individualism and Holism: Studies in Confucian and Taoist Values,* ed. Donald Munro, pp. 199–214. Ann Arbor: Center for Chinese Studies, University of Michigan, 1985.

Mawangdui Han mu bo shu zheng li xiao zu 馬王堆漢墓帛書整理小组, ed. *Laozi: Mawangdui Han mu bo shu* 老子：馬王堆漢墓帛書. Beijing: Wen Wu Publishing, 1976.

Mei, Yi-pao. *Motse, the Neglected Rival of Confucius*. London: Probsthain, 1934.

Mencius. See Yang Bojun 楊伯峻. *Mengzi yi zhu* 孟子譯注.

Mizoguchi Yuzo 溝口雄三. *Chugoku no kō to shi* 中国の公と私. Tokyo: Kembusha, 1995.

Mozi. See Sun Yirang, *Mozi jian gu*.

Munro, Donald. *The Concept of Man in Early China*. Ann Arbor: Center for Chinese Studies, University of Michigan, 2001.

———, ed. *Individualism and Holism: Studies in Confucian and Taoist Values*. Ann Arbor: Center for Chinese Studies, University of Michigan, 1985.

Nivison, David. "Philosophical Voluntarism in Fourth-Century China." In *Ways of Confucianism: Investigations in Chinese Philosophy,* ed. Bryan Van Norden, pp. 121–132. Chicago: Open Court, 1996.

———. *The Ways of Confucianism: Investigations in Chinese Philosophy*. Edited by Bryan Van Norden. Chicago: Open Court, 1996.

———. "Weakness of Will in Ancient Chinese Philosophy." In *Ways of Confucianism: Investigations in Chinese Philosophy,* ed. Bryan Van Norden, pp. 79–90. Chicago: Open Court, 1996.

Nylan, Michael. "Confucian Piety and Individualism in Han China." *Journal of the American Oriental Society* 116.1 (1996): pp. 1–27.

Pang Pu 龐樸. "Kong-Meng zhi jian: Guodian Chujian zhong de Rujia xinxing shuo 孔孟之間郭店楚簡中的儒家心性說." *Zhongguo zhexue* 20 (1999).

———. "Mawangdui boshu jiekai le Si-Meng wuxing shuo gu mi 堆帛書解開了思孟五行說古謎." In *Zhubo Wuxing pian jiaozhu ji yanjiu* 竹帛《五行》篇校注及研究. Taipei: Wan juan lou, 2000.

Peerenboom, Randall P. *China Modernizes: Threat to the West or Model for the Rest?* Oxford: Oxford University Press, 2007.

Pines, Yuri. "Disputers of Abdication: Zhanguo Egalitarianism and the Sovereign's Power." *T'oung Pao* 91.4–5 (2005): pp. 243–300.

Works Cited

———. *Envisioning Eternal Empire: Chinese Political Thought of the Warring States Era*. Honolulu: University of Hawai'i Press, 2009.

———. *Foundations of Confucian Thought: Intellectual Life in the Chunqiu Period, 722–453 BCE*. Honolulu: University of Hawai'i Press, 2002.

Pinker, Steven. *The Blank Slate: The Modern Denial of Human Nature*. New York: Penguin, 2003.

Plaks, Andrew, trans. *Ta Hsüeh and Chung Yung (The Highest Order of Cultivation and On the Practice of the Mean)*. New York: Penguin Putnam, 2004.

Puett, Michael. *The Ambivalence of Creation*. Stanford, Calif.: Stanford University Press, 2000.

———. *To Become a God*. Cambridge, Mass.: Harvard University Asia Center, 2002.

Qian Mu 錢穆. *Xian qin zhuzi xi nian* 先秦諸子繫年. Shijiazhuang: Hebei jiaoyu, 2000.

Raphals, Lisa. "Languages of Fate: Semantic Fields in Chinese and Greek." In *The Magnitude of Ming: Command, Allotment, and Fate in Chinese Culture*, ed. Christopher Lupke, pp. 70–106. Honolulu: University of Hawai'i Press, 2005.

Rickett, W. Allyn, trans. *Guanzi: Political, Economic, and Philosophical Essays from Early China*, vol. 2. Princeton, N.J.: Princeton University Press, 1998.

Robins, Dan. "The Development of Xunzi's Theory of *xing*, Reconstructed on the Basis of a Textual Analysis of *Xunzi* 23, 'Xing e' (*Xing* is Bad)." *Early China* 26–27 (2001–2002): pp. 99–158.

Rosemont, Henry, Jr., ed. *Chinese Texts and Philosophical Contexts*. La Salle, Ill.: Open Court, 1991.

———. "Rights-Bearing Individuals and Role-Bearing Persons." In *Rules, Rituals, and Responsibility: Essays Dedicated to Herbert Fingarette*, ed., Mary Bockover, pp. 71–101. Chicago: Open Court, 1991.

———. "Two Loci of Authority: Autonomous Individuals and Related Persons." In *Confucian Cultures of Authority*, ed. Peter D. Hershock and Roger T. Ames, pp. 1–20. Albany: State University of New York Press, 2006.

———. "Who Chooses?" In *Chinese Texts and Philosophical Contexts*, ed. Henry Rosemont, Jr., pp. 227–263. La Salle, Ill.: Open Court, 1991.

———. "Whose Democracy? Which Rights? A Confucian Critique of Modern Western Liberalism." In *Confucian Ethics: A Comparative Study of Self, Autonomy, and Community*, ed. Kwong-loi Shun and David Wong, pp. 49–71. Cambridge: Cambridge University Press, 2004.

Roth, Harold. *Original Tao: Inward Training (Nei-yeh) and the Foundations of Taoist Mysticism*. New York: Columbia University Press, 1999.

———. "Psychology and Self-Cultivation in Early Taoistic Thought." *Harvard Journal of Asiatic Studies* 51.2 (1991): pp. 599–650.

Sato, Masayuki. *The Confucian Quest for Order: The Origin and Formation of the Political Thought of Xunzi*. Leiden: Brill, 2003.

Schwartz, Benjamin. *The World of Thought in Ancient China*. Cambridge, Mass.: Harvard University Press, 1985.

Scott, Joan Wallach. *Only Paradoxes to Offer: French Feminists and the Rights of Man*. Cambridge, Mass.: Harvard University Press, 1996.
Segal, Jerome. *Agency and Alienation: A Theory of Human Presence*. Savage, Md.: Rowman & Littlefield Publishers, 1991.
Sellmann, James. *Timing and Rulership in Master Lü's Spring and Autumn Annals (Lü shi chun qiu)*. Albany: State University of New York Press, 2002.
Shaughnessy, Edward. "The Guodian Manuscripts and Their Place in Twentieth-Century Historiography on the *Laozi*." *Harvard Journal of Asiatic Studies* 65.2 (December 2005): pp. 417–457.
Shun, Kwong-loi. *Mencius and Early Chinese Thought*. Stanford, Calif.: Stanford University Press. 1997.
Shun, Kwong-loi, and David Wong, ed. *Confucian Ethics: A Comparative Study of Self, Autonomy, and Community*. Cambridge: Cambridge University Press, 2004.
Sivin, Nathan. "State, Cosmos, and Body in the Last Three Centuries BC." *Harvard Journal of Asiatic Studies* 55.1 (1995): pp. 5–37.
Slingerland, Edward. *Effortless Action: Wu-wei As Conceptual Metaphor and Spiritual Ideal in Early China*. Oxford: Oxford University Press, 2003.
———. "The Problem of Moral Spontaneity in the Guodian Corpus." *Dao: A Journal of Comparative Philosophy* 7.3 (Fall 2008): pp. 237–256.
———. *What Science Offers the Humanities: Integrating Body and Culture*. Cambridge: Cambridge University Press, 2008.
Smith, Kidder. "Sima Tan and the Invention of Daoism, 'Legalism,' et cetera." *Journal of Asiatic Studies* 63.1 (2003).
Soles, David E. "Mo Tzu and the Foundations of Morality." *Journal of Chinese Philosophy* 26.1 (March 1999): pp. 37–48.
Stalnaker, Aaron. *Overcoming Our Evil: Human Nature and Spiritual Exercises in Xunzi and Augustine*. Washington, D.C.: Georgetown University Press, 2006.
Sterckx, Roel. *The Animal and the Daemon in Early China*. Albany: State University of New York Press, 2002.
Sun Yirang 孫詒讓. *Mozi jian gu* 墨子閒詁. Taipei: Huaqu shuju, 1987. Cited as *Mozi* in the notes.
Svensson, Marina. *Debating Human Rights in China: A Conceptual and Political History*. New York: Rowman & Littlefield, 2002.
Tang Yu zhi Dao 唐虞之道. In *Guodian Chu mu zhu jian* 郭店楚墓竹簡, ed. Jingmen shi bowuguan 荊門市博物館, pp. 155–160. Beijing: Wen Wu Publishing Company, 1998.
Taylor, Charles. *Human Agency and Language: Philosophical Papers I*. Cambridge: Cambridge University Press, 1985.
———. *Sources of the Self: The Making of the Modern Identity*. Cambridge, Mass.: Harvard University Press, 1989.
Taylor, Rodney. "Religion and Utilitarianism: Mo Tzu on Spirits and Funerals." *Philosophy East and West* 29.3 (1979): pp. 337–346.

Works Cited

Tian jiang da chang 天降大常. See *Cheng zhi wen zhi* 成之聞之. In *Guodian Chu mu zhu jian* 郭店楚墓竹簡, ed. *Jingmen shi bowuguan* 荊門市博物館, pp. 165–170. Beijing: Wen Wu Publishing Company, 1998.

Van Norden, Bryan W. "Mengzi and Xunzi: Two Views of Human Agency." In *Virtue, Nature, and Moral Agency in the Xunzi*, ed. T. C. Kline III and P. J. Ivanhoe. Indianapolis, Ind.: Hackett Publishing Company, Inc., 2000.

———. *Virtue Ethics and Consequentialism in Early Chinese Philosophy*. Cambridge: Cambridge University Press, 2007.

Vinograd, Richard. *Boundaries of the Self: Chinese Portraits, 1600–1900*. Cambridge: Cambridge University Press, 1992.

Vorenkamp, Dirck. "Another Look at Utilitarianism in Mo-Tzu's Thought." *Journal of Chinese Philosophy* 19.4 (1992): pp. 423–443.

Wagner, Donald B. *Iron and Steel in Ancient China*. Leiden: E. J. Brill, 1993.

Wang, Aihe. *Cosmology and Political Culture in Early China*. Cambridge: Cambridge University Press, 2000.

Wang Xianshen 王先慎. *Han Feizi ji jie* 韓非子集解. Beijing: Zhonghua shuju, 1998.

Wang Xiaoyu 王孝魚. *Zhuangzi ji shi* 莊子集釋. Vols. 1 and 2. Taipei: Wan juan lou, 1993. Cited as *Zhuangzi* in the notes.

Watson, Burton, trans. *Basic Writings of Mo Tzu, Hsün Tzu, and Han Fei Tzu*. New York: Columbia University Press, 1964.

———. *The Tso Chuan: Selections from China's Oldest Narrative History*. New York: Columbia University Press, 1989.

Weber, Max. *The Religion of China: Confucianism and Taoism*. Translated by Hans Gerth. New York: The Free Press, 1951.

Webster's New Collegiate Dictionary. Springfield, Mass.: G. & C. Merriam Company, 1979.

Weld, Susan. "The Covenant Texts from Houma and Wenxian." In *New Sources of Early Chinese History: An Introduction to the Reading of Inscriptions and Manuscripts*, ed. Edward Shaughnessy, pp. 125–160. Berkeley, Calif.: The Society for the Study of Early China and The Institute of East Asian Studies, 1997.

Williams, Bernard. *Shame and Necessity*. Berkeley: University of California Press, 1993.

Wong, David. "Xunzi on Moral Motivation." In *Chinese Language, Thought, and Culture: Nivison and His Critics*, ed. P. J. Ivanhoe, pp. 202–223. Chicago: Open Court, 1996.

Wu Xing 五行. In *Guodian Chu mu zhu jian* 郭店楚墓竹簡, ed. *Jingmen shi bowuguan* 荊門市博物館, pp. 147–154. Beijing: Wen Wu Publishing Company, 1998.

Wu Yujiang 吳毓江. "*Mozi gepian zhenwei kao*" 墨子各篇真偽考. In Wu Yujiang, *Mozi jiaozhu* 墨子校注, pp. 1025–1055. Beijing: Zhonghua shuju, 1994.

Xia Yong 夏勇. *Renquan gainian qiyuan* 人權概念起源. Beijing: Zhengfa University Press, 1992.

———. "Renquan yu Zhongguo chuantong" 人權與中國傳統. In *Renquan de pubianxing he teshuxing* 人權的普遍性和特殊性, ed. Liu Nanlai et al. Beijing: Social Sciences Documents Press, 1996.

Xiong Gongzhe 熊公哲. *Xunzi jin zhu jin yi* 荀子今註今譯. Taipei: Shang Wu Publishing, 1990.

Xunzi. See Xiong Gongzhe 熊公哲. *Xunzi jin zhu jin yi* 荀子今註今譯.

Yaffe, Gideon. *Liberty Worth the Name: Locke on Free Agency*. Princeton, N.J.: Princeton University Press, 2000.

Yang Bojun 楊伯峻. *Chunqiu Zuo zhuan zhu* 春秋左傳注, vols. 1–4. Beijing: Zhong hua shu ju, 1995. Cited as *Zuo zhuan* in the notes.

———. *Mengzi yi zhu* 孟子譯注. Hong Kong: Zhong hua shu ju, 1998.

Yang Fanzhong 楊范中 and Zhu Maxin 祝馬鑫. "Chunqiu shiqi Chuguo jiquan zhengzhi chutan" 春秋時期楚國集權政治初探, *Jianghan luntan* 江漢論壇 4 (1981): pp. 104–108.

Yang Kuan 楊寬. *Zhanguo shi* 戰國史. Shanghai: Shanghai renmin chubanshe, 1980.

Yates, Robin. "Body, Space, Time and Bureaucracy: Boundary Creation and Control Mechanisms in Early China." In *Boundaries in China,* ed. John Hay, pp. 56–80. London: Reaktion, 1995.

Yearley, Lee. "Chuang Tzu's Cosmic Identification." In *Taoist Spirituality,* vol. 10 of *World Spirituality: An Encyclopedic History of the Religious Quest,* ed. Tu Wei-ming. New York: Crossroads, forthcoming.

Yü, Ying-shih 余英時. "Individualism and the Neo-Taoist Movement in Wei-Chin China." In *Individualism and Holism: Studies in Confucian and Taoist Values,* ed. Donald Munro, pp. 121–155. Ann Arbor: Center for Chinese Studies, University of Michigan, 1985.

———. *Shi yu zhongguo wenhua* 士與中國文化. Shanghai: Shanghai renmin shuju, 1987.

Zhang Qianfang. "Human Dignity in Classical Chinese Philosophy: Reinterpreting Mohism." *Journal of Chinese Philosophy* 34.2 (June 2007): pp. 239–255.

Zhong Yong 中庸. In *Si Shu Du Ben* 四書讀本, ed. Xie Bingying 謝冰瑩 et al. Taipei: San min, 1991.

Zhou Changyao 周長耀. *Mozi sixiang zhi yanjiu* 墨子思想之研究. Taipei: Zhonghua lunli kexue jiaoyu xiehui, 1974.

Zhou Fengwu 周鳳五. "Du Guodian Chu jian 'Cheng Zhi Wen Zhi' zha ji" 讀郭店竹簡成之聞之札記. *Gu wen zi yu wen xian shi kan hao* 古文字與古文獻 試刊號 (October 1999): pp. 42–54.

Zhu Fenghan 朱鳳瀚. *Shang Zhou jiazu xingtai yanjiu* 商周家族形態研究. Tianjin: Guji, 1990.

Zhu Fenghan and Xu Yong 徐勇, eds. *Xian Qin shi yanjiu gai yao* 先秦史研究概要. Tianjin: Tianjin jiaoyu, 1996.

Zhu, Ruikai 祝瑞開. *Xian Qin shehui he zhuzi sixiang xin tan* 先秦社會與諸子思想新. Fujian: Renmin, 1981.

Zhuangzi. See Wang Xiaoyu 王孝魚. *Zhuangzi ji shi* 莊子集釋, vols. 1 and 2.

Zi Yi 緇衣. In *Guodian Chu mu zhu jian* 郭店楚墓竹簡, ed. *Jingmen shi bowuguan* 荊門市博物館, pp. 127–137. Beijing: Wen Wu Publishing Company, 1998.

Zuo zhuan. See Yang Bojun 楊伯峻. *Chunqiu Zuo zhuan zhu* 春秋左傳注, vols. 1–4.

INDEX

When the text refers to a term most often in Chinese rather than English, the term is listed in Chinese (example: *wu-wei*). Otherwise, the index lists terms in English. When a person and a book bear the same title, the person is listed followed by an entry of textual references.

achieved man: ability not based in social class, 13, 60, 61–62; the achieved sage-king, 9, 10, 18, 20–21, 36–38, 45, 47–48; an advisor to the rulers, 17–19, 154n.77; in *Mozi* (*xian zhe*), 8–12, 26–27, 149n.22; in *Zhuangzi*, 57–61. *See also* meritocracy; upward conformity (*shang tong*)
action theory, xxv
"Against the Ru" (Mohist), 18–19
"Against the Twelve Masters," 87–88. *See also* Xunzi
Aihe Wang, 53, 127, 164n.91
Ames, Roger, xviii
Analects, 3, 45, 50, 90, 147n.1, 149n.13, 155n.9, 156n.16, 180n.34, 181n.88, 186n.6
Angle, Stephen, 134
anti-sovereign school. *See* Primitivist
Asian values and human rights discourse, ix, xi, 131–135
authority: and conformism, xxvi; decentralized authority, 54, 60, 61–62, 63, 74, 102; disparate authorities problem in *Mozi*, 2; ultimate (of Heaven), 124; ultimate vs. proximate sources of, xxvi, 2, 51. *See also* institutional control; moral authority
authority, centralized. *See* sovereign's body; universal cosmic authority
autonomy, 6, 58, 66, 129, 131, 139n.15, 145n.53, 145n.57; and conformity, xxvi–xxviii, 27–28 (*see also* mindful conformity); moral autonomy, 1, 13, 14, 21–22, 49, 146n.1; relational form of, xxvii–xxviii, 121 (*see also* relational individualism)

Berlin, Isaiah, 145n.53
Bloom, Irene, xviii–xix
Bo Yi, story of, 83
bodily agency: deterministic powers, 77–78, 170n.52, 171n.71; visceral connection between human and divine, 86–87. *See also* sovereign's body; *xing* (human nature)
bodily conformity, 30, 48, 54
body (*shen*): needs and desires of, 88–89; as self, xxviii; as the source of cosmic agency, 64, 67, 68, 70, 74–76, 127, 173n.87; wholeness and equilibrium of, 78–84, 108–109
Book of Rites (*Li ji*): *Zhong yong*, 105–108
bureaucratization, xxi, xxiii, 104, 109, 113, 115, 118, 124; of spiritual authority, 115–116

chaos. *See* social chaos
Chen, Alert, 131
Chinese individualism. *See* individualism in early Chinese thought
Cohen, Paul, xviii
"compensatory power," 2, 4, 23
conformity: in early Chinese thought, 128–130; and impersonal authority (paradox of), 36, 41–42; and individual choice, xxv–xxvi, 95, 129; with the political hierarchy, 19–23; Western ideas of, 128.

201

See also bodily conformity; mindful conformity; upward conformity
Confucianism, 33, 139n.15. *See also* Ru texts
Confucius: an advisor to the ruler, xxii; the *Analects*, 3, 45, 50, 90, 147n.1, 149n.13, 155n.9, 156n.16, 180n.34, 181n.88, 186n.6; the "Confucian self," xviii, xix. See also *Laozi*
Cook Ding, story of, 59–60
Csikszentmihalyi, Mark, 30
cultural relativism: comparative method, xvi–xviii; and human rights discourse, 133–134

Dao, the, 29, 36–37, 154n.2, 183n.8; available to all through self-cultivation, 47–48, 55, 125; both internal and external, 107; characterized, 31–36, 57–58; as development of innate agency, 70; external authority and human effort required, 88, 91–93; freedom through, 58–59, 62; human source or possession of, 105–106, 108–109; individually accessing cosmic power, 54, 57–63, 64, 74, 112–114, 124–125. *See also* universal cosmic authority
Dao in texts and teachings, the: guidelines for attaining through *wu-wei* (non-purposive action), 34–35, 38–39, 40–41; guidelines for the sage-king attaining, 32–33, 40, 47, 48, 50, 60, 85–87; Guodian texts, 32–33, 35; instruction to train innate potentials, 105–108; Mohist conception of, 1–2, 10–11, 12–14, 26–28; "recovery model," 126–127; Syncretist on, 112–113; in *Zhuangzi*, 54, 61–62, 64, 112–114. See also *Laozi*
De (virtuous power), 33
de Bary, W. T., xviii
death, 69
decentralized authority, 54, 60, 61–62, 63, 74, 102
dependent agency, 47–51
deterministic powers, 77–78, 102–103; negative and requiring institutional control (Xunzi), 87–93; negative and unchangeable (Han Feizi), 93–95, 97–98, 100, 101
disembodied self, xxix

dualism, Western, xxix
ducal lords, 16, 17, 18, 19, 20, 24

ego/egoism (*wei wo*): as personal salvation, 72–73, 74, 165n.3, 173n.86, 174n.95
embodiment. See bodily agency; bodily conformity
empire formation, 122.
Enlightenment Europe, x, xvii, 129, 138
environmental (external) forces (*shi*), 67, 69, 96
essences (*jing*), 45; as "refined numinosity" (*jing shen*), 109–112
external force or authority (*shi*), 67, 69, 96, 99; institutional control required, 77, 90–91, 95–97, 99–101. *See also* institutional control

Fingarette, Herbert, 130, 146n.1
freedom: through Daoism, 58–59, 62; Western conceptions of, 137n.4

Gaozi: on external sources of morality, 64, 65–66, 67, 68–69, 79
governance, 117–118, 120; based in cosmic authority, 15, 24, 36, 40, 44, 45; spiritual techniques related to, 43, 46, 81, 85–86, 110–118
Graham, A. C., 78–79, 84–87, 172n.79, 172n.81, 174n.92
Guanzi: on the Dao, 36–38; naturalizing moral agency and authority, 65–68, 126
Guanzi chapters: "Inward Training," 31, 32; "Techniques of the Heart-mind," 31–32, 36–37, 38, 40, 43, 45, 46, 51, 156n.14, 185n.34
Guodian excavation, 32, 155n.11
Guodian texts, 43, 153n.63, 164n.1; "proto-Laozi A," 42, 124, 155n.11, 160n.55, 162n.71; *Tian jiang da chang*, 32–33, 35, 43; "Wu Xing," 33; "Zi Yi," 44–45, 48–50, 161n.64, 163n.87

Han Feizi, xxii, 98; on human nature as negative and fixed, 93–95, 97–98, 100, 101, 102–103; influenced by discourse on human agency, 127; institutional control mandatory, 95, 96–97, 99–101
Han Feizi (texts): "Eight Claims," 98; "Measures of the Heart," 99; "On

Problematizing Authority," 99–100; "The Five Vermin," 99
Han period, individualistic ideals during, xix–xx, 122
Hansen, Chad, xviii
health and vitality, 37, 68, 78, 84; cultivation of heart-mind, 32, 55, 56, 69; "Heaven Sends Down the Great Constant," 32–33; the ruler as, 44, 45; of the sovereign's body, 84–87
Heaven's will (*tian zhi*), 1, 4, 5, 7, 8–14, 147n.7, 151n.41, 153n.60; as "compensatory power," 2, 4, 23; in Ru texts, 32; ruling elite as mediator of, 14–19, 20, 21, 27, 32–34; three proofs of (Mozi), 9–10, 150n.32; universal conformity to mandated, 25–26, 33, 149n.17. *See also* universal cosmic authority
hierarchy. *See* socio-political hierarchy
higher power. *See* universal cosmic authority
Hsu Cho-yun, 143n.39
Huainanzi, Yangist thought in, 70, 72–73, 74
human agency: discourse on, xxv, 55, 103, 125, 127–128; through human effort, 91–93; people as dependent agents, 47–51. *See also* internal-external debate over human agency
human agency as innate, 54, 64–67, 77, 91, 95, 98, 125–126, 127, 183n.8; the body as the source of cosmic agency, 64, 67, 68, 70, 74–76, 127, 173n.87; the "inward turn," xix; the *jing shen* (refined numinosity), 109–112; moral motivation as intrinsic and natural, 65–70, 75, 90, 125–126. *See also* bodily agency; individual agency; naturalized cosmic agency; *xing*
human agency as innate: deterministic and largely negative. *See* deterministic powers
human relationship to the divine, 29, 32, 42–43, 55, 86–87, 122–124
human rights discourse: and Asian values, ix, xi, 131–135; cultural relativism and, 133–134; human rights and Asian values, ix, 131–135; universal human rights, ix, x

impersonal authority: and conformity (paradox of), 36, 41–42; sovereign as mediator of, 30–36, 43, 45–46, 52; the sovereign's body and, 30–36
individual, 121, 122, 130
individual agency, xvi, xxiv, xxv, 54, 134–135; in Mohist writings, 4–6, 29; in Primitivist writings, 81–82; in Zhuangzi's "Inner Chapters," 55–63
individualism in early Chinese thought: implicit forms of, 65, 95, 125; incorporated into theories of self-cultivation, xvi, 132; individual agency and, xii, 134–135; integrated (holistic) individualism, xi–xiii, xxx, 129–130, 186n.14; rarely perceived or emphasized, xvi–xvii, xix–xx, 76; relational form of individualism, xxvii–xxviii, 121, 132–133, 139n.15, 145n.57
individualism in individualistic thinking, xv, xix–xxiv, xxvii, 29, 64, 74–76; Han period, 122; in Primitivist writings, 81–82; Qin period, xvi, 122; in Yangist thought, 70–74; in the *Zhuangzi*, 62–63
individualism in individual-oriented institutionalism, 119–120. *See also* Syncretist
individualism in Western individualism, ix–xi, xvii, xxi, 129, 138
institutional control: necessity of, 77, 90–91, 95–97, 98, 99–101; negative powers of the self and, 87–93, 93–95, 96–98, 100; syncretic mixtures with individualism, 104. *See also* Han Feizi; Syncretist; Xunzi
integrated (holistic) individualism, xi–xiii, xxx, 129–130, 186n.14
intellectuals, xv–xvi
interdependence, xii, 48, 106, 115, 129, 187n.14
internal-external debate over human agency, xxiv–xxv, 91, 103, 119, 126; bodily-self as the source of moral rightness (Primitivist), 79–81, 83–84, 86–87; Gaozi on external sources of morality, 64, 65–66, 67, 68–69, 79; Mencius on destructiveness of external sources, 64, 65–66, 67, 68–69, 79; necessity of human effort and external guidance (Xunzi), 89–92; syncretic resolutions of, 104–105, 119–120 (*see* Syncretist; *Zhong yong*). *See*

also external force or authority (*shi*); human agency as innate
"Inward Training," 31, 32. See also *Guanzi*
Ivanhoe, Philip, 126–127, 162n.77, 172n.76

ji (self), 55, 72
jiao (authoritative instruction): complementing human potentialities, 106–108
jing shen (refined numinosity), 108, 109–112

kin-based power, xxi
Kjellberg, Paul, 60
knowledge: as artificial, 81; obtaining, 10–11

Laozi: on the Dao, 31–33, 34, 35, 55, 125; on the ruler's authority and conformity to the Dao, 36–41, 42, 46, 47; self-abnegation in, 38–40; self-cultivation available to all, 47–48, 55, 125; on self-cultivation of the sage-king, 32–33, 40, 47, 48, 50, 60, 85–87; *wu-wei* (non-purposive action) cultivation, 34–35, 38–39, 40–41; *wu-wei* (non-purposive action) in, 34–35, 38–39
Laozi texts: Guodian "proto-Laozi A," 42, 124, 155n.11, 160n.55, 162n.71; Mawangdui versions, 158n.28, 159n.43, 160n.55, 162n.76
Lewis, Mark, 30
Li Kui, xxii
Li Si, xxii
Li Xiangfeng: *Guanzi jiaozhu*. See *Guanzi*
Liezi, 57–58, 72, 173n.84
Liu, Lydia, 133
Liu Xiaogan, 78, 79
Lüshi chunqiu: "Nurture of Life" chapters, 84, 84–87, 102, 177n.38

malleability: as inherent (*gu*), 87, 88, 89, 91, 96
material virtue, 30, 169n.45
Mencius, 73, 171n.62, 172n.76; an advisor to the ruler, xxii; critical of Yang Zhu, 71–72, 73; criticized by Xunzi, 87–88; Daoist self-transformation available to all, 90, 125–126, 171n.71; on destructiveness of external sources of morality, 64, 65–69, 79; on human agency as innate, 66, 170n.52, 171n.71; individualism in, 64–70; naturalizing (internalizing) moral agency, 68, 70, 75, 90, 93, 119, 125–126; Xunzi compared with, 92, 93
meritocracy, 11–12, 13–16, 18, 27, 153n.60; social mobility and, 13–14; socio-political hierarchy and, 13–14, 18, 19, 25–26. *See also* achieved man: in *Mozi* (*xian zhe*); upward conformity (*shang tong*)
metaphors, 151n.36, 172n.77; emptying vessel, 56; masses as the ruler's body, 44, 45, 49; possession and theft, 82–83, 84; state cosmetics, 96–97, 180n.84; vegetative metaphors (willow tree, etc.), 64–65, 115
military meritocracy, xxiii
mindful conformity, 19–25, 150n.24
ming (clarification), 106–107
ming (Heaven's mandate), 4, 6, 81, 82, 148n.12, 149n.13, 159n.34, 176n.19; Mohist rejection of, 4–5
ministers, xxii, 114–115
Mo Di. *See* Mozi
Mohist school, 95, 152n.56; on individual agency, 4–6; individual's relationship to the Divine, 42; rejection of *ming*, 4–5; on upward conformity, 13, 122; upward conformity conception of self-cultivation, 1–2, 10–11, 13–14, 26–28. *See also Mozi*
moral agency: debate over internal vs. external sources of, 126; naturalized, 65–70, 75, 90; potential for requiring training, 105–108
moral authority, 6; dispersed (in the *Analects*), 33, 45; innate cosmic sources of, 120, 139n.14; of the ruling elite, 17, 18, 96; of the sovereign, 14, 16, 19, 49, 50, 149n.21. *See also* mindful conformity; universal cosmic authority
moral autonomy, 1, 13, 14, 19, 21–22, 49, 146n.1. *See also* human agency
morality vs. right behavior, 82–83
Mozi, 7, 8–13, 71–72, 79, 147n.6, 150n.24, 151n.48, 173n.84; an advisor to the ruler, xxii; his three proofs, 9–10, 150n.32
Mozi: "Against the Ru," 18–19; "Shang

tong," 148n.11, 150n.24; "Upward Conformity" chapters, 2, 22, 24, 151n.41; "Xiu Shen" and "Suo Ran" chapters, 96
Munro, Donald, 130, 138n.6

naturalized cosmic agency, 54, 70, 76; in *Mencius*, 70, 75, 90, 93, 119, 125–126; in the Primitivist, 84; in Yangist, 70–74, 75–76, 127, 173n.87. *See also* human agency as innate
neo-Confucian naturalists, 126–127
Neo-Daoist movement, xix
nimbus-like *qi*, 66, 170n.52, 171n.71
non-agency. *See wu-wei* (non-purposive action)
non-instrumentality, 56, 59, 62, 75
non-purpose action: *wu-wei* cultivation, 34–35, 38–39, 40–41
"Nurture of Life" chapters (*Lüshi chunqiu*), 84, 84–87, 102, 177n.38
Nylan, Michael, xix–xx

personal accountability, 42–43
Pines, Yuri, 62
political hierarchy. *See* socio-political hierarchy
Primitivist, 110, 126–127, 202; body as the agent for worldly order, 81, 84; compared with *Laozi*, 81, 84; critical of Yangist orientation, 175n.11; morality vs. right behavior, 82–83. *See also Zhuangzi*
Puett, Michael, 29–30

qi (material force), xxviii, 45, 55, 56, 57, 67, 69, 166n.12; the nimbus-like qi, 66, 170n.52, 171n.71
Qian Mu, 71
Qin period: individualistic theories, xvi, 122; state centralization, xv, xvi, xxi, xxiii, 44, 52, 123; theories supporting rulership, 52–53, 118, 124, 154n.1, 177n.38
Qin Shihuang, 44
Qin state, xxiii, 184n.16
qing (dispositions and emotions), xxviii, 89

"recovery model," 126–127
relational individualism, xxvii–xxviii, 121, 139n.15, 145n.57

responsibility, xxiv–xxv
reward and punishment, 2–3, 22, 26, 117–118
Robber Zhi, story of, 83
Rosemont, Henry, xviii, xxiv, 135, 139n.15, 141n.14, 145n.57, 145n.59
Ru texts, 2, 29, 43, 156n.16, 161n.62; Guodian *Tian jiang da chang* ("Heaven Sends Down the Great Constant"), 32–33, 35, 43; Guodian "Wu Xing," 33; Guodian "Zi Yi," 44–45, 48–49; *Zhong yong*, 105–108. *See also Analects*
ruler. *See* ducal lords; sovereign/ruler
ruler-ruled relationship, 46, 47–48, 50–51, 98–99
ruling elite: mediating Heaven's will, 14–19, 20, 21, 27, 32–34. *See also* socio-political hierarchy

sage-king, 9, 10, 18, 20–21, 36–38, 41, 45, 48; evolving through effort and external guidance (Xunzi), 89–92; self-cultivation of, 32–33, 40, 47, 48, 50, 85–87. *See also* ducal lords; sovereign/ruler
Schwartz, Benjamin, 146n.1
self: embodied (*see also* body [*shen*]), xxix–xxx; embodying the Dao, 41–42; *jing shen* (refined numinosity), 108, 109–112; losing in order to channel the Dao, 38–40, 55, 56, 167n.16; as malleable, 87, 88, 89, 91, 96; non-dualistic, xxiii–xxix; problem of the, 56–58; the selfless self, 125; separation between internal and external, 73–74; spiritual agency of the self, 29–30; universalist conception of, 121
self-abnegation, 33, 34, 35, 38–40, 159n.43; as agency, 36; selfless conformism, 60
self-cultivation: available to all, 13–14, 55, 60, 61–62, 63, 87, 113, 125–126
self-determination, xxi, 2, 130; and conformism, xxvi–xxvii; in Mohist texts, 6–7
selfishness, 33–34, 78, 126, 127, 165n.3; whether Yang Zhu advocated, 73–74, 76. *See also* ego/egoism
Shang Yang, xxii
Shen Buhai, xxii
sheng (life), 85

shi (agent of external authority), 67, 69, 99–101, 166n.6, 170n.58
shi class (educated elite), xv, xxii–xxiii, 15, 61, 128, 143n.39, 168nn.36–37; social mobility of, xv. See also ministers
Sivin, Nathan, 30
Slingerland, Edward, 56
social chaos, 6, 78, 153n.57; and social order, 9, 96
social immobility in Syncretist writings, 185n.39
social mobility, xxiii, 13–14; increase in, xxiii, 121, 143n.39; Mohist texts supporting, 13, 27; of the *shi* class, xv, 125
social order, 11, 46; without external rule, 78, 82; requiring institutional control, 87, 87–93; requiring strict and punitive measures, 95, 96–97, 99–101; sage-king embodying, 38, 45; and social chaos, 9, 96
socio-political hierarchy: conformity of subordinates to, 19–23; and meritocracy, 13–14, 18, 19, 25; and moral authority, 15–16, 17–19. See also ministers; sovereign/ruler
Son of Heaven, 3, 7, 13, 15–17, 23, 85–87, 153n.61, 178n.45. See also sovereign/ruler; sovereign's body
Song Rongzi, story of, 57, 58
sovereign/ruler, 13, 14–17, 43, 51–53; authority contingent on conformity of followers, 22, 24–25; authority derived from harmony with the Dao or cosmic force, 36–40, 86; constrained by cosmic authority, 15, 36, 40, 44, 45, 124; moral authority of, 14, 16, 19, 49, 50, 149n.21; role of, 114–115. See also ruler-ruled relationship
sovereign's body: cultivation of linked to social control, 110–112, 116, 117–118; health and vitality ensures societal benefit, 84–87; mediating cosmic authority, 30–36, 43, 45–46, 48, 52, 102, 123
spiritual agency of the self, 29–30; *jing shen* (refined numinosity), 108, 109–112, 118
spiritual authority: bureaucratization of, 115–116; techniques related to governance, 43, 46, 81, 85–86, 110–118

subjectivity, 165n.3
Sun Yirang, *Mozi jian gu*. See *Mozi*
Syncretist, 109, 119–120, 127, 183n.14, 184n.15, 185n.36, 185n.39; compared with *Laozi*, 111–112; on the sovereign's body, 110–112, 118; on spiritual related to governance, 110–118; *wu-wei* practiced to create social order, 110–113. See also *Zhuangzi*

"Techniques of the Heart-mind," 36, 43, 45, 46, 51, 156n.14, 164n.89, 185n.34; Lower, 36–37, 38, 40, 156n.14, 159n.38, 162n.70; Upper, 31–32, 46, 51, 156n.15. See also *Guanzi*
Tian jiang da chang ("Heaven Sends Down the Great Constant"), 32–33, 35, 43

universal cosmic authority, xv, xxiii–xxiv, 1, 18, 28, 31–32, 123; as Heaven's will (*tian zhi*), 25–26, 33, 149n.17; and the individual, xv. See also Dao; Heaven's will (*tian zhi*)
universal cosmic authority, mandatory allegiance to. See upward conformity (*shang tong*)
universal human rights. See human rights discourse
universalism, 72, 95, 162n.74
upward conformity (*shang tong*): conforming with Heaven's will, 17, 19, 23–24, 25, 35, 148n.11, 149n.21; early Mohist writings on, 1–4, 12, 122; in Guodian texts, 35; individual self-determination in, 4–7, 150n.24; Laozian notion of *wu-wei* and, 35; types of, 13–14. See also meritocracy
"Upward Conformity" chapters, 2, 22, 24, 151n.41. See also Mohist school; *Mozi*

vitality. See health and vitality

Wang Xiaoyu: *Zhuangzi ji shi*. See *Zhuangzi*
Warring States period, xvi, xxi, 30, 71, 78, 140n.5, 153n.63, 173n.84; changing conceptions of the individual, xxi–xxii, xxvii, 120, 121, 127–128, 129; changing conditions in, xxiii, 53, 142n.31. See also internal-external debate over human agency

Index

wei (human effort), 91–92
Wei-Jin period: individualistic ideals during, xix–xx
wei wo. *See* ego/egoism (*wei wo*)
Western conceptions of individualism, ix–xi, xvii, xxi, 129, 138
Wu Qi, xxii
Wu-shi, 162n.75
wu-wei (non-purposive action) practice bringing about social order, 34–35, 81; as purification of the *xing* (Primitivist writings), 85; related to spheres of governance, 110–111, 113–114; and *you-wei* (possessing activity), 112–118
"Wu Xing," 33

xin (one's heart-mind), xxviii
xing (human nature), xv, xxviii, 68, 78, 85, 164n.1; as base (Xunzi), 87–93, 93–95, 96–98, 100; complemented by *jiao* (authoritative instruction), 106–108; embodying the sacred, 66, 170n.52, 171n.71; moral motivation intrinsic to, 68–70, 125–126; positive powers of, 77–78; violation of, 83–84. *See also* individual; internal-external debate over human agency
Xunzi: an advisor to the ruler, xxii; on bodily needs and desires, 88–89; on deterministic negative powers requiring institutional control, 87, 87–93, 102–103; influenced by discourse on human agency, 127; Mencius compared with, 92, 93; on the self as malleable, 87, 88, 89; on self-cultivation, 88, 90–93
Xunzi: "Against the Twelve Masters," 87–88; "Zheng Ming" (Reification of Names), 92–93

Yang Zhu, 172n.78, 173n.84; individualism in, 126, 174n.94; on the material body as the source of cosmic agency, 70, 74, 75, 75–76, 127, 173n.87; on the self (*ji*), 72–73, 74; sources of his thought unclear, 70–71; whether advocating selfishness, 73–74, 76, 78, 126–127, 159n.42, 174n.95
Yangist school, 165n.3, 173n.84, 174n.92; in the *Huainanzi*, 70, 72–73, 74; in "Nurture of Life" chapters of the *Lüshi chunqiu*, 84–87, 172n.79; Primitivist on, 175n.11
Yao, Emperor, 88, 89–90, 91, 100, 112, 153n.63
yi (justice), 3, 12, 122, 128, 170n.51; sources of, 6–7, 8–9, 91–93. *See also* authority; Heaven's will
yi (rightness), 66
you-wei (possessing activity), 120; and *wu-wei* functioning as spheres of agency and social control, 112–118
Yu, Emperor, 9, 35, 88–89, 90, 91, 96
Yü Ying-shih, xix–xx

Zhang Qianfang, 7, 151n.42
"Zheng Ming" (Reification of Names), 92–93. *See also* Xunzi
zhi cheng (correct fulfillment), 108
Zhong yong, 105–108
Zhou state and period, xxi, 9, 16, 44, 49, 124, 164n.91; cultural authority of, 33
Zhuangzi, 182n.1, 183n.14; the attained individual, 57–61; Daoist self-transformation available to all, 55, 125; dating of, 29, 174n.4; individual access to cosmic authority and power, 54, 55–63, 74, 124–125; individualistic thinking in, 62–63; on *jing shen* (numinosity) and spiritual agency, 108, 109–112; on the problem of the self, 56–58; on the self, 54, 61–62, 64, 112–114
Zhuangzi (texts): "Current Times in the Human World," 59–60; "Inner Chapters," 55, 57, 58, 61
Zhuangzi (texts) "Nurture of Life" chapters, 84, 84–87, 102, 177n.38; rejecting external authority, 79–81; on violation of *xing* (human nature), 83–84; visceral connection between human and divine, 86–87; on *wu-wei* purifying the *xing*, 85; *xing* as sacred, 79, 80
Zhuangzi (texts) "Outer Chapters," 108, 119–120; politics irrelevant in, 60, 61–62, 63, 74. *See also* Primitivist; Syncretist
"Zi Yi," 44–45, 48–49; criticized by Xunzi, 87–88
Zuo zhuan, 131

About the Author

Erica Fox Brindley received her doctorate in East Asian Studies from Princeton University. Her publications include numerous journal articles on the issues of human agency, the self, ethnicity and identity, and theories of music in early China. She is presently an assistant professor of history and religious studies at The Pennsylvania State University.

Production Notes for Brindley | *Individualism in Early China*

Cover design by Wilson Angel

Text design by University of Hawai'i Press production staff
 with display and text type in Sabon

Composition by Terri Miyasato

Printing and binding by The Maple-Vail Book Manufacturing Group

Printed on 60# Maple Recycled Opaque, 426 ppi